POPULAR LITERATURE IN VICTORIAN SCOTLAND

AUP Titles of Related Interest

THE LAIRD OF DRAMMOCHDYLE AND HIS CONTEMPORARIES
or Random Sketches done in outline with a burnt stick
William Alexander
Edited with an Introduction by William Donaldson

TEN MODERN SCOTTISH NOVELS
Isobel Murray and Bob Tait

GRAMPIAN HAIRST
An Anthology of Northeast Prose
Edited by William Donaldson and Douglas Young

LITERATURE OF THE NORTH
Edited by David Hewitt and Michael Spiller

THE CLYACK SHEAF
Sketches of Life and Characters in Northeast Scotland
David Toulmin

A BLASPHEMER AND REFORMER
A Study of Lewis Crassic Gibbon
William K Malcolm

FROM THE CLYDE TO CALIFORNIA
Robert Louis Stevenson
Edited and Introduced by Andrew Noble

THE LUM HAT AND OTHER STORIES
Last tales of Violet Jacob
Edited by Ronald Garden

THE CONCISE SCOTS DICTIONARY
A comprehensive one-volume dictionary of the Scots Language
from the 12th Century to the present day
Editor-in-chief Mairi Robinson

POPULAR LITERATURE IN VICTORIAN SCOTLAND

language, fiction and the press

WILLIAM DONALDSON

ABERDEEN UNIVERSITY PRESS

First published 1986
Aberdeen University Press
A member of the Pergamon Group

© William Donaldson 1986

The publisher acknowledges subsidy from the Scottish
Arts Council towards the publication of this volume

British Library Cataloguing in Publication Data

Donaldson, William
  Popular literature in Victorian Scotland:
  language, fiction and the press.
  l. Press—Scotland—History—19th century
  I. Title
  072'.911   PN5134

  ISBN 0 08 034513 1
  ISBN 0 08 034515 8 Pbk

PRINTED IN GREAT BRITAIN
THE UNIVERSITY PRESS
ABERDEEN

Contents

List of Illustrations vi

Acknowledgements vii

Introduction ix

One *Organ of the Scottish Democracy*
  The Press and its Public, 1840–1900 1

Two *The Scoatch Depairtment*
  The Press and the Vernacular 35

Three *To Instruct as well as to Amuse*
  Didactic Fiction in the Scottish Press 72

Four *A Prophet . . . and from Galilee*
  The Novels of William Alexander 101

Five *Swallowed up in London . . .*
  A view of the Kailyard with Some
  Conclusions and a Postscript 145

Notes 151

Glossary 173

Index 183

Illustrations

Hoe Double Supplement Perfecting Machine   8

Facsimile of the top portion of Page 1 of the first issue
  of the *People's Journal*   12

Sir John Leng   13

The Offices of the *Dundee Advertiser* and *People's Journal*
  from 1802 to 1859   22

The *Dundee Advertiser* and *People's Journal* Office (*c.* 1908)   23

Certified Circulation of the *People's Journal* (*c.* 1890)   27

W D Latto (Tammas Bodkin) in a characteristic attitude   46

David Pae   78

Dr William Alexander   103

Acknowledgements

I have incurred many obligations during the course of this study. Without the generous assistance of many individuals, institutions, companies, libraries and archives throughout Scotland the work could not have been completed.

First and foremost I would like to thank the Leverhulme Trust whose generous award of a fellowship enabled me to undertake the full-time research on which the book is based. Acknowledgements are also due to Grampian Regional Council who kept a job for me to return to, the University of Aberdeen who made me an honorary fellow, and the British Academy who gave me a grant to help prepare the manuscript for the press.

I am indebted to D C Thompson & Co Ltd for their support.

I wish to thank the staff of Aberdeen University Library, in particular Mrs Myrtle Anderson-Smith, and Miss Mary Williamson of Special Collections; the staff of the local and reference sections of Aberdeen City Library, the Ewart Library Dumfries, the Central Library Dundee, the Glasgow Room Mitchell Library, Hamilton District Library, the Dick Institute Kilmarnock, Kirkcaldy District Library, the North East Fife District Library Service, the Central Library Paisley, Peterhead Public Library, and in particular Mr G Miller, the staff of the National Library of Scotland, Wick Public Library, and the Sir John Anderson Library, Woodside.

Descendants of W D Latto and David Pae have gone out of their way to supply me with information; I wish particularly to thank Mrs Christian Buist, Mrs Judith W Cooke, Mr David G Pae, and Mr John R Watson.

Of the many friends who have helped me with information and advice I am especially grateful to Mr Thomas Crawford, Mr William Findlay, Ms Caroline Macafee, Dr Ian Olson, Mr D J Withrington, and to Professor Peter L Payne and my colleagues in the Department of Economic History at the University of Aberdeen.

Introduction

This study is a modest introduction to a large subject. It aims to extend our knowledge of popular culture during a period of revolutionary change by focusing on the medium which acted as its principal agency, the newspaper press.

Although regarded as an invaluable source of information, the press has received relatively little attention as an institution in its own right. Within the last decade, indeed, there has been a quickening of interest in the English press, but the situation in Scotland remains unsatisfactory. There are a number of 'house histories' of various journals, differing widely in extent and quality, but only one book-length study treats the Scottish press as a whole, R M W Cowan's pioneering survey, *The Newspaper in Scotland a Study of its First Expansion 1815–1860* (Glasgow 1946). Cowan is painstaking and well-informed, but his picture of the press in Scotland is hardly representative of the nineteenth century as a whole. His concentration on politics tends to obscure the diversity of the medium, and by ending his study in the mid 1850s he avoids the implications of the most important single event in newspaper history, the repeal of the Stamp Act in 1855 which laid the foundations of a whole new popular press.[1]

The press is a paradigm of Victorian enterprise. Virtually a cottage-industry in 1800, it developed by the end of the century into a large-scale capital-intensive business of considerable technical sophistication. The growth of the railway network led to unprecedented expansion in circulation, newsgathering was transformed by electric telegraphy, and the introduction of steam power permitted the development of high-speed rotary presses which revolutionised productive capability. A whole complex of social changes took place at the same time, including a great extension in functional literacy, the creation of a new reading public, and the rise of a mass popular literary market. It was in the second rather than the first half of the century that these things came to pass.

As an agency for disseminating culture, the press has been neglected almost completely. The traditional view of its main function as the shaping of political opinion has encouraged a narrow concentration on the leader columns of the larger dailies, despite a growing awareness that the links between politics and the press are neither simple nor direct. The present study focuses on the weekly press, in particular the new wave of penny papers like the *People's Journal* which catered first and foremost for the working class. These were not newspapers as the term would nowadays be understood, but an intriguing hybrid form combining a wide-ranging news function with many of the attributes of a popular literary miscellany.

There had long been an overlap in Scotland between the press and the

more traditional world of letters. The reader may perhaps recollect that
James Watson, compiler of the *Choice Collection of Comic and Serious Scots
Poems* (Edinburgh 1706-11) and a key figure in the eighteenth century
vernacular revival, also founded the *Edinburgh Courant* in 1705. The critic
and historian Thomas Ruddiman was a newspaper proprietor, owning in
his day one of the longest running Scottish papers, the *Caledonian Mercury*
(1720-1867). Sir Walter Scott was an owner and contributor to the
Edinburgh Weekly Journal which was edited by his friend James Ballantine;
his *Minstrelsy of the Scottish Border* (1802-3) was printed on the presses of
the *Kelso Mail* which Ballantine also edited. 'Christopher North', J G Lockhart, William Edmonstoune Aytoun, and James Hogg were contributors to
the *Edinburgh Evening Courant*. Hugh Miller was editor of the Free Church
paper, the *Witness*, which had the largest circulation in Scotland in the
decade following the Disruption, and his celebrated autobiographical study
My Schools and Schoolmasters first appeared in its columns. William
Alexander, the doyen of North-East prose literature, and author of *Johnny
Gibb of Gushetneuk* (Aberdeen 1871) was editor of the *Aberdeen Free Press*
and it was there that the novel first appeared as a serial in 1869-70. In more
recent times both Lewis Grassic Gibbon and Hugh MacDiarmid began their
careers in the press, Gibbon with the *Aberdeen Journal* and MacDiarmid
with a number of papers, most notably the *Montrose Review*.[2]

Newspapers aimed at a readership in the lower-middle and 'respectable'
working classes dominated the popular market during the second half of
the century, and they published original writing, poetry, prose fiction,
memoirs and reminiscences, biography, history, folklore and popular
musicology in enormous quantities. By the end of the period more than two
hundred separate titles were appearing every week in Scotland, and many
of them had been publishing such material with unflagging diligence for
upwards of half a century.

To these considerations of scale must be added the obscurity of the
original source material. In this field the ordinary tools of enquiry are of
relatively limited use. General bibliographies and library catalogues tend to
record books and pamphlets only and even specialist guides like the
Wellesley Index to Victorian Periodicals tend to confine themselves to middle
class 'literary' magazines like *Blackwood's* or the *Edinburgh Review* which
existed in a different world from the popular press. Surveys such as Joan P
S Ferguson's *Directory of Scottish Newspapers* (Edinburgh 1984) and Lionel
Madden and Diana Dixon's *The Nineteenth-Century Periodical Press in Britain*
(New York & London 1976) are becoming available, giving some indication
of the physical whereabouts of newspapers with information on dates,
titles and extent of holdings; in a number of places, too, the daunting task
has begun of indexing specific papers, but it is probably still true to say that
on the whole the Scottish Victorian press exists in a bibliographical
wilderness.

Newspapers present a number of additional problems not always encountered in other fields. The source material is scattered and sometimes
inaccessible. Some papers are still in the hands of their publishers; some are

deposited in libraries of various sorts all over Scotland; some are available only in the British Library's Newspaper Division in Colindale, North London. Sometimes runs are complete, sometimes not. Some newspapers are represented merely by one or two tattered copies; some have failed to survive at all. Although technical standards were generally high in the Victorian press, the paper, after the passage of a century or so, is often fragile and requires to be handled with care. Heavy use and indifferent storage conditions often means that the newspapers are dirty and they are normally bound in unwieldy annual slabs which grow ever larger as the century advances. To this must be added the densely compact character of the text which makes extended reading taxing from a physical and psychological point of view.

If for a variety of reasons, therefore, I have had to be selective in my sampling of the original source material, I have, at the same time, been able to consider a spread of papers published throughout mainland Scotland and the northern isles, including the *Aberdeen Weekly Journal*, the *Airdrie & Coatbridge Advertiser*, the *Ardrossan and Saltcoats Herald*, the *Ayr Advertiser*, the *Ayrshire Post* (Ayr), the *Banffshire Journal* (Banff), the *Blairgowrie Advertiser*, the *Buchan Observer* (Peterhead), the *Buteman* (Rothesay), the *Dumfries & Galloway Courier*, and *Dumfries and Galloway Standard*, the *Dumfriesshire and Galloway Herald* (all of Dumfries), the *Dundee and Perth Saturday Post*, the *East Fife Record*, the *Eskdale and Liddesdale Advertiser* (Langholm), the *Evening Express* (of Aberdeen), the *Fife Free Press*, the *Fifeshire Advertiser* (both of Kirkcaldy), the *Glasgow Weekly Herald*, and *Glasgow Weekly Mail*, the *Hamilton Advertiser*, the *Inverness Courier*, the *John O'Groat Journal* (Wick), the *Kilmarnock Standard*, the *Kirkcaldy Times*, the *North Briton* (Edinburgh), the *North of Scotland Gazette* (Aberdeen), the *Northern Advertiser* (Aberdeen), the *Northern Ensign* (Wick), the *Orcadian* (Kirkwall), the *Paisley & Renfrewshire Gazette*, the *Penny Free Press* (Aberdeen), the *Perthshire Advertiser* (Perth), the *Peterhead Sentinel*, and the *Wishaw Press and Advertiser*.

Two newspaper groups have been chosen as the main focus of enquiry: the Leng papers published at Dundee including the *Dundee Advertiser*, the *People's Journal*, the *People's Friend* and the *Evening Telegraph*, concentrating on the *People's Journal*, the greatest popular weekly newspaper in Scotland; and the *Free Press* group of Aberdeen whose publications included the *Daily Free Press*, the *Weekly Free Press*, and the *Evening Gazette*, with particular reference to the *Weekly Free Press* (the title by which it is referred to throughout, although the actual wording tended to vary). Unreliability of circulation statistics makes it difficult to generalise about relative scale, but there is no doubt that the Leng group was one of the biggest in Scotland during the second half of the nineteenth century as well as being, arguably, the most innovative and exciting newspaper business in the country. The *Free Press* group was selected because it permitted discussion of William Alexander, one of the most distinguished authors in Victorian Scotland in his own right, and a leading representative in his generation of the new breed of professional pressmen created by the newspaper revolution.

According to the prevailing view of Scottish culture, the nineteenth century after the death of Scott was a period of decline and failure in which Scottish writers, recoiling from the spectre of industrialisation, immersed themselves in rural fantasy following Sir James Barrie, 'Ian Maclaren' (Dr John Watson) and other writers of the 'Kailyard School'. The present study seeks to modify this view, suggesting that Scottish culture was (and is) a popular culture, and that its major vehicle during the period was not the London-dominated booktrade, but the Scottish newspaper press, owned, written, and circulating within the country. It suggests that in the Scottish context fiction published in the press was more significant than fiction published in book form as well as being infinitely greater in extent. It suggests further that use of the Scots language was much more extensive and important than might otherwise be concluded on the evidence of a book-culture produced for an all-UK literary market, and that during this period popular newspapers provided the environment for a vernacular prose revival of unprecedented proportions. It suggests, finally, that as well as giving a unique insight into the condition of the people of Scotland during the second half of the nineteenth century the popular press played a major role in a communications revolution of lasting significance for contemporary Scottish culture.

UNIVERSITY OF **ABERDEEN**
Centre for Continuing Education
Centre for Scottish Studies
Thomas Reid Institute for Cultural Studies

SCOTTISH LITERATURE: NE - SW

A HALF-DAY

CONFERENCE

Saturday 8 May 1993   9.00 am - 1.00 pm

Fraser Noble Building, Old Aberdeen

SCOTTISH LITERATURE: NE - SW
Enrolment Form

Saturday 8 May 1993

I wish to enrol for the above conference

Title Dr/Mr/Mrs/Miss/Ms ....

Surname ....

First Name ....

Address ....

....

.... Post Code ....

Telephone Number (Day) .... (Evening) ....

Additional names enrolled on this form:

....

....

Number of place booked ....

Conference Fee: £5.00. This includes coffee.

Cheque/Postal order enclosed for £...

Cheques should be crossed and made payable to **The University of Aberdeen.**

Please return this form, together with payment to:
Centre for Continuing Education
University of Aberdeen
Regent Walk
ABERDEEN   AB9 1FX

Telephone: (0224) 272449

SCOTTISH LITERATURE: NE - SW

A Half-Day Conference

Saturday 8 May 1993

Fraser Noble Building, Old Aberdeen

PROGRAMME

0900	Enrolment
0930	The Historical Ballads of the North East *Professor David Buchan*
1015	NE Language and Literature, and the Wider Context *Dr William Donaldson*
1100	Coffee
1130	English in its Underwear: Writing from a West of Scotland Background *William McIlvanney*
1215	Questions and Discussion
1300	Close

The Chair will be taken by *Dr David Hewitt*,
Reader in English and Head of the Department of English,
University of Aberdeen

SCOTTISH LITERATURE: NE - SW

The speakers in this half-day conference will explore aspects of the literature belonging to two distinctive Scottish regions. To varying degrees, they will also comment on the problem of the relationship between regional and national literature.

The Speakers

Professor David Buchan a native of the NE and an Aberdeen University graduate, is Research Professor of Folklore at Memorial University, Newfoundland. Among his many publications is the *The Ballad and the Folk*. During this academic year, he has been visiting Research Fellow at the Thomas Reid Institute for Cultural Studies and the Department of English.

Dr William Donaldson, also a native of the NE and an Aberdeen University graduate, is a teacher of English at Harlaw Academy and a Tutor-Counsellor of the Open University. He is an Honorary Research Fellow of Aberdeen University's Department of History and Economic History, Among a wide range of publications is *Popular Literature in Victorian Scotland.*

William McIlvanney was born and raised in Kilmarnock, and taught in Ayrshire secondary schools for seventeen years after graduation from the University of Glasgow. Among his novels, mostly set in the SW, are *Laidlaw*, *Docherty* (winner of the 1975 Whitbread Award for fiction), *Walking Wounded*, *The Big Man* and, most recently, *Strange Loyalties* (Winner of the 1992 Glasgow People's Prize). He is currently Writer-in-Residence at the University of Aberdeen.

The Thomas Reid Institute for Cultural Studies is a focus for international collaboration in research across a wide range of disciplines. It aims to encourage research and debate involving both the academic community and the public at large. The Director is Dr Joan Pittock Wesson.

ONE

Organ of the Scottish Democracy

The Press and its Public, 1840–1900

Newspapers had existed in Scotland from about the middle of the seventeenth century, and in 1845 there were about eighty of them.[1] Basically they were advertising media (as so many of their titles imply), moderately profitable offshoots of existing printing and publishing businesses in the cities and in larger town like Dumfries or Perth where there was a sufficient concentration of population to make them viable.

They were small scale businesses requiring little capital and employing few people, with an unhurried work-rhythm based on a once-weekly pattern of publication and using simple machinery which had altered little in design for several generations. When Alexander Sinclair who was to become one of the leading figures in the Victorian Scottish press became office-boy at the *Glasgow Herald* in 1845, the editorial and reporting staff numbered just two: George Outram the editor, and his assistant James Pagan. The business side of the paper was managed by a solitary cashier whose method of accounting was, apparently, to carry his loose change in one pocket and the paper's petty cash in the other. Nearly all Scottish papers were produced on hand presses driven by human muscle, and successful ones like the *Glasgow Herald* or the *Aberdeen Journal* might have a circulation of three to four thousand copies a week.

From an editorial point of view scissors-and-paste methods were still common and newsgathering was rudimentary. The *Glasgow Herald*, quite typically, got its British and international news from the London papers, and its Scottish news from other Scottish papers. Local intelligence was supplied by correspondents and there was little actual reporting. Newspapers sold within a narrow social range, made most of their profits from advertising, and avoided thrusting their opinions upon the reader.[2]

The *Dundee Advertiser* provides a fairly typical example of the ethos prevailing in the Scottish newspaper world before the repeal of the Stamp Act in 1855 triggered off a period of revolutionary growth. It was a long-established city paper which later became one of the great Victorian dailies with premises in Bank Street which were the envy of the British press. In 1845, however, it was housed in a battered old tenement in the Overgate, and inside looked like this:

> The editor's room, which was occupied for two hours on two days of the week, was plenished with furniture and fittings made, it was said, in the reign of Queen Anne, and handed down by the ducal house of Argyle as heirlooms to the then proprietors . . . The cashier's department was just large enough for two seated at the desk and one on a chair. All the furnishings in the case and

press rooms were of the most original and unique kind, and had been in constant use for 50 years, some of the frames being held together with ropes . . . In the press-room there was the press which was said to have printed Prince Charlie's proclamation in 1745. Along with it was a bank and nothing in it. On it again was a wooden horse, which was propped up on two legs because the proprietors were too poor to give it four. The literary department produced two columns of leaders each week . . . the selecting and arranging of the general news was all gone through at one of the compositor's frames in the case-room. The reporting, for which a brilliant staff of one was retained, was all done in the press-room . . . thus . . . the *Advertiser*, which for long had held the first place among newspapers in Dundee.[3]

The reason for this stagnation lay in the climate of state control within which the press had long been accustomed to operate. The history of Government attempts to influence the press by such means as direct payment, farming of official advertising, and various restrictive statutes is long and involved, but it is necessary to consider some of the chief constraints at least in outline. These were basically three in number: a tax on advertisements which effectively limited newspaper revenue, ensuring that papers would be expensive and therefore few: a stamp duty which restricted circulation by obliging publishers to purchase, in advance, a special stamp for each copy of any paper defined as containing 'news', which enabled it to be posted and re-posted free during seven days following publication, which in turn tended to created multiple subscriptions and organised chains of readers, especially in country areas. Unfortunately the Government fixed the price at a very high level. The average weekly newspaper cost about sevenpence and fourpence of that went on the Stamp alone. At a time when the average working man earned somewhere between ten shillings and £1 per week, the price was prohibitive, and meant to be so. Finally, the State made sure that raw material costs remained high by imposing a tax upon paper at a certain rate per pound. These, then, were 'the taxes on knowledge', and the story of their repeal is inseparable from the revolution in popular publishing that took place in the generation after 1855.[4]

Abolition proceeded from a variety of considerations: on the one hand there was an admirable desire to improve the condition of the working class by means of a cheap wholesome popular press; on the other, and less admirably, was a desire to destroy the radical underground by exposing its illegal unstamped papers to the free play of market forces; underlying both of these ideas was a general dislike of restrictive taxation inspired ultimately by the movement towards free trade with its attendant principle of *laissez faire*.[5] Scottish newspaper proprietors were mainly opposed to repeal, and when they presented their case to the Select Committee on Newspaper Stamps in 1851, their spokesman was Alexander Russel, editor of the *Scotsman*. Russel questioned the wisdom of making a cheap newspaper press available to lower classes at all, and then went on to make a number of predictions: the number of newspapers, he said, would greatly increase; their relationship with their readers would change; a local newspaper press would come into existence, and it was here that he saw the main danger—in his view, it would have to operate in so restricted a market that it could never hope to maintain its independence or its breadth of view. The press would become parochialised and trivialised.[6]

In terms of simple arithmetic at least, the figures seem to confirm Russel's analysis: twenty-five Scottish burghs had a newspaper in 1845; by 1860 this had doubled, and the newspaper world had come to be, in Alexander Sinclair's phrase, 'like a new creation'.[7] The figures doubled again by the turn of the century. There was a threefold increase in numbers of papers of all kinds in the period up to 1910.[8] But a simple generalisation based on numbers of titles hardly gives an accurate picture in view of the massive increases in periodicity and volume that occurred at the same time.

Repeal immediately halved the price and made it possible to contemplate publication more than once a week. Many papers developed a bi- or tri-weekly pattern during the 1850s and 1860s as an intermediate step towards daily publication at 1d. which became the prevailing city pattern. A single title might be in existence throughout the period, therefore, but involve a vastly different scale of operations at different times. When it started in 1853, for example, the *Aberdeen Free Press* was a weekly with a circulation hovering around the five or six hundred mark. Thirty years later it was the most important paper in the north of Scotland coming out six days a week with a popular week-end edition, and a related evening paper selling heavily in the city of Aberdeen and its immediate neighbourhood.[9]

What the combined circulation was is difficult to say. Most newspapers were privately owned and under no obligation to keep proper accounts or issue public statements. Even the ones which were limited companies played their cards close to their chests and either indulged in extravagant claims or else maintained a cryptic silence on the whole subject—at least in public. The reason, of course, was the need to maximise advertising revenue. It was here that the battle for profitability was won or lost. Competition quickly brought the price of a typical daily down to a penny and that simply met production costs. Profits came through advertisements. A successful paper might have 40–50 per cent of its column space given over to them, and this had an important side-effect because it determined the social boundaries of the readership. When the price dropped the great expansion into the working class began to take place—but not into the working class as a whole. The poor were excluded; not because they might not be able to afford a paper, or read it once they had bought it, but because their purchasing power was so small that it was useless to advertise goods and services to them—they couldn't afford them. The new press aimed itself, typically, at the upper working-class—the decent respectable working men and women with a little disposable cash in their pockets and their white-collar cousins in the rapidly expanding lower middle class.[10]

Amongst papers which were already in existence at the time of repeal, the *Falkirk Herald* and the *Stirling Observer* show a fairly typical pattern, growing out of existing publishing concerns diversifying to meet changing needs. Between them the towns formed the hub of the popular literature market, where packmen and pedlars had long filled their wallets with chap-books and song-slips to satisfy the country trade, and newspapers were the next logical step for printers with spare capacity. The *Stirling Observer* came from the Randall and Macnie press, one of the leading chap-book publishers, and the *Falkirk Herald* from those of the Johnston family with a similar background. There is an interesting line of continuity here; the popular newspaper was in many ways the natural successor to the chap-book as a vehicle of popular culture.[11]

The new wave of post-repeal papers created their own patterns. Some owed their existence to individual entrepreneurs, but often they were founded by groups, local law firms sensing a political opportunity in the expanding urban communities, businessmen brought together by similarity of outlook and a sense of the limitations of existing journals. One, the *Buteman*, was founded by a mutual-improvement society, the Rothesay Young Men's Literary Association, who caught the prevailing mood and felt it was time the town had a paper. They had no capital, no experience, and little knowledge of printing or publishing. But they borrowed some money, bought a handpress, and selecting one of their number, a spinning-worker named Robert McFie as editor-elect, induced Blackies of Glasgow to employ him while he learned something about the business.[12]

By such means Scotland began to be covered by an extensive network of papers serving specific local areas. They tended to be based in towns and cities, of course, but they also circulated in surrounding country districts. Each paper's territory was clearly defined, and defended against interloping rivals with an almost feudal vigilance. The *Hamilton Advertiser*, for example, staked out its private domain on its masthead, laying claim to no fewer than forty-four towns and villages—by name—in the west central Lowlands.[13]

In some places, though, especially in outlying areas, 'local' papers might be produced entirely outside the community. The *Orkney and Shetland Chronicle*, for example, was compiled and published in Edinburgh. But this was regarded as unsatisfactory in several ways, especially when bad weather cut the islands off from the mainland. It was felt too that the local community ought to be able to exert a direct influence on the papers which served it and when the *Orcadian* started up in Kirkwall in 1854, the fact that it was the first paper actually to be produced on the island was seen as a major recommendation. Its publisher wrote that

> his chief reason in this undertaking is to supply to the County of Orkney &. Zetland the long felt desideration of a local newspaper, thus affording an advantage to the inhabitants to be obtained only through a medium of communication printed and published amongst themselves and over which they will exercise adequate control . . .[14]

The *Orcadian's* jobbing department was quickly transformed into a vigorous little local publishing house, issuing books on a wide variety of regional topics, a pattern repeated by many local newspaper presses as the century advanced.[15]

When the *Peterhead Sentinel* began in 1856, it introduced itself with typical modesty:

> The promoters do not claim to great pretensions and will not guarantee their Newspaper to be one conducted with first rate ability and talent. Nay, the public need not look upon it in that light at all, but rather the reverse. It is . . . simply a Newspaper written in a common-sense matter-of-fact style. It is not established for the purpose of agitating national topics, but published for the purpose of devoting its columns to local subjects . . .[16]

Within a few years, however, electric telegraphy and specialist press agencies transformed new gathering, and by giving unrestricted access to world and general UK news, made it possible to edit a 'national' style paper from practically anywhere in the country. By the later 1860s, the *Sentinel* had attained a high standard in coverage of local news, but there was also a strikingly greater concentration on national and international affairs, signalled by eloquent and cosmopolitan leading articles of great sophistication and breadth of view.

Perhaps this is not so surprising, bearing in mind the high quality of recruitment into journalism at this time, as post-repeal expansion began to make it attractive as a career in its own right. Two of the most distinguished Victorian journalists, Sir Hugh Gilzean Reid and James Annand, MP, laid the foundations of their careers in Peterhead on the *Sentinel* and its rival the *Buchan Observer*.[17] Before they became large and technical organisations, Scots papers often had editors who had done something different first. A number of them like R S Rintoul of the *Dundee Advertiser*, or William Naismith of the *Hamilton Advertiser* came up through the printing and bookselling trade.[18] Some were lawyers like James Hedderwick of the *Glasgow Citizen*, or James Bell who founded the *Edinburgh Weekly Chronicle*.[19] There were quite a number of schoolmasters, most notably William D Latto, former master of the Free Kirk school at Johnshaven, Kincardineshire, and editor of the *People's Journal* for nearly forty years. People came into newspaper work from élite trades where to some extent work-rhythms could be controlled and there might be time for reading, reflection, and discussion. William Scott of the *Montrose Review* had been a weaver, and W H Murray of the *Falkirk Herald* a shoemaker to trade; but beyond this the pattern begins to fragment: James Bridges the editor of the *Perthshire Advertiser* was a former railwayman, Henry Alexander of the *Aberdeen Free Press* an engineer, while William McCombie, the founding editor of that paper was, and continued until his death to be, a farmer.[20]

McCombie's relationship with his paper shows what a basically leisurely and dignified pursuit newspaper editing could be until well into the post-repeal period. The role was also very loosely defined. As we have seen, McCombie had a quite separate alternative occupation; indeed his distinction as an agriculturalist did much to help sell his paper outside the city where it challenged and eventually broke the long-standing monopoly of the *Aberdeen Journal*. In addition, he suffered relatively poor health for a number of years after the paper started, and did not even live in Aberdeen. Once a week his leading article and other literary 'copy' arrived through the post from the Howe of Alford, but he might well not appear in the office for weeks on end. He relied upon his assistant William Alexander to discharge his administrative duties (he would have nothing to do with the 'business' side of the paper) and many of his editorial ones as well.[21] His opposite number, William Forsyth, was basically a poet and angler who edited the *Aberdeen Journal* as a kind of afterthought. His presence in the office was also a fairly hit or miss affair, and anyway he preferred to work mainly at home; but at least his home was in Aberdeen.[22] In 1872, however, his pleasant bookish existence was shaken to its foundations; the *Free Press* went daily.

For a big city paper it came round to the idea rather slowly. The *Scotsman* had already published daily since 1855, the *Glasgow Herald* since 1859, and the *Dundee Advertiser* since 1861. The underlying factor was probably the way the population was distributed within its area. Aberdeen still lagged significantly behind Dundee in terms of growth, and the demographic balance between city and countryside was still heavily in favour of the latter. The *Free Press*'s proprietors, however, had come to the conclusion that the pace of civic activity had recently shown distinct signs of increase, and that the city might just be big enough to support a daily paper. After its initial difficulties, it had begun to prosper, and was now a considerable property. At first, many of the booksellers and stationers who normally held newspaper agencies refused to take it because of its radicalism, and an alternative distribution system had to be created based on different outlets—such as druggists, saddlers, general merchants, bank and law agents—anything which served as a focus for a community life. In the intervening twenty years, however, there had been an important change in the political loyalties of the North-East. The Tories lost ground progressively from the mid 1860s onwards, and for a generation thereafter the region was one of the bastions of northern Liberalism. In this more favourable climate the *Free Press* began to outdistance the *Aberdeen Journal* even in its own rural strongholds. The new daily was to be edited by the experienced and able William Alexander who was in the forefront of the new breed of professional journalists in Scotland. Born in the Garioch in 1826, his early life as a farm servant gave him an intimate knowledge of the agricultural scene which he put to outstanding journalistic and literary use. He had turned to writing following a serious injury, and when the *Free Press* began in 1853, William McCombie invited him to join the staff. Although McCombie stamped his personality strongly upon the paper, he was basically an absentee, so that when Alexander stepped into his shoes in the early 1870s, he already had twenty years of running a newspaper behind him in everything but name.[23]

Even at this period, though, papers did not rely exclusively upon their small professional staffs for their supply of 'copy'. They tended to act as outlets for a whole range of like-minded people. In its early days, much of the *Free Press* was written by its proprietors, notably the businessman David Macallan, who regularly (too regularly in Alexander's view) contributed articles on subjects like Voluntaryism and Temperance reform in which he had a particular interest. Likewise the *Aberdeen Journal* often carried pieces by conservative university professors and the higher clergy in the city.

This cosy, unhurried, faintly donnish atmosphere disappeared at a stroke when a paper went daily. To move from 40–50 to somewhere around 200–plus columns a week—assuming a six-column four-page format with retention of the separate weekly edition—demanded a considerable increase in what the Victorians called the 'literary department'; that is editorial, sub-editorial, and reporting staff; larger and more powerful printing machines, probably one or more of the new high-speed rotary presses fed by miles-long webs of paper, and a bigger staff of compositors and pressmen to service them; an expanded commercial department to deal with the advertising and distribution side, and, of course, a whacking increase in capital investment to pay for it all.

Sometimes management functions were split, with the editor retaining responsibility for the 'literary' part of the paper while the business and production side was controlled by a general manager. Some editors combined both functions, and they were very busy people. A Victorian daily required the almost hourly personal presence of its editor, although work patterns did tend to vary. Some editors would come into the office for a while in the morning and then disappear until early evening when the real work of the day began. Others arrived about mid-afternoon and worked straight through. It was said that a conscientious editor didn't leave the premises until he had a copy of the next day's paper actually in his hands as the first edition came off the press at, perhaps, three o'clock in the morning. And this happened six days a week. The pressures of the job increased almost indecently, and to cope with them at all required large quantities of energy and business acumen, a detailed practical knowledge of the technical production of the paper, an ability to manage large groups of subordinates working under acute pressure, and a virtually unbreakable constitution.[24]

One of the early casualties was the gentle William Forsyth of the *Aberdeen Journal*. He was born at Turriff in 1818, and studied medicine at the University of Edinburgh. For him as for Alexander, illness was the gateway into writing and a newspaper career. He contracted jaundice and occupied the recuperation period writing poetry, some of which was published in the *Aberdeen Herald*. On the strength of this, such was the casual nature of recruitment at this period, he was offered a post by Robert Carruthers on the *Inverness Courier*. As soon as there was a vacancy on the *Herald*, its editor James Adam asked him to fill it, and he returned to the city as sub-editor of that paper. It was not the mundane parts of a job which, in any case, 'were not other than an easy-going man might overtake,

Hoe Double Supplement Perfecting Machine. *Source: How a Newspaper is Printed.* Reproduced by courtesy of City of Dundee District Council.

without much waste of midnight oil', that gave him his professional standing, but his skill as a poet and essayist. He wrote for many of the leading periodicals of the day, *Blackwood's*, the *Cornhill*, *Punch*, and his poetry won him a solid if minor reputation when it was published in collected form under the title *Idylls and Lyrics* (Edinburgh 1872).[25] In 1848 he became editor of the *Journal* and was in post when the paper went daily in 1876.

The reason why this happened was quite simple. It was to counteract the pernicious influence of the Liberal papers by starting up a penny daily in the Conservative interest. The driving force behind the venture was Col Thomas Innes of Learney, one of the most active Tory lairds in the North-East. He saw clearly enough how Conservatism had lost its hold on the region, and he spelled it out in a series of letters to his neighbour Alexander Irvine of Drum:

> The most important omission, was not being alive to the great change which within the last few years, has been coming over the tenant constituency . . . The construction of a system of Railways in the county centering in Aberdeen, & the Penny newspapers have converted them from a most passive & docile into a most active & jealous constituency and they cannot be managed thro' their lairds as formerly . . . (31 May 1866)

Or again:

> At present the Radicals have got the ascendancy. And how? By Penny Newspapers. (5 June 1866)[26]

By the later 1870s, however, few individuals could contemplate financial outlay on such a scale: the cost of building up a newspaper from scratch was becoming prohibitive. In the spring of 1876, therefore, Learney and a consortium mainly of fellow lairds formed a joint stock company called the Aberdeen and North of Scotland Newspaper and Printing Co Ltd and bought out the proprietors of the *Aberdeen Journal*. The price was £8,500, £2,500 of it in the new company's stock. The name of the new paper was intended to be the *Northern News*, but tradition prevailed, and as the summer advanced the *Aberdeen Journal*, the oldest paper in Scotland, was enlarged and reconstructed to meet the challenge of the new age.[27]

Immediately Forsyth found himself plunged into a maelstrom; things happened with bewildering rapidity, and there was a new and oppressive financial stringency. He had long been accustomed to little luxuries like correcting from printed proofs; that went—no more costly re-setting on grounds of mere style. And then, various parts of his job were taken away and given to other people. A manager appeared, called John Thomson, late of the *Bradford Chronicle*, who was given authority over all aspects of the paper including Forsyth himself. Responsibility for news was taken from him (little to his regret—it was an aspect of newspaper work he regarded without relish: indeed he once declared 'he didna gie tippence for't'), and placed in the hands of an assistant editor named Archibald Gillies, a journalist of large experience and a former editor of the *Aberdeen Herald*. But the arrangement proved cumbersome and inefficient. There was continuous squabbling amongst the top three about who did what and who reported to whom. It got so bad that members of the Board had to sit in on daily business meetings to make sure that the paper ran with any degree of smoothness and efficiency. It was soon obvious that one of them would have to go, and in January 1877, Forsyth was sacked. Gillies took over his duties, but still found the going hard. There were complaints about overspending, inefficiency, failure to meet sales and advertising targets, and it was clear following the departure of the old editor that a lot of life had gone out of the paper. In the first year there was an operating loss of five and a half thousand pounds.

The *Free Press* had been observing this with some interest, waiting patiently for the new venture to bite the dust through a fatal mixture of undercapitalisation and muddle. When it became clear during the following summer, however, that the *Journal* had received a fresh injection of cash from its backers, it stepped in to deliver the *coup de grace*, arranging for its own private telegraphic wire (a costly manoeuvre, meaning more and fresher news, giving it a distinct technical edge), and doubling its size up to eight pages for the same price of a penny.

The *Journal* fired Thomson, hired Forsyth again, and appealed to the Scottish Conservative Association which was putting together a package of telegraphic and newsgathering support to help the Tory press peg back the Liberal lead in Scotland. There followed one of the best-documented newspaper wars in Scotland, which included the technical bankruptcy of the original Aberdeen and North of Scotland Company in 1884, and which flared into life intermittently thereafter until the amalgamation of the two papers in 1922.

The strain of all this proved too much for Forsyth. His health deteriorated and in November 1878 he felt compelled to tender his resignation. The Board recorded their appreciation of the valuable services he had rendered to the Party. Seven months later he was dead, at the age of sixty-one.

His death marks a watershed of a kind. The Scottish press had completed the first phase of its post-repeal expansion and had achieved its definitive Victorian pattern: a network of local papers based on the middling to large towns and following in the main a weekly pattern of publication; the bigger city papers with a more regional market but also enjoying to a varying degree an element of 'national' sales, which typically appeared in daily form six times a week together with a separate weekly edition. The new dailies were very much 'newspapers' as the term would nowadays be understood; but the weeklies were different. Although their growth is inextricably bound up with that of the daily press, they tended to perceive popular literature, and especially serial fiction, as a central feature of their activities, and in the decades following 1855 they developed into the major vehicle of popular culture in Victorian Scotland.

The weekly press in Scotland was diverse in origin, in type, and in scale of operation. Some papers were mere summaries of the week's news, but others, especially if they had a predominantly working-class readership, evolved into a distinctive new form, half newspaper half popular miscellany that was to become the most characteristic feature of the popular market during the second half of the century. One paper in particular whose name became synonymous with working-class aspirations and culture grew in little more than a decade from obscure local beginnings into a major national concern. It was the brainchild of John Leng, the young and energetic managing proprietor of the *Dundee Advertiser* who was on the lookout for fresh opportunities as the press revolution gathered momentum.[28] He brought out two new titles: the first, a daily version of the parent paper selling at ½d., disappointed his hopes—but the second, a new weekly sharing the *Advertiser's* advanced Liberal opinions and combining an efficient news service with a prominent popular literary element succeeded beyond the wildest expectation. On 2 January 1858, the first number of the *Dundee, Perth, and Forfar People's Journal* issued from the office in the Overgate. It marked the beginning of an era.

The prospectus declared:

Innumerable complaints having been addressed to us respecting some of the cheap papers which have sprung up since the abolition of the stamp, as being utterly unworthy of the intelligence and character of the respectable portion of the working-classes, we have resolved on publishing this the first number of a new people's journal of large size, well printed, on good paper, price one penny.

In this new journal our aim will be not to write *down*, but to write *up* to the good sense of the working-classes, whose interests will be carefully considered, and a considerable portion of space devoted to the discussion of questions in which they are specially concerned. By freely publishing letters and communications from working-men, reporting their meetings, epitomizing the newly published biographies of men like Livingstone and Stephenson, who have raised themselves from poverty to lofty reputations, replying to the questions of correspondents on points beyond their information, and co-operating generally in every movement having for its end the intellectual and social advancement of the people, we hope to justify the honourable name of the *People's Journal*.

We shall not, however, confound discrimination with dullness, but shall endeavour to be both merry and wise. There are always tears more than enough; we shall join the laughing side, and laugh whenever we can do so, that those we laugh *at* may also laugh *with* us. Private life shall be sacred from remark, but public foibles may fairly contribute to public fun.

By a careful compilation of the local, district, and general news of the week, we shall endeavour to make the *Journal*, as a newspaper, a favourite at the people's firesides.

Having made arrangements to secure for the *Journal* a large circulation throughout the County, it must prove an excellent medium for advertisements intended to meet the eye of many thousands of the working-classes both in town and country.

Facsimile of the top portion of Page 1 of the first issue of the *People's Journal*. *Source: The Jubilee of the People's Journal.* Reproduced by courtesy of City of Dundee District Council.

Sir John Leng. *Source*: *The Jubilee of the People's Journal*. Reproduced by courtesy of City of Dundee District Council.

Leng's venture was one of many new-style working-class papers struggling into existence and it was by no means first in the field. Just the year
before, the *Falkirk Herald* had responded to the quickening pace of industrialisation in its area by bringing out a special Saturday edition at a penny
while the radical Glasgow weekly, the *Workman* and the *North Briton* of
Edinburgh both anticipated the *Journal's* social and cultural preoccupations
by some years.[29]

The real pioneer was William Chambers, whose magazine the *Edinburgh
Journal* had dominated the popular market during the previous generation.
It was published weekly, cost just 1½d. because it carried no news, and
although one of the first fruits of the Useful Knowledge movement in
Scotland, it was a very bright and readable publication. It contained short
stories, and poems, and jokes and anecdotes, lots of accessible Scottish
history and biography, and articles on popular antiquities. It used
vernacular Scots frequently in dialogue in stories and in anecdotes, and
mixed it freely with the text in discursive passages. It was racy and of the
soil. And it enjoyed a great and deserved success. And this was the
problem: it began to sell well in England and it is clear that by about 1840 it
was finding most of its readers there. It developed a bland and centrist
tone, and a lot of the vigour seeped out of it, a not uncommon fate of
Scottish periodicals whose readership or headquarters (or both) drifted
south.[30]

But the newspaper press did not follow this example. Scottish papers
sold—and very profitably—within Scotland; they did not have to attract an
English readership as a basic fact of their existence. At the same time as
'official' literary culture appeared to decline with the Scottish book trade
dropping as a percentage of the UK market, and the Scottish bourgeoisie
increasingly absorbed in a London-dominated all-British middlebrow
culture, there emerged on an extensive scale a new popular literature
based on a distinctively Scottish newspaper press, owned and produced,
within the country with the outlook and tastes of a Scottish audience
specifically in mind.[31]

The *People's Journal* was in the forefront of this revival. It adopted
Chambers' original formula, added a comprehensive news service to it, and
introduced a new element which had much to do with its later success: the
idea of reader-participation. The *Journal* sought, not as a cheap stunt, but in
sober earnest, to obtain as much material as possible from the pens of its
readers and to pay them properly for it. Tentatively at first, and then with
greater assurance, the paper probed its expanding readership for signs of
intelligence, imagination and literary ability. Precedent supplied guidelines
for most other aspects of the paper, but this was a gamble—or an act of
faith—and the omens were not propitious.

The ignorance, brutishness and incivility of the less 'respectable' portion of
the working people of Scotland was almost axiomatic in educational and

reformist circles at this time, and the prospect of leisure increasing as a result of technical change was occasioning concern.[32] Pressure-groups like the Society for the Diffusion of Useful Knowledge believed that what the people did with their spare time must be controlled, and the provision of carefully-compounded morally bracing cheap reading matter began to be perceived as an urgent priority. Into the breach, accordingly, rushed various publications, amongst them the *Buchan Clown* of Peterhead. It styled itself 'A Moral and Literary Miscellany' and was published monthly at 1½d. It was explicitly reformist in tone, dwelling continually on the coarseness of the common people. The short stories which formed a prominent part of the *Clown's* contents were clearly intended to instil the rudiments of sensitivity and the finer feelings, a crash course in moral education diguised as general literature.[33] It was not a new tactic, of course; arguably it is still happening in every English classroom in the country. At any rate, the *Clown* confronted the matter squarely in the opening issue: how, it demanded, were the people to be advanced?

> The time is not yet far gone by, when the men, after being exhausted with thrashing out the corn, and the women after performing the drudgery work of the house and dairy, had to spend their winter evenings in the wearisome occupation of knitting stockings. It is quite obvious that, in this state of things, the country people could not cultivate their minds, for they had not the necessary time. Now, however, matters are changed. The introduction of thrashing machinery has transferred to brutes or (what is still better) to the inanimate powers of matter, what had formerly to be effected by the human hand; and weaving-looms have, as completely, liberated the females from the continual labour of the 'shank', by outstripping them in the market, both in the quality and the cheapness of the article executed. By this means, several hours each day have been reclaimed, and the question which we wish to press home on our readers is simply this. How have you employed these hours? Is it possible that you have wasted them in listless inactivity, that you have acted as if *mind* formed no part of your nature, as if you were akin only to the beasts that perish? This is, we are persuaded, the case only with a few; the necessity of action and excitement is strongly marked in the human constitution, and, in order to gratify this principle, it is probable that you have had recourse to the gaming table . . . There is still another way in which we are sorry to observe it is become not uncommon for young men to spend their evenings, and that is to assemble in considerable numbers in an alehouse or dram-shop. This is to be lamented above all things. Nevertheless, it is just what is to be expected—for man is a social being, and can only secure full enjoyment from the society of his fellow-men. Instead, therefore, of railing at the associating principle, we shall endeavour to convert it to useful and ennobling purposes. Now, how could time be better spent than in the acquisition and diffusion of knowledge . . .?[34]

The problem with the *Clown's* programme as it came rather ruefully to perceive, was that for it to be effective, the projected audience had to have the inclination and the ability to read. And there appears to have been considerable market resistance. One of William Alexander's early series in the *Free Press* called 'Sketches of Rural Life in Aberdeenshire' deals directly with this point. In the issue for 7 January 1853, for example, his two main characters, the 'maister' of an unendowed school and a tenant farmer called Peter Stark, discuss the availability of cheap reading matter and its effects upon the rural population. The dominie begins:

> So ye're to stand by yer auld text: ye say we've gained in knowledge, but, Peter, this knowledge has never yet reached the masses in sic measure as to mak them, generally speakin, intelligent men. Ye ken yoursel . . . a new wardle's been opened up t'ye—the wardle o' letters, namely; for, however little progress you or I have made in literary pursuits, we've acquired some taste for reading, and can at least read a book or newspaper intelligibly. Noo, this canna be said o' the greater part of our ploughmen and labourers: to confine them an hour at a book is just like condemnin the criminal to an hour o' the treadmill; they baith tak muckle about the same interest in the occupation. Noo, I say, though our means o' gettin information be abundant, and daily becomin mair accessible, yet, if we shun them, and hoot at them, hoo can we expect to derive ony benefit fae them?[35]

One reason for this state of affairs was the generally poor standard of public schooling. Teaching was poorly remunerated and, except in a few favoured middle-class schools, was barely considered to be a profession in its own right. It was seen either as a stepping stone to better things, something a young clergyman might turn his hand to for a year or so while he waited for a kirk, or as a refuge for the inadequate. In pre-compulsory days, poor children went to school more or less as it suited their parents for whom the child's ability to earn might well be an important consideration. The common course lasted for about three sessions, but the effectiveness with which it was taught and the time it took to complete it varied enormously. Irregular attendance often made it impossible to pursue a connected or coherent course except with a few children. It was a pedagogical nightmare, and one of the main stumbling-blocks to the social reformer.[36] As one anonymous correspondent wrote to the *Free Press*:

> Though Lord Brougham has done much to popularise the opinion that 'The schoolmaster is abroad,' I am afraid that his Lordship, in uttering this saying, was merely dreaming; unless we accept it as meaning that the Dominie is out of the country altogether . . . I have been a worker ever since I can remember, and would be the first to defend my workman-brother, if unjustly assailed. But after 50 years' experience, or nearly so, of working men, I unhesitatingly affirm, that an infinitesimal number only owe the Schoolmaster anything . . . many of those who have been benefitted by education . . . cannot attribute it to their school-training, but rather to their own indomitable energy, in over-coming the want of it . . . What does the education of the labourer's family generally consist in? It is in the purest sense rudimental—reading, writing, and cyphering, and that generally not pursued beyond two or three or four quarters at school, each at long intervals, so that on entering the fourth quarter, they start not from the close of the third, but have to return and walk over the same ground trodden in the former three, and which is now trodden for the fourth time . . .[37]

The rote methods of instruction which were used tended in any case to produce no very deep impression upon the children and the perception began to grow that the mere technical ability to read, write and count, might indicate relatively little about the intelligence, moral worth, or cultural attainments of their possessor. This point was forcefully made by William D Latto in the *People's Journal* in June 1858 near the beginning of his long association with the paper. He knew what he was talking about. He had been brought up in poverty in rural Fife, and was himself largely self taught. At the time of writing he was a serving schoolmaster:

Noo, when I charge the ploughmen in this coontry wi' ignorance, I dinna mean to say that very mony of them are sae far back as to be unable to sign their ain names. I believe the maist feck o' them wad be able to do that. Neither do I mean to say that the airt o' readin' is a' thegither unknown among that class. Na, I'll even admit that they do, in some instances, manifest a certain familiarity wi' the science o' numbers. But I maun be allowed to say that a man may hae a certain proficiency in a' thae departments o' learnin' withoot bein' in the proper sense o' the term an intelligent or a moral man . . . in estimatin' the amount o' popular intelligence has it no been hitherto ower aften the practice to confoond the means wi' the end—to measure a man's moral principles by his ability to read, wreat, an' cipher? . . . does the mere mechanical ability to write ane's name afford only guarantee whatever that the individual so qualified is capable o' practisin' virtue, or o' distinguishin' atween gude an' evil? Na, na; something far mair intellectual is requisite to put a man in possession o' self-government that the knack o' tracin' a few crooked lines upon a piece o' paper, for that is the haill extent to whilk the airt o' wreatin' is cultivated by the maist feck o' ploughmen. Let them sit doon to compose a letter, an' the paucity an' incongruity of their ideas will at ance become apparent. The fack is they canna string thegither three lines o' common sense on ony subjeck whatever. I've even kenned some o' them when determined to wreat a lang letter, under the necessity o' makin' atonement for their ain lack o' ideas by copyin' a wheen verses o' the Sang o' Solomon or the prophet Jeremiah! An' education o' that meagre description canna be dignified wi' even the character o' intellectual. The plain truth is, it is naething ava . . .[38]

Such failures, of course, did not spring entirely from shortcomings in the education system. There may well have been positive resistance to the acquisition of literacy skills especially in rural communities with a vigorous oral tradition and limited possibilities for social mobility or in urban areas where language formed an audible line of demarcation between social classes. A character in one of William Alexander's serial novels alludes to this when he says:

Awat, mony ane's fesh'n their craag to the woodie wi' vreetin' . . . Cep' a dominie, or maybe a tradesman to get a skance o't, there's little eese for vreetin' aiven to loons; an' for lassies to hae ocht adee wi't's gaun clean oot o' reel.[39]

It is difficult to make general statements about literacy because it is so hard to measure, but in principle it would seem that two thirds to three quarters of the adult population were notionally literate by the middle years of the century. Even so, the distribution of reading and writing skills was extremely uneven, with levels in the Highlands and the industrial areas falling considerably behind the rest of the country. The Scots often boasted that they had the best-educated population in Europe, but contemporary notions of what constituted reading skill were so primitive that much concealed illiteracy may lie beneath the surface. In 1915, David Hershell Edwards of the *Brechin Advertiser* recorded an interview with a local woman called Margaret Thomson, when she was then nearly eighty which would certainly tend to support this view:

> 'Dod, min,' she often said, 'my mither dee'd fin we were a' young, and as I was the auldest I had to bring up my brithers an' sisters, an' get them a' marriet an' into hooses o' their ain. Sine I marriet Rob Thamson, an' brocht up my ain bairns, an' got them a' oot into the warld. I got unco little time at the schule, and never could write mair than my ain name, for ye see that fin I was to be marriet I was telt that I wad hae to sign my name, an' I managed it, though it took me a month to learn the scrawl. I never was a coonter.' And this was evident from the fact that, when asked the number of her family, she made reply—'I cudna tell ye, just a puckle by guess. But I wis countit the best dancer in the Muirside and the best hand at trampin' blankets in the parish.'[40]

In his 'Enquiry into the Reading Habits of the Working Classes in Scotland' Alastair R Thompson attempted to calculate the ratio between 'active' and 'passive' literacy in the early Victorian population, an actively literate person being defined as one 'who can read so easily and intelligibly as to read for instruction and amusement', the passive or merely technically literate person being one 'who could read but with difficulty and with limited comprehension'. Thompson came to the conclusion that the actively literate proportion of the population might be as low as ten per cent.[41]

Between about 1850 and the early 1870s, however, conditions appear to have improved quite markedly. Once again it is difficult to quantify, but climbing newspaper circulations and the undoubted expansion in other branches of popular publishing would seem to argue for a distinct amelioration in the situation; and if the correspondence columns of contemporary papers form any kind of guide, then it is clear that public anxiety about illiteracy and semi-literacy was at a significantly lower level by 1870 than it was in 1850.[42]

The gradual invasion of society by the printed word itself prompted the urge to read, and people often taught themselves from whatever came to hand, as William Lindsay did, whose life illustrates so many aspects of working-class experience at this time. He was publisher of the Aberdeen editions of the *People's Journal* and one of the leading radicals in the city with a career covering the whole gamut of populist politics during the middle years of the century. He was an early Socialist: an active campaigner in the Ragged Schools movement; Aberdeen correspondent of the Anti-Taxes on Knowledge Association; a moral force Chartist and friend of Lovett, Collins and Ernest Jones; a member of the Anti-Corn Law League through which he came to know Cobden, Bright and Thomson; a temperance reformer and founding member of the Northern Co-operative Company; Aberdeen delegate to the National Association of United Trades, Liverpool, May 1848, and Chairman of the Edinburgh Conference, Spring 1852, which formulated the policy of the Scottish Advanced Liberal Party; Secretary of the Scottish Forty-Shilling Freehold Association; and Aberdeen delegate, Workmen's Peace Association Conference, Paris, 1875. He also taught himself to read, from advertisements.[43]

He was the son of a shoemaker, and was born in 1821 at Newhills near Aberdeen. His father moved into the city when Lindsay was still an infant, and his business prospered; he employed a number of journeymen and his shop in the Hardgate became a place of local resort. As a result of this his window was much sought after by advertisement canvassers and was usually covered with bills and posters. The tax on advertising severely restricted the newspapers as an outlet so alternative means of display had to be found: there was a curious caravan-like contraption, for example, which was wheeled around the streets of Aberdeen and whose canvas sides were covered by colourful advertisements; at night it was illuminated from the inside by candles so that the words could still be read.[44] People used to congregate at Lindsay's father's window at meal times and in the evenings to read and discuss the bills. As he watched them it began to dawn on the young Lindsay, then aged about four, that reading was fun; so he cut the letters from discarded posters until he got the whole alphabet; and then he learned it higgledy-piggledy a letter at a time. His mother got him a card with three-letter words on to show how the symbols were combined, and then began to teach him herself. By the time he was seven, he could read most of the New Testament. He attended school for a few sessions and then, from about the age of twelve, earned his living as a reader. This was a common practice in the workplace at that time, especially amongst skilled trades. The journeymen would open a joint subscription to newspapers and other popular journals, and while the rest of the men worked, one read to them, and his wages were made up later by his colleagues.[45] A cheaper alternative was to hire a literate child, and this is what his father's workmen did. For a small weekly sum Lindsay read to them from the *Aberdeen Journal*, the *Aberdeen Herald*, and the radical *Weekly Dispatch*. He became friends with some of the local mill-girls, and when he discovered that many of them could neither read nor write, invited them round in the evenings after their shift, since cobblers often worked well into the night especially during the winter, and they would sit with their sewing or darning while he read:

> The girls manifested a real interest in these proceedings, and I had now become so entirely their 'guide, philosopher, and friend' that I was frequently asked to read their love letters for them, they being quite unable to do so for themselves, in many cases . . . I kept, for many years, a copy of a letter written by a young lad, and another as it was dictated to me by a young girl. I think I can still reproduce them as they were originally expressed. Here is what Willie Brown said:

My dear Annie,
You say your father winna lat you gang wi' me tae the theatre, that's a pity,
because I'm sure there wid be nae ill o't . . . but we canna help it. There's
anither thing I wid like ye tae speer at yer father. A fortnight after this
there's tae be a gran' masons' ball in the Mutton Brae Hall. Oor Charlie's a
mason, an' he's promised tae get twa tickets tae me, he says it's tae be a
splendid affair, an' I wid like weel to get you for my pairtner. Jimmy
Robison an' me wid baith see ye hame afore it was ower late. Wid ye meet
me next Sunday mornin' aboot aucht o'clock at the Sillerton Gate in St.
Andrew Street, an' we'll hae a walk roon by Cornhill an' get a flow'r till ye
afore we come hame.

Your affectionate freen,
Willie Brown

This was how Mary Ross directed me to write and scorch her lover with the
fire of her indignation:

Tell him that I wint neen o's insults. He gart me stan' at the fit o' College
Street last Fiersday nicht an' the win' blawin' on me till I thought ma nose
wid come aff. He needna say that he wis keepit ower lang at's work, oor
Tam saw 'im gaun up his ain clossie an 'oor afore I wis waitin' him, wi's
han's in his jacket pooches, whistlin' a' the road. Tell him gin he's nae
wintin' me I'm nae wintin' him, I can get plenty o' lads, mair than I ken fat
tae dee wi' . . . Tell 'im there wis a lad up at oor hoose yestreen, bigger an'
better looking' gin him, so you can jist tell 'im gin he's nae to meet me at the
exact time that he promises, nae tae come back to oor house ava, bit if he
dis wint tae see me he can come to oor back green neyst Seterday nicht an'
haave up a starn san' at oor window, an' I'll ken it's him.[46]

In the country districts likewise, the newspaper became the principal
vehicle of the printed word, and in many districts there was a recognised
'reader'. His neighbours would assemble at the house to which the paper
was addressed and duly hear it read through; then there would be
discussion. People often formed clubs to help them buy a paper, and at the
annual settling up, the person at the end of the chain would bring in the
copies for the year and they would be divided up equally amongst the
members.[47] How the newspaper was read varied of course from household
to household, but in the more enlightened ones it is clear that it was used
for mutual instruction:

There are mony systematic peculiarities in newspaper readers which are
worth bein' noticed, as from them we may form a general outline of a man's
disposition. I could tell you the names of men (that is, gudemen) whose habit is,
on the evening of the newspaper, to appropriate a' the readin' to themselves.
Observe this individual fu he sets himsel' up in his corner wi' the air o' an
oracle, puts on his spectacles, draws the lamp close by himsel', an', haudin' the
paper in sic a way as to screen the lave fae the rays o' that luminary, he reads
aff 'hale wheel,' shapin' the unmanagable words in's ain caums; while his
hearers, nae bein' incommodit by the ootward brilliancy, are the mair apt to be
mentally enlightened . . .
There's anither kin' o' reader still mair intolerable than this man—we mean

him who pounces upo' the paper as seen's the laddie feshes it hame. He sits an' reads as lang at ae side as he might gae owre it a', yet never announces a word o' the intelligence, nor would he divide the paper in twa to accomodat anither; an' sud ony ane venture to luik owre his shou'der, he snarls as a snappish cur does if ony ane interferes wi' him fan he has something that skites better in's cheek than mealy sids . . .

But do dee justice to the readin' public, there are a few men o' real sterlin' honesty. O' this num'er is the man who can tak a peep o' the paper fan the family are nae met, but fan they're gather't roun the ingle he hands it to a boy and tell him to 'read *alood*'.

Noo, the laddie reads clearly an' distinctly, an' should a hard word occur, the dictionary is leukit, so that naething is lost—the haill circle, be it muckle or little, gatherin' information, and, maist o' a', the min' o' the youthfu' reader is led to expand . . .

Few things make a chiel mair blate-like than the want o' a newspaper, especially in the time o' some notable movement like the present war; yet there's mony ane would wus for a paper, regalarly, that canna get it. We canna afford a paper oor leen, an' though some ane, at twa miles distance or so, would tak a share, the intermediate neibor is nae a reader o' newspapers, nor onything else; so we maun gie up the proposal. But lately, I heard a person say concernin' a neibour that he would never mention 'paper' to him again, as he had formerly broken up an excellent club fan he had the paper quite handy the second day, at the rate o' three shillins a year. Noo, fat would ye make o' a man like that? An' considerin that the same individual has a family comin' fast to years o' discretion, hoo are they likely to be educated?[48]

The paper which took its role as a popular instructor most seriously and took most pains with its distribution system to make sure that country areas were properly served was the *People's Journal*. Its sheer ubiquity crops up again and again in the literature. An old business acquaintance of William Lindsay told him, years afterwards, that although he disliked the paper's politics, he felt bound to testify that after a lifetime travelling in the north of Scotland, he had seen it in places where he had never seen a leaf of printed matter before, an opinion which many schoolmasters had confirmed, especially in the remoter parts, and added as his conviction that it had done more to stimulate the people to read and think for themselves than anything else he knew.[49] One of the *Journal's* correspondents added:

. . . in many country districts and villages in the north of Scotland a new era may date in the civilisation and manners of the people. Instead of the Saturday evening alehouse there is the Saturday evening fireside—instead of the excited or half-sottish 'jaw' there is the 'news' of the week, with a fresh supply of wholesome literature. But this is not all. A love for reading is thus engendered among communities of good average intelligence, where, strange as it may seem, before the introducton of the *Journal* in dozens of families no trace of any volume could be found but the Bible, the Church Record, and the children's school-books. But now such communities are fast introducing 'penny readings', the weekly reports of which stimulate other communities to adopt the same, and everything bids fair for a complete revolution in the educational standards of our country.[50]

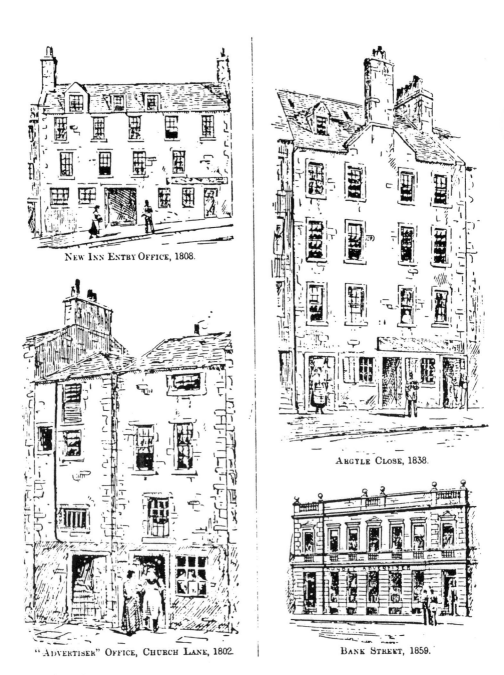

NEW INN ENTRY OFFICE, 1808.

ARGYLE CLOSE, 1838.

"ADVERTISER" OFFICE, CHURCH LANE, 1802.

BANK STREET, 1859.

The Offices of the *Dundee Advertiser* and *People's Journal* from 1802 to 1859. *Source: How a Newspaper is Printed*. Reproduced by courtesy of City of Dundee District Council.

Of course, the *Journal* was never squeamish about self-advertisement, but some of the testimony, especially from children seems transparently sincere, like the little girl who wrote in November 1869, 'If it had not been for the *People's Journal* I never would have learned to read.'[51]

In 1858 the *People's Journal* was very much a local paper based on the Dundee/Perth axis and selling mainly in the northern half of the Tay basin. Leng had laid his preparations well, and the *Journal* began with a sound advertising base and a claimed circulation of around 7,000 copies a week. It was a city paper and devoted itself assiduously to urban affairs; but it treated the country market seriously as well, and this as much as anything was to lay the foundation of its later success. As a radical paper it encountered the usual problems with the established agencies. It started with thirteen country agents, mainly booksellers, but including a saddler, a butcher, a postmaster and a shoemaker, and its geographical boundaries were defined by Montrose in the north, Coupar Angus in the south, and Perth and Blairgowrie in the west. The first phase of expansion took place as infill within this original territory; in a few months the number of agencies had increased twofold, and the circulation doubled in a year. In 1859 came the first of the district editions, which was to become the basic strategy for the whole subsequent growth of the *Journal* and the means by which it increased its coverage geographically until it achieved the status of a national paper—arguably the first in Scotland.

Fife was long-established *Dundee Advertiser* territory, and it was only natural that when the new paper was launched it too should go on sale in

The *Dundee Advertiser* and *People's Journal* Office (*c.* 1908). *Source*: *The Jubilee of the People's Journal*. Reproduced by courtesy of City of Dundee District Council.

the Kingdom. In order for this to be done, however, it had to be parcelled up, loaded on to the ferry, sailed across the Tay, unloaded at the other side, and then carted to Cupar in a horse van.[52] One way round these difficulties would be to create a separate edition and print it in Fife. This was put to Leng by the enterprising bookseller and printer Alexander Westwood of Cupar, who added that he himself should edit and publish it. Leng agreed at once, and so began a business connection that was to last for nearly half a century. As a radical and a former weaver, Westwood's credentials were sound, and his earlier years as a book-canvasser for Chambers had given him an intimate knowledge of the county and a large number of business contacts within it. He was likewise given sole responsibility for appointing agents and correspondents, and thus equipped he proceded to open up Fife as a sphere of influence for the *People's Journal*. Two ideas were brought into play here that marked all the paper's subsequent operations: firstly, maximum availability, using every link in the existing communication and distribution network, railways, coaches, the postal service, carriers and carters and packmen and pedlars, to get the paper to the people; and secondly, taking on and beating established papers in their own back yard by means of saturation local news coverage.[53] In the ensuing eighteen months, total circulation almost doubled again. By 1862 it stood at 37,500, the biggest for any weekly paper outside London—a position the *Journal* was to hold until 1914 at least.

A key figure in the national growth of the paper was the group's commercial manager and general circulation wizard James Littlejohn. He was born in Perth in 1822, it may be assumed in fairly humble circumstances, since he spent some years as a pupil-teacher in a local school which was a common channel of upward mobility for bright lower-class children. He progressed to the University of Glasgow with the intention of studying for the ministry, but his health broke down and he turned to journalism for a living. He worked on the *Perthshire Courier*, and did some freelancing for the *Dundee Advertiser* on the side. Leng liked his style and offered him a job, probably in 1854, quickly realised that his gifts were administrative rather than literary, and within a year Littlejohn found himself in charge of the business side of the paper. It was he who created the urban agencies for the *People's Journal* from which the whole rural network grew, and superintended the major changes in the system of distribution when the parent paper went daily in 1861.[54]

The internal records of John Leng and Co do not seem to have survived, so that we do not know how the decision was taken to extend northwards after Fife had been consolidated. Aberdeen had lain within the general orbit of the *Advertiser* for a number of years, it is true, but relatively poor communications with the north as well as the formidable opposition of the Aberdeen papers, had limited expansion in this direction. In the old days copies for the northern city had to be taken to Forfar in order to catch the Perth mail coach, but even after the coming of the railways parcels for Aberdeen were carted more than twenty miles by horse-van to Guthrie station about half way between Arbroath and Forfar where the Caledonian

Railway Company's line from Perth joined that of the Scottish North-Eastern Company completing the main route north.[55]

A major thrust into the North-East must have seemed a logical, indeed even an inevitable, step if the paper was to entertain serious ambitions beyond the boundaries of Strathtay, just as William Lindsay must have seemed the obvious choice to handle the Aberdeen end if he could be induced to take it on. As a business opportunity, the attractions were considerable: there was no serious competition at the price—the *Free Press* at this period of its existence was one of the most beautifully produced papers in Scotland, but it was still selling at 3*d*. unstamped; politically it offered a chance to challenge East Coast Conservatism in its very bastions. Above all, perhaps, it was an opportunity to break into the biggest pool of readers of any rural area in Scotland. In 1863 an act passed through Parliament to unite the Dundee and Arbroath Railway with the Scottish North-Eastern. This meant a single set of freight tariffs for the north line and brought Aberdeen and its hinterland within effective range of Leng's presses.[56]

Shortly afterwards, Lindsay received a visit; indeed, two visits, and both of them were of interest:

It was the late Mr, afterwards Dr, William Alexander, the author of 'Johnny Gibb', who first asked me if I sold the *People's Journal* at my shop in Gallowgate. I replied that it had not been, but that some of the flaxdressers at Broadford had ordered copies, and that I was enquiring about it. A few evenings after that conversation, a gentleman called at my place of business . . . I was much interested in his appearance. His countenance expressed keen intelligence, mixed with a vein of playful humour. He at once began conversation, not on any specific business, as I expected, but on the current topics of the day, keeping on a running commentary on things in general, by which I saw that my visitor had public affairs quite at his finger ends. After a bit, he broke in with the question, 'Do you know the *People's Journal?*' I said 'only imperfectly', and mentioned that a gentleman connected with the Press in Aberdeen had asked me the same question a few evenings before. So far as I can remember, he replied to this as follows: 'Well, I have come to Aberdeen to make you acquainted with it, and to make you make a great many other people acquainted with it. The Proprietors of the *Journal* have been enquiring about who would be the likeliest person to become their local publisher, as they mean to print a local edition for Aberdeen, and Mr John Leng, one of the Proprietors, and myself, have come to the conclusion that you are the man we want.' He then proceeded with business details all of which seemed to be so fair and reasonable, that I felt that that was all right. Our interview ended, however, with me asking a week to consider the matter. This was ultimately agreed to. The time passed away. My friend put in an appearance at the end of the week, and to make a long story short, a formal agreement constituting me their Aberdeen publisher, was completed.

The gentleman who carried through this transaction was the late Mr James Littlejohn, the then Commercial Manager of the *Dundee Advertiser* . . . During the seventeen years that we wrought together in business, we travelled over many parts of the country, establishing agencies, appointing correspondents, and, generally, promoting the circulation of the *People's Journal* in the North of Scotland.[57]

And so the Aberdeen, Banff, and Kincardine *People's Journal* came into being. At first, and for a number of years, it was split printed. That is verso pages (numbers two and four) were printed in Dundee and were standard with the Dundee edition, while recto pages (numbers one and three) were left blank for Lindsay to complete with local advertisements and news on his presses in Aberdeen. As one would expect there was detailed news coverage of the towns and villages of the North-East heartland, but the inclusion of places like Inverness, Wick and Stromness, indicated the territorial ambitions of the paper. Aberdeen was intended to be a springboard for the whole North of Scotland. And so it proved.

In the Spring of 1864 the combined circulation of the *Journal* stood at slightly over 58,000 copies a week. Within two years it topped 100,000 and a further three district editions were launched, two—one each for Perth and Forfar—within the original hinterland, the third, the so-called 'South' (but actually Edinburgh) edition marking a further extension of territory to include the whole of the eastern half of Scotland. Aberdeen developed separate city and country editions the following year,and the *Journal* was already beginning to be perceived as a national paper.[58] By 1875, circulation was approaching 130,000 copies a week. A continuous increase in productive capacity took place, most of it concentrated in Dundee where the bulk of the *Journal* was printed; that year two rotary web presses were installed with a combined capacity of 30,000 copies per hour.[59] The paper itself grew bigger; by 1875 the Dundee edition was eighteen columns wide when opened out and had become almost unmanageably large.

By 1890 sales were being authenticated by outside accountants, and the paper was claiming the biggest certified circulation in Scotland.[60] It had also broken into the industrial Midlands and the densely populated West Central Lowlands with separate editions for Glasgow and West of Scotland, and Stirling and Clackmannan. There were now eleven of these in all, including the two just mentioned: Aberdeen City, Dundee, Perthshire, Fife and Kinross, Northern Counties (Inverness, Caithness, Sutherland and North Isles—printed by William Lindsay in Aberdeen), the North-East Counties edition for Aberdeenshire, Banffshire and Kindcardine; a Forfarshire (East Coast) edition, including Montrose, Brechin, and Arbroath, and a Forfarshire county edition.

By 1914, circulation stood at around a quarter of a million copies.

The Glasgow and Edinburgh papers had been fused into a single 'National' edition; there was now also an Irish edition and two separate pictorial editions, making thirteen in all. During the period two new titles had been started, the enormously popular literary miscellany the *People's Friend* in 1869, and the leading Dundee evening paper, the *Evening Telegraph* in 1877. The headquarters of Leng & Co had grown to encompass more than forty thousand square feet of space. It was five storeys high and a street long. Its great presses were capable by 1900 of producing four-page papers at the rate of 164,000 copies an hour. One issue of the *People's Journal* alone weighed twenty-five tons, and was available for sale in some twelve thousand newsagents. Pasted together end to end its weekly columns

The Certified Circulation of the PEOPLE'S JOURNAL is
219,545 Copies Weekly.

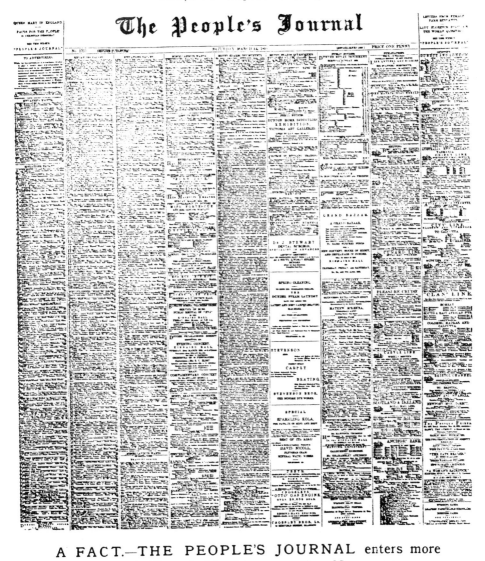

A FACT.—THE PEOPLE'S JOURNAL enters more
Scottish Households than any other Newspaper.

Certified Circulation of the *People's Journal* (c. 1890). *Source: How a Newspaper is Printed.* Reproduced by courtesy of City of Dundee District Council.

stretched for almost 9,000 miles.[61] And the business was profitable, judging at least by the elegant houses some of the partners and senior staff contrived to raise for themselves along the pleasant shores of the Firth. Considered in this light, it is perhaps surprising that the political stance of the *Dundee Advertiser* group remained as consistent as it did.

Yet when John Leng stood for Parliament in one of the Dundee seats in 1889, his programme was as radical as any then available in Scotland, including payment of MPs, triennial parliaments, universal adult suffrage, free education, poor law reform, disestablishment of state churches, and nationalisation of the land.[62]

The *People's Journal* reflected the views of its creator, and remained in the forefront of advanced Liberalism throughout the period. It was strongly Abolitionist, and supported the North during the American Civil War—unlike many Scottish papers. It was anti-Imperialist while Leng lived, and supported Gladstone through the Home Rule crisis and the split in the Liberal Party; it campaigned ceaselessly for extension of the franchise, and a whole range of social and economic reforms, particularly those affecting the working class with whose interests the paper remained identified throughout. The views of the editor William Latto also influenced the paper strongly during the thirty-eight years he guided its affairs. These consisted of powerful class-identification based on a long-term involvement in radical politics; and Latto did not have to rely on his imagination when he came to depict the problems of the poor. He had experienced them at first hand.[63]

He was born in the parish of Ceres in Fife on 27 June 1823, and received only the most rudimentary schooling before becoming a herd at about the age of ten. He was apprenticed to a handloom weaver and set up his own loom in Ceres village at the age of fourteen. His interest in politics was awakened early and he studied contemporary affairs assiduously. He listened eagerly to wandering Chartist orators and became a strong supporter of the 'Six Points'. He was all for Feargus O'Connor and 'physical force', and on one occasion was chosen to lead the Ceres contingent to a great Chartist rally on Monkstown moor carrying the banner, a young tree upside down and bearing the legend 'Let tyranny be uprooted'. The 'Ten Years' Conflict' was then reaching its height and Latto became one of the first members of the new Free Church in Ceres when it was formed in 1843. Before long he also became involved in the Free Trade movement and began to write bits of prose and verse for the reforming papers in Fife. He had meantime been pursuing a vigorous programme of self-improvement (he was in many ways a typical Victorian autodidact), studying English grammar while he worked from a text book attached to his loom. A number of neighbours helped him, and the Free Kirk minister taught him Latin and lent him books.

His efforts bore fruit and in the summer of 1846 he became master of a small subscription school in the neighbourhood. He worked there for the next two years, educating the children by day and himself by night, scraping together some savings, and starting to find his feet as a writer with pieces appearing in the *Fife Herald*, *Hogg's Instructor*, and the *Northern*

Warder of Dundee. He won a small bursary which enabled him to attend the Free Church training college at Moray House in Edinburgh, and on qualifying he took a post at Johnshaven near Inverbervie, where he taught for the next eleven years, apparently with considerable success.

When the *People's Journal* started up Latto became a paid contributor and he supplied a fortnightly letter in the vernacular on a wide variety of social and political subjects. Soon he was writing leaders and reviews for the *Journal* and the *Dundee Advertiser*, and when the latter went daily in the winter of 1860–61, he became editor of the *Journal* in his own right. He kept up his public involvement in radical politics for some years thereafter. For example he addressed the great rally on the Magdalene Green at Dundee during the agitation to extend the franchise to county house-holders; he was secretary of the East of Scotland Reform Union working to promote manhood suffrage and the ballot, and, of course, he dealt with the whole spectrum of politics, international, national, and local in the columns of his paper for a period of nearly forty years.[64]

On the domestic front he focused attention on working-class movements and social issues affecting the working classes such as the housing of the poor, the evils of the bothy system, trade unionism and unemployment, work conditions and wages, education for children and adults, emigration, and co-operation.

To Latto probably more than anyone else the paper's most distinctive feature is due: its unique openness to its readers, its eagerness to act as a platform for their opinions and experiences, its genuine readiness to enter into dialogue with them. It is this that gives the *Journal* its status, perhaps unique in literature of this type, as a working-class paper which was not simply intended to be purchased by lower social classes, but was to a significant degree intended to be written by them. Nor was their contribution confined to the correspondence columns, although these were prominent and printed under the heading 'The People's Opinion' immediately next to the leaders; reader opinion was assimilated into the central identity of the paper by the commissioning and printing of leading articles by working men, and there was a lot of other material from the same source.

From Latto too came that enthusiasm for Scottish popular culture which was so marked a feature of the paper.[65] There was a lot of the vernacular in it; it was, after all, the language of the people—and he ran his own column in Scots for many years under the pseudonym 'Tammas Bodkin'. There were frequent series on things like Scots proverbs and popular songs, and long and detailed pieces on Scottish history, both national and local, often very ambitious in scope. For example in 1868 there was a special series by George Gilfillan entitled 'Eminent Scotchmen, being a New Series of the Scots Worthies' which taken altogether amounted to a political and literary history of Scotland of quite amazing range and fullness. Among the people who featured in it were Wallace, Bruce, James I, James IV, early Scottish authors including Thomas the Rhymer, Barbour, Wintoun and Blin Hary—with extensive quotations in modernised spelling—James V, William

Dunbar, Gavin Douglas, Sir David Lyndsay (again with large quotation from the originals), Mary Queen of Scots, George Buchanan, John Knox, Andrew Melville, Drummond of Hawthornden, the Marquis of Montrose, Graham of Claverhouse, Fletcher of Saltoun, and so on; and there was a lot of material like this in the *Journal* during the second half of the century. Nor was its concern with the collective past limited to orthodox history. It took a pioneering interest in what was then called 'popular antiquities'—a useful phrase, covering what would nowadays come under the headings of folklore and social and economic history—conditions of everyday life amongst the common people in former times, their social organisation, work methods and techniques, their systems of value and belief (especially abberrant ones like witchcraft, ghosts and fairy lore). An excellent example of this was a series which ran through most of 1876 with the title 'Life in Two Worlds in Perthshire' which dealt with the social life and popular culture of the area including articles on popular poets and ballad writers; domestic life at the end of the eighteenth century; the housing of the agricultural population; 'shank night' and other marriage customs, including 'feet washing', 'the send' and penny weddings; items of popular diet; beggars; schools and schoolmasters and the influence of the bible and catechism on literacy; other popular reading matter like Boston's *Fourfold State*, *Pilgrim's Progress*, and chapbooks like 'Thrummy Cap', 'The History of Simple John', 'The Life of George Buchanan', Hary's 'Wallace' and 'Satan's Invisible World Discovered'; the circulation of printed ballads in country districts, including 'Sir James the Rose', 'Gregor's Ghost', 'The Dowie Dens o' Yarrow' and various Robin Hood ballads: it spoke about cockfighting; funeral customs; lykwakes and resurrectionists; smugglers; the decline of hellfire Calvinism; army recruiting; harvest and harvest homes; and the growth of interest in secular politics among the common people in the wake of the great Reform Act of 1832.[66]

It was with imaginative writing, however, that the *Journal* recorded its greatest success in the field of reader-participation, leading to a degree of literary collectivism quite possibly unique in the annals of the British press.[67] The first poetry competition was announced within a fortnight of the paper's start, and got a good response. 'Nothing', Leng declared, 'has ever gratified us more than to have placed in our hands such a body of evidence attesting the intelligence of the classes whom we specially address, and the right feeling which pervades them. . . . Our wish is that the *People's Journal* should be as much their own production as possible.'[68] The winning pieces were printed in the paper and a second competition at once announced. It got nearly fifty entries.[69]

Next Leng offered a complete Shakespeare for an 'Original Tale of Scottish Life' not exceeding four thousand words, the winner to be published. There were seven entries.[70] But each successive competition brought a larger response. Within a year there were cash prizes ranging from 10 shillings to 50 shillings and about three dozen story scripts each time. He tried various methods of assessment, and called in outside experts or even teams of experts as the scale of participation grew. George Gilfillan judged the poetry in this way for a number of years.[71] He even enfranchised the readers, publishing a leet of stories or poems, and then printing voting slips in the *Journal* so that the people could pick the winners for themselves.[72]

The paper actively sought out imaginative writing from its readers over and above the competition system, and would print it if considered good enough. There was a column 'To Correspondents' which was addressed mainly to the authors of rejected manuscripts, telling them in no uncertain terms why their piece had found its way into the editorial bin, but often as well pointing helpfully to what was good in their writing and offering detailed technical advice. Latto had a talent for this and the column was popular, often the first thing general readers looked at. Over the years it built up in to a useful correspondence course in creative writing.[73] In 1866 Latto ran a competition for an original Scottish song, just the words, it was not necessary to supply the tune. There were four hundred entries, and the announcement of the prize-list had to be delayed for weeks while the adjudicator grappled with them. On the 29th of December he finally presented his report:

It has been affirmed that the present age is not favourable to the development of the poetic faculty. People are said to be too deeply engrossed in mere money-getting now-a-days for having the leisure necessary to the cultivation of the imagination to its fullest extent. The voice of the Delphic oracle, it is alleged, has been drowned amid the roar of the factory, the shriek of the steam whistle, and the ear-splitting rattle of the railway train. We have been taught to expect henceforth nothing worthy the name of poetry—nothing, at least, fitted to compete with the great masterpieces of the poets who flourished in bygone ages. There is, perhaps, a certain amount of truth in these averments. This is emphatically a 'fast' age. We travel at railway speed. We make haste to be rich. Competition has penetrated into every pursuit, even into the meditative haunts of the poet. Formerly, a great poem was the work of a lifetime. Now, it must be written impromptu. The sons of song are no longer content to 'cultivate literature on a little oatmeal'. There is a ready market for their wares, and, seeing they are but men, it is not wonderful that they should be eager to transmute their crude ores of thought into 'money current with the merchant'. What we lack in the quality of our modern poetry, however, we have in quantity. There never was a time probably, when poetry of a certain kind was more plentiful than it is at present. Every second person one meets has at one period or other of his life essayed to climb Parnassus. Our own columns, from week to week, bear ample testimony to the truth of this assertion. We mow down whole swathes of embryonic poets every time we lift our critical sickle. Yet no sooner is one tuneful regiment smitten down than another is ready to take its place. We do not complain of this persistency on the part of our youthful songsters. The rather do we rejoice that they possess so much pluck and perseverance. It is something to get working men and women to write anything—even bad verses. In order to do so they must think, and a habit of reflection once formed may lead to valuable results. . .[74]

A few years later, there was a competition for original melodies, settings of the first three Christmas prize poems of 1874. There were more than three hundred entries.

Latto introduced Christmas and New Year story competitions during the sixties to mark the holiday with a special fiction supplement. It did much to revive the idea of Christmas as a special day in Scotland throughout large parts of which it had ceased to be celebrated. Conditions were announced in the Autumn and writing for it became a popular activity—the more so as prize money increased. In 1866, for example, it was £5 for first. The example of Dickens was fatally present in many of these stories over the years: a lot of them were set in London and had Cockney-speaking characters (or as nearly so as could be contrived), but they sometimes possessed considerable accuracy, freshness and vigour if their creators could be persuaded to stick to New Year, stay in Scotland, and write about something they had actually experienced. There is a pleasing example of this in the issue for 31 December 1870, a little courtship story sent in by a writer in Ontario. It is set in the North-East in midwinter, and the hero is determined to deliver his father's newspaper to the next reader in the chain because he loves his daughter, but he is too bashful to say so and the paper is his only excuse to go. The snag is that a full blizzard is raging outside. He falls in the river and is discovered outside his sweetheart's door a speechless pillar of ice with the *Aberdeen Journal* frozen in his hand. They thaw him out, and as the goodwife prises the paper from his fingers she remarks, philosophically, 'Waesucks for ye, Davie Chalmers—they'll hae gleg een wha reads ye the nicht.'

A separate Christmas supplement had to be issued in 1868 because the paper could not hold everything Latto wanted to print, and next year the problem became even more acute. He got half a hundredweight of entries: two hundred and twenty-five short stories, six hundred and five poems, and two hundred and thirty-five letters. It was a terrible job just processing the stuff because of the precautions the anxious authors had taken to ensure it got safely through the mail:

> The mere opening of the letters and packages, and the jotting down of titles, etc., occupied us for about eighteen hours. The process involved close attention and hard manual labour. A bushel of packages to open at a down-sitting is no joke. And then, too, the opening process was rendered unnecessarily difficult in a good many instances by the 'siccar' way in which they had been sealed, pasted and otherwise closed up. Sealing-wax, common bees'-wax, rosin, weavers' dressing, glue, gum, tape (red, white, and blue), cords of all sizes, from common twine to cart ropes, brass wire even, were some of the fasteners made use of in order to prevent the outside world from knowing what the package contained.[75]

The *Journal* had opened a Pandora's Box of popular literature and become completely overwhelmed by the response; a separate publication, the *People's Friend*, had to be started to contain the overspill. At first it appeared monthly, but even this was not enough so on 5 January 1870 it was re-issued as a weekly with its own editorial staff.[76] Unlike the *Journal*, the *Friend* did not draw attention to itself or celebrate its own success: ten years of publication, the thousandth issue, the half-jubilee all passed without comment; there was no leader or other significant editorial statement, so far as I am aware, at any time during the nineteenth century. All of which gives a particular interest to the introductory remarks 'Our Design and Purpose' written by Leng for the first of the new series.

> In issuing the first number of the New Series of THE PEOPLE'S FRIEND, we desire to present to our readers a clear and full explanation of the aim we have in view, and the object we desire to accomplish. The idea of the periodical, as well as the nature of it, was suggested by the pleasing result which attended the Prize Competitions which have from time to time taken place in connection with THE PEOPLE'S JOURNAL. The great and wide-spread interest which these excited, and the surprising amount of literary talent which they elicited, showed us that it wanted but the establishment of a regular and suitable medium to call forth a wide manifestation of mental power which was lying dormant, and to provide literary entertainment which the masses of the people would welcome with eager avidity. This impression was fully confirmed by the success which a year ago attended the production and publication of our Christmas Number. The large number of excellent productions sent in from all parts of the country, the immense circulation which the sheet attained, and the many hearty expressions of approbation which reached us, made us resolve at once to follow out the idea we had formed, and forthwith was commenced 'THE PEOPLE'S FRIEND'.[77]

The *Friend* introduced a fixed rate of payment, and this principle was in time extended to the *Journal*. As the century advanced contributions became more sophisticated; by 1900 the latter was offering £100 for a 60–80,000 word serial novel, and ten guineas for a short story.[78] The paper itself became more diverse in its perception of its readers' needs and the demands it made upon them. Jokes and 'Varieties' were introduced; a ladies' column and a problem page, conducted by that doyenne of Scots lady journalists Jessie King, late of the *Perthsire Advertiser*;[79] a children's column; free medical and legal advice, a service for finding missing relatives; a chess and draughts section; sports reports; cartoons, including cartoon strips which although not a regular feature pre-date by some years the *San Francisco Examiner's* 'Little Bears and Little Tigers' usually considered the earliest example of the form;[80] illustrations, firstly by means of plaster engraving and then zincography; and finally even the 'new journalism' with its obsessive interest in the private lives of actresses and its instinctive preference for the picture to the word as a means of communication.[81] As Latto entered his sixties, the *Journal* began another long period of rapid growth. It got bigger and more complicated, and he was unable to impose his personality on it as he had before, but the 'new journalism' he resisted to the end. He retired in December 1898 aged 75, and died the following summer. 'The Journal was fortunate in its first editor, W D Latto', a later contributor wrote. 'He stamped his strong Scottish personality upon the People's Journal . . . From the first it showed the greatest sympathy with the workers, and constituted itself champion of the working man . . . the policy of the paper was founded on personal freedom, political rights, and international peace . . . [he] made it the organ of the Scottish democracy.'[82]

The principal feature of his long tenure of the editorial chair was his reverence for the printed word, not just as a thing in itself, but as an agency of great and transforming power. Of course he was not alone in this view; it can be encountered during the period almost wherever one cares to look—but one of the most memorable expressions of it in the Scottish press comes from the Rev Dr Norman MacLeod, minister of the Barony Kirk in Glasgow and editor of the popular weekly *Good Words*, in a speech delivered to the letterpress printers of Glasgow at their annual *soirée* on 14 January 1860, with Mr James Hedderwick of the *Glasgow Citizen* in the chair:

> I cannot imagine anything on the face of this earth so wonderful as printing or so wonderful as books. Why, it is no exaggeration to say that the men now before me print every single morning in Glasgow more words, produce more matter, in twenty-four hours than was ever written by the hand during twenty-four centuries before the invention of printing. (Hear, hear, and applause.) Only think what an extraordinary thing this thing called a book is? Surely printing is like the power of witchcraft. Here, for example a man is multiplied ten thousand times ten thousand over. You have such power over him that he never dies. He is in a hundred places at the same time, and he lives on from generation to generation. You so multiply the man—you invest him with such extraordinary powers of immortality, that he lives in every house, and dwells, it may be, in every cottage in the land. The poorest man may have the greatest authors that ever lived to delight him. In the middle of the night the greatest poets that ever breathed come and recite to him their most beautiful poems; the noblest dramatists will repeat their dramas; the finest orations which ever issed from the senate or the bar are placed within his reach; and the noblest and most eloquent preachers that ever preached will recite again to him their sermons. He has this power, that he can summon travellers from the centre of Africa or from the North Pole, and relate their travels; and in this Republic of Letters the mightiest man will come down and speak to the poorest artizan with the same noble language that he addresses to kings and emperors. Nay, those very kings and emperors will come to where the artizan lives, and tell all or many of the state secrets, and open their hearts to him . . . I can state assuredly that the press is one of the greatest powers under God for the advancement of the civilisation of man. (Hear, hear.)[83]

Latto's ghost would echo 'amen' to much, probably all of this. It is central to the philosophy of the *People's Journal* while it was edited by him—with this difference. He would never have allowed the common man to be so passive; Latto's artisan would have talked back, introduced evidence from his own experience, referred to notes drawn from the leading authors of the day, and finally, who knows . . . have transformed the argument into a serial novel and sold it to a newspaper?

TWO

The Scoatch Depairtment

The Press and the Vernacular

One of the most striking things about the popular press in Victorian Scotland was its readiness to use the language of the people—vernacular Scots. This took place on an extensive scale and in some respects was pioneering, indeed revolutionary, in its implications. A whole new vernacular prose came into being with a range and diversity unknown for centuries.

According to the standard accounts, the Scots prose tradition disappeared in the early seventeenth century, after the Reformation. The main line of the vernacular tradition continued in poetry with Ramsay, Fergusson and Burns, while Scots prose assumed a subsidiary role in the dialogue of novelists like Scott, Hogg, and Stevenson, whose principal medium was standard English.

But the language of the law and of public administration retained a significant amount of Scots features for at least a century after 1603, and it was long before they disappeared entirely from the Kirk. Scots continued to be the preferred vehicle for large areas of life as public records, diaries, sermons and the popular tale collections known as chapbooks bear witness. The chapbooks are particularly important because they formed the staple secular reading-matter of the great majority of Scots until well into the nineteenth century.[1]

The survival of spoken Scots has also been underestimated. The editors of the *Concise Scots Dictionary*, for example, appear to consider it practically defunct by the time of the Union: 'It is doubtless possible to exaggerate the length things had gone by the late seventeenth century, and individuals no doubt varied, as they do today. But the overall impression must be that . . . from this time onwards, forms of speech which mostly favoured traditional Scots usages were identified with conservatives, eccentrics and, especially, with the common people'[2]—i.e. about 95 per cent of the Lowland nation.

Attempts to reform spoken idiom in Scotland by agencies like the elocution movement have received some emphasis, but there is little evidence that they made much headway. The example usually cited is the course of lectures delivered by Thomas Sheridan who harangued audiences in Edinburgh in the autumn of 1773 on the finer points of English pronunciation—in a rich Irish brogue.[3] But elocutionism was often associated with blackguardism and imposture, and the general run of practitioners seem to have been pretty doubtful characters: such as the notable professor of a later generation who fell foul of the Aberdonian scandal sheet *The Squib*, and was 'papered' as follows:

MALCOLM ROBERTSON, *Professor of Elocution and Rope-Maker*, for Elocution Pamphlet. We do not depreciate the merits of Elocution, but we would rather hear the cash which he owes us tinkling in our coffer, than listen to him bellowing out 'Dinna shak' your gory locks at me man.'[4]

Although thanks to the chapbooks the Scots common reader was familiar with a wide range of standard and non-standard written forms, he had little direct access to English as a sound-system until the broadcasting network expanded during the present century. English orthography gave an uncertain guide to pronunciation, and the reading learner was heavily dependent on the teacher's own usage, as the following example may show:

> 'And how did you contrive to communicate the pronunciation when you taught the English language . . .?'
>   'I lait it a doon ba rool, ye see, an' re-ad it ba exampal.'
>   'In the case of o o?'
>   'I taul them for a constant rool that twa o's soon'it ay the voual u; for instance, g,o,o,d, *gweed*.'[5]

The evidence seems clear that in elementary education generally during the first half of the nineteenth century, the printed symbols of standard English were matched to the sound-system of spoken Scots. The folklorist Walter Gregor gives an example of this in a lesson from Banffshire which probably dates from about 1840:

> The pronunciation was the broad northern: muckle aw, little aw, beh, ceh, etc. The system of teaching the alphabet, if not by all, at least by some, was truly mnemonic—e.g.:
>
> *Teacher* 'Faht is't yer mither pits ona hir nose t' lat 'ir see?'
> *Scholar* 'Geh' (g being in shape somewhat like old-fashioned spectacles).
> *T.* 'Faht it's it flees ow'r the kirk?'
> *S.* 'Keh' (the jackdaw being called the 'keh').
> *T.* 'Faht is't it's roon like the meen?'
> *S.* 'O'
>
> No attempt at explanation of the lesson was ever made. it was, read and commit to memory and nothing else. On rare occasions, an explanation was ventured on, as the following shows:
>
> *Scholar* 'Werse forteent. But not long aifter there arose agins' it a tempestyis ween called . . . Eh--eh--eh?'
> *Teacher* 'Spell the word, ye gowck.'
> *S.* 'Eh--uh--airr--o--ceh--aill--y--deh--o--ainn.'
> *T.* 'Ehrehchlydin. That's the place the ween comes oot o'; myne that noo.'
> (*Acts* xxvii. 14.).[6]

Until well into the century Scots was the normal medium of instruction in many schools, and there is abundant evidence that this was so. A moment's reflection will make it clear why. The aural experience of the majority of children ensured that a Scots or Anglo-Scottish idiom had to be used if a basic understanding was to be achieved. The following lessons, probably from Angus or Forfarshire, and dating from about 1860, illustrate this well:

'Noo, laddies . . . Noo, point oot Ameriky! That's no Ameriky, ye gowks; gae awa to the tither side o' the warld wi' ye . . . Aye, yer com nearer't noo. Aweel, that's whaur Charlie Donat's faither's till . . .
Ameriky's a great big place . . . but it disna a' belang till itsel'—we have big lump o't ca'ed Canady. Point oot Canady!' Here the pointers clattered all over the sheet, to North, South, East, and West, but as far from 'Canady' as possible. 'Eh, that's awfu'!—Jock Stewart's *hettest*!'—instantly every stick claimed kinship with Jock's—'but ye're a' *cauld* yet. Up a little—tuts! that's owre far; doon! doon yet—easht noo. Div ye no' ken your richt hand frae your left? The tap North, the boddam Sooth, the richt hand Easht, an' the left hand Wast—pit doon your pointers an' say that a' thegither . . .'
Sclates were dear and *skilie*, or slate pencil, was scarcer here than was straw in ancient Egypt. But neither were much missed under [our] system of elementary arithmetic, the materials for developing which consisted simply of the clay floor of the school-room, and a bag of marbles which, doutbless, had been pilfered by the ruthless dominie from past generations of scholars, under such specious pretences as their lawful forfeiture by carelessness, bad conduct, etc. The youngsters squatted on the floor, and, each being supplied with a few marbles, the 'lesson' began . . .
'Put down fowre bools! D'ye ca' that fowre, Johnnie? I've anither name for'd. Weel dune, Tammy! ye'll be a man before your mither yet. Tak' them a' up but twa, noo! Did ye no' hear fat I said, min? Gin I come owre your fingers *twice*, I'll learn ye to coont *twa* some better. Noo, lift ane, an' leave ane. Fat's your fingers made o', Bobbie? at' ye lat a' your bools gae scatterin' owre the flure that wye. Your fingers is a' thooms, I'm dootin'. Tak them a' up noo! Put down sax! Coont them ane by ane, min! Confoond ye, canna ye stop when ye come to sax! Tak' them a' up, an we'll try again. Ane—Geordie, I'll ha'e to gi'e ye a lickin', I doot. D'ye ye no' ken fat ane is? Hoo mony heids ha'e ye?' and so on . . .[7]

In middle-class burgh schools and private academies, much instruction was probably going on by mid-century in what passed for English, although even here Scots was used occasionally,[8] but in parish schools (even of the best sort) Scots continued in use as the basic mode of instruction. This appears in an extended passage in Neil N MacLean's classic study *Life at a Northern University* (Aberdeen 1906) which depicts the writer's preparations for the Latin papers in the bursary competition of 1853 under the supervision of James Lyall, an alumnus of Marischal College and for thirty-four years parish schoolmaster of Peterhead. The discourse is highly technical, concentrating on attitude and examination technique, and is couched in vernacular Scots (and Latin) throughout. Although some of the bourgeoisie were consciously trying to avoid items of Scots lexis in speech, it is clear that in many cases their success was relatively partial. The idiom and phonology of spoken Scots was highly resistant to the encroachment of book-English.[9]
The middle-classes were still largely bilingual at the end of the century,

especially in country areas. Gavin Greig the folk-song collector is a typical case. He was a graduate of Aberdeen, and headmaster of the school of Whitehill near New Deer in Aberdeenshire, a writer and musician playing a leading part in the cultural life of the North-East, a magistrate and a fellow of the Educational Institute of Scotland. He used Scots habitually in everyday life, including to his colleagues.[10] There are many indications of its widespread use by the Scots bourgeoisie during the period, including several examples cited in other contexts in this book, but perhaps one other instance may suffice here. It comes from a serial story which ran in the *Weekly Free Press* in the summer of 1894 with the title 'Cross Purposes: or, The Links o' Cullen', and the hero is a clever local boy, a typical 'loon o' pairts', who has completed his theological studies and is about to enter the ministry. The heroine, his sweetheart, is equally able and has just completed her training as a teacher. At one point the young ordinand bids her farewell with the following words: 'Weel, aw doobt aw maun rin; aw'm tae preach for Mr Mackintosh the morn, an' aw hinna lookit oot ma psalms yet.'[11]

It was into such a setting that on 2 January 1858, the *People's Journal* introduced the first of its vernacular correspondents.[12] He was identified simply by the pseudonym 'Sandy', and he was the first of a whole new school:

> MISTER EDITUR,—I canna say that I'm verra weel pleased at ye gie'in sae little notice to the public in general, and ye're humble freend Sandy in parteekelar, o' ye're meanin' to publish the 'People's Journal.' It tak's a gude deal to pit me oot o' my ordiner' canny way, but I maun honestly say that I was a wee bit dumfoundered this mornin' when my auldest laddie cam rinnin' in cryin', 'Faither, there's anither new penny weekly paper to be published in Dundee, and it's to be oot the morn's mornin', an' they ca'd the "People's Journal".' 'Hoots, laddie,' says I, 'gae wa' wi' ye, ye're haverin', man; ye've made a mistak' this time, for as gleg's ye are at readin' bills on the wa'.' But the younker stuck fast up for his correckness, an I wasna lang o' findin' oot that the laddie was richt, an' o' making' mysel acquent wi' a' the oots an' ins o' the matter . . . I made up my mind to gie'd a fair trial, an' besides tellin' ye a bit o' my mind on the subjeck, to offer ye a letter noo an' then, as I can find time frae my wark, telling ye in a plain, even doon way my thochts on the passing subjecks o' local or general interest. I mean, of coorse, to write to ye in the same way as I wud dae if I were crackin' wi' ye ower the fireside, using my ain auld Doric for the maist part, no because I couldna' maybe manage to write gae an' fair English, if I were to pit mysel' till't in earnest, but jist because I think my ain hamely Scotch to be every bit as expressive, or even far mair sae, than what is ca'd 'pure' English, while it comes easier and mair nat'ral to me, and'll maybe find its way readier to the hearts o' many o' your readers who are accustomed every day to speak it, and who, I hope, often tak' delight in readin't, no as it's shamefully carikatured and murdered in ower mony o' oor modern cheap prints, but as it's to be fund in the pages o' oor ain honoured Scotch poet, Robbie Burns.[13]

The main purpose of the letter was to give a detailed account of a local strike, an account strongly favourable to the men, and this concept—of ideas and ideals existing in real communities—was to be at the centre of the new vernacular prose. The column was placed immediately next to the leaders and linked to them typographically, giving it an implied 'official' status, and as the weeks went by 'Sandy' and his colleague 'Jock Clodpole' began to write what amounted to alternative leading articles in Scots. The vernacular became part of the editorial identity of the paper and as the *Journal* grew in influence, Scots became again, to an extent, one of the languages of authority.

It was well suited for dealing with local subjects; in the issue for 15 January, for example, after a brief excursion into the subject of pulpit oratory, Sandy went on to discuss the rival candidates for the Provostship of Dundee, alleged irregularities in a public drainage contract, and the management of the Dundee poorhouse funds. The local aspect was never entirely forgotten but the vision of the column progressively widened until a whole range of social and political issues came within its compass, including regular comment on Parliamentary and international affairs.

Although he invoked the name Burns, Sandy departed significantly from the standard literary Scots of his day using a degree of orthographic freedom to represent specific features of the local sound-system. This can be seen in the retraction implied by the spelling of 'Editur', the elision of 't' in words like 'correckness', 'subjecks', 'conduckin'; and the way in which standard English spellings are modified to suggest a particular intonation, as in 'carikatured', and 'freend'. There is, admittedly, no trace of the initial fricative as in 'fat', 'far' and 'fan' ('what', 'where' and 'when') which was still apparently, a feature of local speech at that time,[14] but a genuine attempt seems to have been made to represent on the page a speech-based idiom owing at least as much to contemporary usage in the city of Dundee as to literary precedent either from the serious or the popular branches of the tradition. As 'Sandy' himself said: 'I mean . . . to write to ye in the same way as I wud dae if I were crackin' wi' ye ower the fireside . . .'

One of the problems with Sandy was that he was a city-dweller, and could hardly speak for the growing numbers of country readers. There was a clear need for a rural correspondent, and on 27 February 1858, 'Jock Clodpole' made his appearance, the alter-ego of William D Latto, the greatest exponent of epistolary vernacular prose in Victorian Scotland:

Mr EDITUR,—Ye'll no ken me na, but I'm second cousin to ye're droll freen' 'Sandy', although I meikle dreed he winna look upon a puir unedicat' body like me as fit to be considered his equal, seein' hoo I've been born an' brocht up a' my days in the country, an' am therefore nae sae weel versed in a' ye're toon manners an' ways o' thinkin . . . Hoosomdever . . . I cam' to the resolution that I wad pit twa or three paragraphs thegither by way o' experiment, an' should this letter, whilk is the result o' the foresaid resolution, prove acceptable to the readers o' the *People's Journal*, an' please a' parties, they may expeck to hear frae me ance i' the fortnicht at least. Only, Mr Editur, ye maun tell the printers to keep a strict e'e on my spellin' an' correck a' mistak's, else I meikle dreed the reader will be sometimes at a loss to ken whilk end o' my words is upmost, for, when I got my edication spinnin' wheels were as rife in Scotland as hurdy-gurdies are said to be among the Tyrolese, an' every ither cotter hoose ye passed was an academy forsooth, in whilk sax or aucht sprauchin' urchins sat squattin' roun' an auld toothless dame, decked up in a frowdy mutch, joost for a' the warld like a wheen chickens roun' a clockin' hen. The feint a schule book was to be fund in thae seats o' learnin' but the single carriches an' the Proverbs o' Solomon, for at the time I'm speakin o' Barrie's Spellin Book and Collection had na penetrated into these parts, an hoo the auld crones could get the wee bit chafts o' the bairnies to gang roun' Baptism an' the Lord's Supper, surpasses a' human comprehension. Some o' them, I ken, had an unco cute plan o' surmountin an orthographical difficulty, as my ain instructress for instance, for whenever she encountered a meikle jaw'breaker, she said wi' an air o' the maist profound erudition that it was joost the name o' some ootlandish toon in Sooth Ameriky, an' bade the reader pass ower to the next word.

Losh! if it wad na be ower sair a tax on the reader's patience, I could tell an unco queer mischanter that befell the worthy dame aforesaid, in whilk mad prank I, to my shame be it spoken, had a leadin' hand, an' it is the mair memorable to me that it had the unexpected effeck o' bringin' my academic trainin' to a premature, if not a violent conclusion. The story is shortly this. I had got a bawbee frae uncle Tam, an' what did I do, think ye, but ran awa like a fule, as I was, and waired it upon gun poother—the mair shame to Deacon Scales for sellin' it to me—an' of coorse I was a great man amang the scholars that day, for I had a bawbee's worth o' poother i' my pouch. We got an auld key, an' filed a touch-hole in't, an' had joost let aff the first shot when, lo! Granny Effie, as we ca'd the mistress, dreeled us in to oor lessons, an' spoiled a' oor sport, meikle to our chagrin, ye may be shure. There was at that time a meikle ill-contrivin' halian at the schule, wi' a towsy tap like a water dog, an' a bubbly nose, ca'd Rob Tamson, an' whether it sprang frae his ain native talent for mischief brewin' or some evil speerit put it into his noddle, I canna tell, but he advised me to slip doon a pickle o' my poother below the chair on whilk she sat an' span, wi' a sprinklin' a' the way frae the chair to the ace-hole. Weel, I was simple eneuch to do his biddin' withoot thinkin' o' the upshot. Nae sooner, hooever, had Granny tane her seat at her wheel, puir body, than up gets Rob, the vaig, gangs to the fire, an', it bein' an unco cauld forenoon, tak's the poker an' redds the ribs, a' the while an expression on his coontenance o' the most profound innocence. Of coorse, afore ane could say Jack Robinson, the poother played pluff, an' besides singin' a' Effie's nether garments, an' raisin' a deafenin' skirl amang the weans, it set fire to the flowers o' lint that were strickin' a' ower the wheel, an' at last the 'devoorin' element' as you newspaper folks ca' it, seized haud o' the rock itsel' whilk it reduced to black ace in less than nae time. The haill catastrophe was the wark o' a few seconds. I kenned na what to do nor what to think. Effie was nearly mad wi' fricht an' anger, an' as sune as she saw there was nae danger o' the conflagration spreadin', she banged doon the strap that hung at her lug in a convenient situation, an' ca'd a cooncil o' war instanter. Rob Tamson was tane into custody as the Guy Fawkes o' this gun-poother plot, he bein' the loon that set lunt to the train. I guessed in a twinklin' that my name wad be before the cooncil next, for weel did I ken that Rob wad na scruple to turn queen's evidence the moment that he had to choose between that an' a sair hide, an' therefore I tane up my position so that happen what micht the wheel should stand betwixt me an' a' skaith. I didna wrang Rob in the least wi' my uncharitable surmise, for joost as the strap was aboot to alicht on a maist vulnerable part o' his body, oot cam the truth wi' a lee at the tail o't to bear it company, 'It was Jock Clodpole', he cried oot like a bull o' Bashan 'that had the poother, an' I kenned naething o' its being laid below the chair.' I didna deny it an' Effie sprang towards me with an awfu' bellum, but somehoo or ither I aye managed to keep the wheel between her an' me. Hoo lang we ran roun' the wheel, Effie the greyhound an' I the hare, I canna pretend to calculate, but at length an' lang, as chance wad hae it, a hole in Effie's apron caught haud o' the temper pin. Doon gaed Effie an' the wheel aboon her, an' I, deemin' discretion the better part o' valour, tane the opportunity o' boltin' to the door, while my antagonist was gatherin' hersel' oot o' the floor. I never stayed to say fareweel, but scoured aff awa hame as fast as my locomotives wad serve my purpose. As soon as Effie could gather her fins frae aneath the *debris* o' her wheel—for it was a' dung to crockanition accordin' to her account, though I sairly jalouse she made things look a sicht waur than they really were, in order to mak' my offence appear the mair heinous— up the auld sorra banged the rock, wi' black aizles o' the lint still adhering till't, an' strauchtway tane the gate at my heels as fast as her auld legs could carry her, an' threatenin' vengeance against me a' the way. A droll sicht it must hae been to see her an' me rinning' up the Lang Loan i' the direction o' oor hoose, but weel-a-wat it was nae funny affair to me, for weel kenned I what was awaitin' me. Of coorse Effie, in lodgin' her complaint wi' my faither, wha was an unco strick disciplinarian in his way, didna mak' the business appear ony better than the plain simple truth, an' my certie! if he—honest man, peace to his ashes noo that he's gane the way o' a the earth—didna make Uncle Tam's bawbee the dearest to me that ever I had in a' my born days, he did naething . . .

As for my edication I may as weel state that I was to hae been padded aff again to the schule in the afternoon, but Effie said she wad never mair allow sic a menseless rapscallion as Jock Clodpole to darken the door o' her academy. Thus ended my schule edication, when, as I aften heard my mither remark afterwards, I wanted joost four days o' seven years an' sax months auld. Nae wunder, then, that my spellin' is a wee thocht gleyed at times, seein' the kind an' extent o' the instruction I got in my bairnhood . . . In gude troth I've been mair behadden to my ain native haivens an' industry for the little I ken o' beuk lear than to ony o' my youthfu' instructors. My haill design in makin' mention o' the defects o' my edication was joost to forewarn the printers no to pit in a' my words *verbatim et literatim*, I think they ca' it, an' also to guard the reader against lookin' for ony thing frae my pen half sae bricht an' learned as they get frae cousin Sandy . . .

Considering that the passage is a rhetorical *tour de force*, the exaggerated humility of the opening and closing sections is perhaps a little overstated. Yet the contrast shows an important feature of Latto's technique. He plays the clownish element implicit in his nom-de-plume to the hilt, but not for its own sake; it forms a springboard for the brilliantly opportunistic anecdote which makes up the central section and provides the piece with a tellingly ironical frame. These elements are, to some extent, traditional, but the skill with which they are used is remarkable. Latto's creative temperament was ideally suited to the freely-ranging discursive essay in Scots, and in the early numbers he vigorously pushed the form around to see what he could make it do. The second letter, for example, was given over entirely to national and international politics and delivered a sustained attack upon repression and hypocrisy at home and abroad:

> ... the maist common verdick come to by ony o' my acquaintances hereawa wha are capable o' formin' an opeenion o' their ain, is that Pam [Palmerston], in bein' cowpit aff his seat, has got nae mair than what he well deserved, an' what he has been evidently workin' for ever sin' the conclusion o' the Rooshian war . . . a cheenge o' ministry had become an indispensible needcessity, baith for the honour an' weelfare o' the nation, whether at hame or abroad. Joost see, for instance, hoo the twa engineers, Wat and Park, puir chields, hae been abused by that miscreant Bomba an' his myrmidon crew, and yet oor bauld Premier never aince made what was worth ca'in an effort to deliver them 'oot o' the land o' Egypt, oot o' the hoose o' bondage'. Na, na, I suppose he was feared for endangerin' oor amicable relations wi' the perjured Emperor o' Austria . . . I wad ask . . . what the result wad hae been, gif instead o' Bomba it had been the King o' Greece or Mr Commissioner Yeh, or any ither feckless or far awa potentate that had been sae far left to himsel' as to daur the snarl o' the Breetish lion by clappin' twa o' his whalps into an iron cage for seven or aught months withoot either provin' them to be guilty or gi'en them an opportunity o' clearin' themsells frae the imputations cast upon their characters? . . . on a' considerations o' equity, the same measure o' joostice that has been meted oot to Yeh sud hae been meted oot to the Neapolitan Nana Sahib as weel. Aha! but Bomba is the very *beau ideal*—the maist perfect eemage an' exemplar o' absolutism an' oppression that we hae in Europe, an' of coorse his big brithers o' a like kidney wi' himsel' wadna stand by an' see him sair bamboozled an' belawbered without squairin' their neives in his defence. The fact is, that Bomba is sae far convenient to the ither tyrants o' Christendom that he keeps them a' in coontenance; for, hoowever deeply they may sink into the mire o' depravity, he will be aye sure to keep a wee bit below them, sae that they can aye say in self-defence, 'We're no sae bad as his Majesty o' Naples at ony rate . . .[15]

In subsequent weeks there were further episodes of autobiography mixed with discursive pieces on a variety of subjects: the education of the poor—which dealt with the damaging effects of youth employment upon learning and mental culture; the improvement of cottar houses, including a fierce denunciation of greedy lairds and farmers; illegitimacy in country districts; adult education; the defects of the bothy system, and reform of the franchise. Latterly the column concentrated increasingly on social evils in the rural economy, becoming virtually a serialised history of nineteenth century argiculture, and all in vernacular Scots.

The letter of 5 June entitled 'Clodpole's first interview with Mrs McBean', is probably the most impressive of these early pieces. It is an 'autobiographical' sketch which continues the story—after several weeks—of Clodpole's early life and education. Following the debacle at the Dame school, his father has undertaken his schooling personally, but with little satisfaction on either side. Then one fine spring morning the situation is resolved by the arrival of a *deus*—or rather *dea-ex-machina*. The main part of the narrative is prefaced by an astonishing mock-heroic invocation to the spring in which Scots invades the heartland of English pastoral in a spirit of swashbuckling verbal play:

Weel do I yet remember the day whereon my destiny for life was irretrievably fixed. A saft, sun-lit, heart-thrillin' mornin' it was, towards the latter end o' April, when Nature, wakin' up frae her lang, cheerless torpitude, obedient to the summons o' Nature's God, divests hersel' o' the hoary garb o' Winter, an' bedecks hersel' anew in the flowery garniture o' Spring. A clump o' young trees doon in the dell, a bowshot or sae frae my faither's hoose, the scene o' mony a bird-nestin' expedition, was vocal wi' the ringin' sang o' the black-bird. Far awa' on the Cauldhame Hills could be dimly descried a flock o' sheep, seemin' in the distance to be 'scarce sae gross as beetles'. Frae the serene cerulean vault aboon, the spreckled sangsters o' the lea, Nature's earliest choristers, were chantin' in mingled harmony their mornin' hymns o' praise, that fell on the ear like a transitory emanation frae the upper Sanctuary. Eastward on the whinny muir were heard the pertinacious wailin' expostulations o' scores o' noisy peeweets, busy in the performance o' their wild harliquinades in middle air, noo skimmin' awa to a great distance, as if gien' themsels' up to despair, an' then, as if havin' plucked up fresh courage, dartin' back again wi' strange capricious somersaults, an' makin' a harsh whizzin' sound wi' their wings, as if they were aboot to fa' doon dead or wounded. By sic like artfu' demonstrations does the puir peesweet manifest his displeasure wi' those wha presume to disturb the quiet o' his rural domains; an' by these tokens it was that I jaloused some intruder to be abroad on the whinny muir on that bonny spring mornin'. The scene in a' its details yet remains distinctly stamped on memory's tablet, as if it were but a thing o' yesterday. I had been abroad that mornin' by the skraigh o' day, in order to see a brood o' infantile chucks that had come into existence durin' the precedin' nicht. It was while standin' viewin' the puny cheepers, wi' admirin' raptures, roon' at the barn door, wi' naething on me but the breeks, an my wee Kilmarnock, that my attention was arrested by the clamours o' the angry peesweets. Castin' a glance in the direction o' the whinny muir, I there perceived a movin' object in human shape, aroon' whilk the peesweets' attention was evidently centred, but whether it was man or woman, I couldna at first joost exactly determine. Gradually, however, it becam' mair an' mair distinct, until I was at last able to discern its ootline to be that o' an auld woman, arrayed in a coarse grey hame-spun woollen cloak, an' a cockernonie o' the genuine sow-backit description, begirt wi' a yellow silk handkerchief . . .

The darting, improvisatory quality in Latto's prose is illustrated by the sudden introduction of a passage—to all appearances quite coincidental upon the formation of annals in rural parishes:

Of coorse, onything in the shape o' humanity was, in that ootlandish neuk o' creation, quite an object o' the maist intense an' pryin' curiosity to the simple inhabitants o' Hungryhole. Indeed, a phenomenon o' that kind was o' very rare occurrence in sic a desert place, an' therefore when it did happen it was generally seized on as an era whence to date succeedin' events, until another phenomenon equally important appeared to occupy its place. In the chronology o' Hungryhole, for instance, it was noted that 'Bruckie calved the broon stirk joost that day aucht days after the Hielan' piper cam' ower the muir playin' Shantrews', or that 'Jock brunt his mou' lickin' the parritch spurtle on the identical mornin' that Sandy Blawthree rade past on the braw new bawsand naig that he coft frae the Yorkshire Jockey at Fiddler's Tryst.' Archbishop Usher wad hae been rather a 'leetle' puzzled wi' sic a primitive system o' chronology, but then, if the chronology was simple, sae also, it maun be confessed, were the events whase dates it was employed to fix an' determine. True it is, in a historic point o' view, it micht do unco little towards settlin' sic knotty questions as whether

> Cheops or Cephrenes was architect
> Of either pyramid that bears his name?

but it was nevertheless quite adequate to a' the requirements o' Hungryhole an' its unlettered inhabitants.

The central section starts here, and we see something of the redoubtable Mrs McBean, and something else, too, about Latto as a writer—his interest in the variety of Scots, its regional and class dialects:

> 'Losh, Mrs McBean, this is no you, is't?' quoth my mither, as soon as the frowdie cam' within speakin' bounds; 'A sicht o' you is surely gude for sair een! Hoo's a' wi' ye, woman? an' hoo's the gudeman?'
>
> 'Teed, Mrs Clodpole,' was the reply, 'I'm unco prawly, muckle opleedged t'ye, an' Tonald, she was weel eneuch fan she was last apoot ta pit placie ower py, but she'll hae gaen awa twa tree tays syne till oor nain coontry to speer for ta praw Laird o' Tillyquhassle—aye will she, puir man. Tonald an' ta Laird will be cousins joost sax times removed, ye ken, teed will they, an' tere's aye been an unco freenship petween them twa; ugh aye.'

Now we reach the artfully postponed climax. As the women gossip it emerges that Mrs McBean needs a herd laddie. Clodpole's father appears and volunteers the services of the narrator:

> 'I think I could save ye a gude hantle o' trouble as weel as travel, Mrs McBean,' said my faither, wi' a consideration for her auld Heilan' shanks that I couldna approve o'; 'I've a bit callant o' my ain to spare, joost a wee thocht ootheady an' rebellious in his natur'—Gude be thankit for the afflictions as well as for the manifold mercies that he sends us—but gin ye haud the strap gaen on'm wi' reasonable vigour, I've nae doot but he'll grow main complowsible under the visitation. Wadna this bit callant suit your purpose, d'ye think?'

In the negotiations which follow, the chronology motif returns, and we begin to realise why it was introduced in the first place: the narrator's lot is already fixed—it was implicit in his relationship with his parents from the outset; and so, with a neatly circular movement, the essay draws to its conclusion:

> 'Fu wad ta pit callant suit wi' us, tid ye'll pe speerin, Mr Clodpole? I'm no that ferra sure, put we can be crackin' apoot it. Fu auld wad he pe?' inquired Mrs McBean, e'ein' me frae head to fit.
>
> 'Auld eneuch to be worth his arles an' his bit o' meat at ony rate, forbye twa or three shillin's o' wauges I'se warrant. He'll be nine year come Lammas, I think. Eh! gudewife, what say ye? Look the meikle Bible.'

'That's joost the eild o' 'm to an oor,' quoth my mither, raxin' doon the Haly Book, an' turnin' up the family register therein recorded, 'The year o' the big spate as ever was, whan Francie Baird's farrow-sow, an' thirteen as dainty grices as ever ploughed a midden, were drownit i' the Brig Hole.'

'He'll hardly be pig eneuch for oor pits o' jobs; put fu meikle silder wad ye pe for askin' for him?'

'I sanna be misleared wi' ye, Mrs McBean, as ye're an auld acquaintance—joost his bit o' meat and' a pair o' shoon at the term,' was my faither's modest proposal.

'Weel, weel, wese no pe castin' oot apoot ta pits o' progues,' quoth Mrs McBean, 'Here's ta arle-penny, an' noo ta pit loonie is my Gillie frae Beltane till Martinmas tay.'

Thus it was that I was sold into the hoose o' bondage afore I could weel discern atween my richt hand and my left . . .

In retrospect, the extravagant opening seems at least as much a celebration of lost youth and innocence as a literary pastiche, just as the amusing digression which follows it turns out not to be a digression at all, but a method of linking the whole piece together; a kind of double focus is created which allows the reader to enter both the initial state of innocence and the sense of betrayal at the end; a chain of implication is also set in motion which establishes the materialistic narrowness of the community in a highly effective manner: when Clodpole's mother consults the ha-bible to establish his age and links his birth with the death of a family of pigs, she creates the impression that the latter event is as significant to her as the former, if not more so, a bleakly revealing comment on the mental and emotional poverty which could conceive of such a linkage in the first place. The pun which follows, 'He'll hardly pe pig eneuch for oor pits o' jobs' is obviously not accidental. The essay is also linked together at a more subtle linguistic level. The pull and surge of different registers is felt within the very fabric of the language: not just between 'Scots' and 'English', but between different idiomatic levels within each, and from this tightly constructed pattern emerges a highly elliptical and laconic sense of pain and loss. The ultimate perspective is provided by the form itself: this essay is one of a series whose main purpose was to expose abuses like the one shown happening here; the fact that there is no direct allusion to it makes it doubly telling. This is sophisticated writing.

Latto's powers as an essayist reached their fullest development in the 'Tammas Bodkin' column which he began to contribute to the *People's Journal* shortly after he became its editor. The Bodkin papers present a number of interesting textual problems. First is their sheer extent. They began on 16 February 1861, and ran intermittently for more than thirty years. Sometimes there were little clusters of essays, sometimes lengthy and continuous ganglia stretching over several months at a time; sometimes there were gaps within series, and of course there were gaps—sometimes for years—between series. But taken together, they must amount to at least three quarters of a million words.[16]

Some sixty essays are available in book form, revised by Latto himself, under the titles *Tammas Bodkin: or the Humours of a Scottish Tailor* (Edinburgh 1864), *The Bodkin Papers* (second series, Leng, Dundee, 1883), and *Tammas Bodkin: Swatches o' Hodden-Grey* (Hodder & Stoughton, London, 1894). The Edinburgh edition of 1864 and the related London edition of 1894 are the more important, as well as being the most widely available— indeed, only one copy of the 1883 edition appears to have survived. The book editions are by no means a straightforward re-print from the columns of the newspaper with which, indeed, their relationship is intriguingly indirect. For a start the content dates from an early period. There was nothing after 1863 in the first collection, and the London edition added only a handful of later pieces to it (as well as omitting several interesting early ones). Most of the 1864 text, moreover, was written expressly for book publication with, as the preface makes clear, a predominantly middle-class audience in mind.[17] Less than a quarter of the contents originated in the newspaper, and even these had undergone significant changes in the process.

There are two different 'Tammas Bodkins', the protagonist of the book, and the protagonist of the column. The book Bodkin stands squarely in the Scotch mannerist tradition of Galt and David Macbeth Moir whose *Mansie Waugh, Tailor in Dalkeith* (Edinburgh 1828), a study of the sayings and doings of a small-town tradesman, enjoyed a considerable influence during the nineteenth century. Tammas

W D Latto (Tammas Bodkin) in a characteristic attitude. *Source*: '*The Jubilee of the People's Journal*'. Reproduced by courtesy of City of Dundee District Council.

Bodkin is mentioned in the book as Waugh's apprentice, and although the Latto persona is not identified with him (he is stated to have been a cousin, one of the Lothian branch of the family), the debt to the older school is still explicit. Various aspects of Bodkin's earlier career are narrated, and, upon the whole, they are conventionally conceived—there is a comic howdie, the infant hero is mistaken for a changeling, he outwits a succession of schoolmasters, causes a catastrophe at a diet of catechising, later courts a local farmer's daughter, marries, and becomes a manufacturing tailor in Dundee. He is shown at the end of the book standing in the churchyard of his native parish looking back over what is obviously rather a long life. The text comes to about 160,000 words, and more than three-quarters of it are occupied by his experience in childhood and youth; the rest is treated in a very episodic and fragmentary way.

The writing possesses considerable vigour, and in one respect at least it is significantly innovatory. While Galt had favoured a Scots-influenced English as his narrative medium, and Moir had mixed vernacular dialogue with standard English connecting prose, Latto used Scots throughout. And yet, on the evidence of these volumes it is difficult to see what the Victorians got so excited about. And they did get excited. Although he was known only by his pen-name, Latto's reputation as a Scottish—perhaps *the* Scottish writer—was almost unrivalled during the second half of the nineteenth century. But of course contemporaries could read him in his original form in the weekly columns of the *People's Journal*, where he appeared to much greater advantage. Book format provided a restricted canvas little suited to the zestful amplitude of his natural style. Some of the Clodpole material, for example, was revised for incorporation in the Bodkin text of 1864, and there is obvious stylistic loss. This is still more true of the edition of 1883, despite the author's expressed hope that the pieces might actually gain by condensation.[18] In the London edition the process was taken still further. Although based on the Edinburgh edition of 1864 and containing a similar number of essays, the Hodder & Stoughton text was just over half its length, the prose being brutally cut to bring it within the publishers' limits. This is the version most likely to be found in British libraries.

The book Bodkin was strongly conditioned by existing, basically bourgeois, literary conventions. But in the working-class market in which the *People's Journal* existed there were few precedents for what Latto was doing, except possibly in the chap-books, which typically lacked the intellectual breadth or the moral concern which formed the essence of the Bodkin persona. Latto created his own conventions within the specific context of the popular newspaper, and the original text must form the basis of any assessment of his achievement. In the *Journal* Bodkin was developed with much greater originality and scope—even having a different biography, which included foreign travel, the inheritance of great wealth, and many other things unrecorded in the books. Still more importantly, perhaps, he acted in the newspaper as a vehicle for ideas: he analysed the Game Laws, discussed trade unionism, agitated the Nine Hour Question, and a whole range of class-related social issues. He delivered political harangues at election times, and commented upon many aspects of national and international affairs. In Latto's hands, vernacular Scots became a channel which opened out into the whole contemporary world. He was the first prose writer to be completely alive through the medium of the language since the seventeenth century. Compared with the Bodkin of the newspaper, the Bodkin of the book was a headless wonder.

As the original text is extensive and inaccessible, I have selected a series of essays on the Great Exhibition at Paris which appeared in the *Journal* in 1867, and which show a mixture of wit, intellectual vigour, and cosmopolitan ease which marks the new style at its best. The Paris episodes (some two dozen in number) were set within a lightly-sketched narrative framework. In the spring of that year, Bodkin received a letter from a certain Ezekiel Eleizer Twentyman, Mechanical Inventor, Buncombe Street, New York, inviting him to answer various questions about his links with the recently extinct American branch of the family. These proving satisfactory, he was notified that he had inherited the fortune of the wealthy James Bodkin of New York, and invited to complete the legal formalities in Paris where Twentyman was to be exhibiting. After various minor contretemps, Bodkin and his wife Tibby duly arrived in the city and ensconsed themselves in their hotel, *La Grenouille Couchant* in the *Rue L'Escargot*. Next morning they got their first real taste of life in France:

> Havin' dressed oorsels, we ordered breakfast, or a *déjeuner* as the Frenchies ca' their mornin' meal, never dreamin' nor anticipatin' but we wad get tea an' toast, an' maybe a couple o' eggs, or a bit gude ham or cauld meat, but judge o' oor disappointment when the garçon brocht in twa cups o' *café au lait*—that is to say, coffee an' milk in' t—wi' twa wee rolls, or *petits pains* as he ca'd them, an' feint foondit besides!
>
> 'My man,' quo' I, 'is there no sic a thing as tea an' toast to be gotten in this pairt o' the ceeveleezed warld?'
>
> But I micht as weel have addressed mysel' to the stanes o' the wa'—the puir creature did not understand a single syllable o' what I said till him.
>
> 'Parle voos Anglais?' quo' I.
>
> 'Nong, Monsieur!' quo' he, an' he shook his head dubiously. I was wae for him.
>
> 'Parle voo Français?' quo' he.
>
> 'Nong, Monsieur,' quo' I, an' I also shook my head dubiously, while he seemed wae for me. Oor pity was, therefore, mutual . . .
>
> 'Tibbie,' quo' I, 'this will never do. There's to be naething but hunger an' herschip here, I see. That's hoo the French folkies are sic wee ill-grown warrochs; they dinna get their meat. An' they ca' *this* a breakfast, do they? Gude help them, puir bodies, for they're greatly to be pitied.'[19]

In search of proper nourishment as much as anything else, the couple began their exploration of the city:

> In a city o' palaces like Paris the difficulty is to ken not whaur to begin' seein', but whaur to leave aff. Whaur everything is worth seein' ye can begin onywhere. We landit in the Boulevard de Sebastopol, a wide an' elegant street,

that rins north an' sooth through the very centre of the city . . . I was greatly
interestit in the Boulevards. They are very wide, an' the hooses, bein'
comparatively new, an' built o' a fine licht coloured stane, are very elegant. On
the ooter edges o' the foot pavements there are raws o' trees, intermingled wi'
elegant lamp-posts, kiosks for the sale o' newspapers, an' circular pillars,
shapen somewhat like the wee turrets on the Albert Institute, an' whase uses I
will not here tarry to describe in detail . . . There is neither fog nor reek in
Paris to obscure the brilliancy o' the scene, an' really the sicht is grand—that is
the only word I can find in my vocabulary fit to describe it. An' then the
shops—they are perfect marvels o' elegance; an' the gudes desplayed in
them—they are masterpieces o' taste an' skill. Gowd and silver and precious
stones—gude-life, I never saw onything equal til't! . . .But what diverted me
mair than onything was the sicht o' the *cafés* an' *restaurants*, an' their name is
Legion. Ye canna gang twenty yards in ony direction in some o' the principal
streets an' boulevards withoot seeing a *café*. Ye look through the window—an'
the whole front o' the hoose is a window for ordinar'—an' ye see croods o' folk
sittin' at little roond tables sippin' coffee, or beer, or wine, or cognac—some o'
them playin' at cards, some at dice, some at dominoes, some at billiards, an'
some at the dambrod—an' the whole fraternity o' them keepin' up an incessant
chatter, chatter, chatter, insomuch that it is, to a douce, taciturn auld chap like
me, the greatest marvel in creation to conceive what in a' the earth they can get
to talk aboot. I jalouse that much o' their conversation is thin an' watery, and
little calculated to minister to edification . . . A Scotchman wad think shame if a
stranger saw him takin' his food, an' mair especially if he saw him takin' aff his
toddy; but the Parisians are destitute o' ony feelin' o' that kind, they eat an'
drink an' gamble—they do almost everything, in fact, in public. An' for smokin'
an' spittin', ye ken, they cow the gowan![20]

The day continued with a drive down the boulevards to the Madeleine 'a
splendid kirk, modelled after the Parthenon at Athens, an' surroondit by
Corinthian pillars . . . ', the Place de la Concorde, the Place de la Bastille and
the Tuileries.

As the visit continued the comic contrasts between Scots and French
manners, although never entirely forgotten, tended to become lost in
genuine admiration for the city. There followed detailed and vivid accounts
of the opening ceremonies and of the Exhibition park and its environs:

The Champ de Mars . . . is a lairge sandy plain lying on the left or sooth bank o'
the river Seine, aboot a mile an' a half or twa miles doon frae the
Tooleries . . . At the end o' the plain furthest frae the river stands a noble
buildin' ca'd the Ecole Militaire, wherein the young sogers learn to cut human
throats upo' the maist scientificalest principles extant . . . Across this said river
stretches a stane brig exactly fornent the centre o' the Camps de Mars, an' ca'd
the Pont d'Iena, built by auld Nap. in commemoration o' his great victory ower
the Prussians at Jena in auchteen hunder an' five. It has five eliptic arches, ilk
ane o' them ninety feet in span, an' is decorated wi' statues o' colossal
dimensions. In aughteen hunder an' fourteen, when the Prussians were in
Paris, auld Blucher threatened to blaw up this brig, as he looked upon it in the
licht o' a standin' insult to his nation, but it was saved frae destruction by Louis
the Auchteenth, wha threatened to stand upon't an' gang up i' the air alang wi't
if the auld ruffian daured to carry oot his vengefu' threat. The destruction o'

the brig wad certainly have been a great calamity—a wanton flingin' awa' o' gude stane an' lime—but Louis himsel' was for little ither use than makin' a grand experiment wi' in the science o' projectiles . . . A short distance frae the north end o' the brig o' Jena . . . is . . . the famous Bois de Boulogne, whaur the fashionable warld disports itsel', flirts, an' mak's love

'Upon a simmer's afternoon,
Awee afore the sun gangs doon.'

This plateau is ca'd the Place du Roi de Rome, the said Roi de Rome wha has lent his name to the Place havin' been the son o' the First Napoleon by his second wife Maria Lousia. As for his bein' Roi o' Rome, he was nae mair that than he was Roy o' Aldivalloch . . .

Turnin' to the left as ye enter the Park frae the Brig o' Jena, ye enter the territory allotted to Great Britain. There, amid windin' walks, ye wend yer way, meetin' wi' fresh curiousities at every stap. There stands a shed, filled wi' warlike gear, frae Woolwich—great guns an' sma' guns, an' swirds, an' so forth; there ye'll see a hoose ereckit by the Bible Society, whaur spiritual artillery are fired aff free gratis for naething, in the shape o' tracts an' copies o' the Gospels in a' languages. Haudin' straight forrit, ye enter Morocco, wi' its curious tents; America, wi' its log huts; Persia, wi' its kiosks; Tunis wi' its Bey's Palace, cafe, an' barber's shop; China wi' its porcelain tower an' bazaar; Siam, wi' its grove; Egypt, wi its Temple o' Edfou; Turkey, wi' its mosques; Russia, wi' its imperial stables, containin' real live horse—splendid lookin' animals; Sweden, wi' its model o' the hoose wherein lived Gustavus Vasa; Switzerland, wi' its elegant chalets; Austria, wi' its models o' Syrian, Wallachian, Tyrolese, an' Hungarian hooses; Spain, wi' its Moorish farms and cottages; Germany, wi' its beer shops; Holland, wi' its Java villages an' diamond cuttin' warks; an' lastly, France itsel, wi' its grand conservatory, an' hothooses, an' model farms, an' model cottages, an' pavilions, an' an iron lichthoose twa hunder feet high, an'—but this sentence is ower lang already, an' mair I will not add to it, except to remark that fully to describe every object o' interest in the Park wad be the wark o' a life-time, whilk I do not intend to bestow upon it, as I've got sundry ither little bits o' jobs I wad like to accomplish afore I gang hence . . .[21]

The American stand was still not officially open. Twentyman's machines were in packing-cases, and Bodkin found himself waiting in the pavilion with increasing unease, when

. . . I felt a hand upon my shoother, an' lookin' roond, I was confrontit by an indovidooal o' the male specie, wha, like Heather Jock in the auld sang

'Was lang an' thin,
Fine for gaun against the win'.'

On his head he wore an enormous wideawake felt hat that had evidently been a stranger to the brush an' the smoothin' iron since the day when it left the hands o' its fabricator; on his lang, lank limbs he wore a pair o' white an' black tartan slacks—dambrod pattern—that wad hae been an' inch or twa wider in the legs, an' three or four inches langer, if I had been his tailor; on his back there was a lang frock coat that wad hae looked rather mair fashionable, not to say respectabler, had it been a wee thocht shorter; while atween his waistcoat pouch an' his button-hole there was stretched an enormous gowd chain that must have cost a very considerable soom o' money when it was new. The man had a head o' hair upon his shoothers that micht hae saired a Samson or an Absolom. It was of a sandy colour, an' hung doon his back ten or twal inches at least. His chin was also weel supplied wi' a vast crap o' the same material. All this I perceived at a single glance, an' all this I have been particular to describe, because wi' this said gentleman I'll hae occasion to haud not a little intercoorse an' communion afore I leave Paris an' the Great Exhibition. I've remarked that he laid his hand on my shoother, an' that I turned an' confrontit him . . .

'Lord bless me! Ye dinna mean to say . . . Is yer name Twentyman—?'

'I guess it's abeout that same,' quo' he, 'Mr Ezekiel Eliezer Twentyman, mechanical inventor, Buncome Street New York. That's about my name, pretty consid'ble—yes sirr.'

Twentyman is the direct ancestor of Desperate Dan, a comic Yankee of rumbustious energy and beguiling turn of phrase who galravages round Paris with Bodkin for a period of several months. The inheritance turns out to be perfectly *bona fide*, and includes a gold mine in Idaho, large deposits in trusts, and a splendid mansion in New York. Bodkin is rich and Twentyman and his agent, Julius Caesar Pilkem, immediately arrange a celebration at the *Hotel Tout le Mond* during which the hero is introduced to several novel and potent drinks à *l'Americaine*:

I am indebted for the following facts to the retentive memory an' observant e'e o' my respected pairtner in life. It is scarcely necessary to premise that, as she did not partake o' the lickers . . . so neither did she participate in the infirmity o' memory an' motive power that paralysed me durin' the latter part o' my sojourn at the Hotel Tout le Monde, an' also in a greater or a lesser degree, throughout the whole o' the succeedin' nicht.

Accordin' to Tibbie's account, then, we had a 'consid'ble' variety o' drinks over an' above the champagne I had ordered an' paid for, an' it is needless to remark, *en passant*, as the Frenchies wad say, that said drinks were brocht in, not at my dictation, but solely at the instigation o' my American freends, wha, it wad appear, were greater adepts at 'likerin' up' than I hae ony pretension till. This was subsequent to the consumption o' the champagne, hooever, an' after it had begun to exert its malign influences upon oor intellectual faculties. Had I been perfectly *compos mentis*, of coorse, nae amount o' temptation an' persuasion that my American freends could hae brocht to bear upon me wad hae led me astray frae the paths of sobriety an' uprichtness, but ye see, when wine's in wut's oot . . . A gless or twa o' champagne seemed a very harmless indulgence, especially after the transaction o' sic wechty business as is involved in the servin' o' ane's sel' heir to a fortune o' twa hunder an' fifty thousand dollars, inclusive o' a gowd mine amang the cannibalistic Injins o' Idaho, but see what it led to! I sanna dilate further on the subject by way o' pointin' a moral or adorning a tale, but will proceed to set doon a succinct narration o' facks, drawn, as I've already said frae the storehoose o' Tibbie's memory.

'I say, July,' quo' Mr Twentyman familiarly addressin' Mr Julius Caesar Pilkem, 'them European drinks air'nt nothin' like ourn they ain't.'

'Wall I guess not,' quo' Mr Pilkem, 'poor wake stuff they are—wouldn't go deown in our country, Zekel, nohow, 'cept in the very perlite cirkles. People as likes to be thought summat oncommon may perfess to like 'em, but for all that they aint the sort o' tipple for this 'ere chile. No, sirr.'

'Jist suppose we have one or tew of them things?' quo' Mr Twentyman.

'Wall,' quo' Mr Pilkem thochtfully, 'the idear has a sort o' refreshin' look abeout it. Yes, sirr, it have; but I guess we can't have the rekisite liquids in this here cuss of a place like as we cud have in New York, and eout West genn'ly. But we're coves of an inquirin' turn of mind—we air; we'll jist ax the *garçon.*'

So the *garçon* was ca'd in an' put through his carritches, an' the outcome o' the conference was that an assortment o' bottles, containin' divers kinds o' lickers, soon made their appearance upo' the table . . . Mr Twentyman, as I've said, is famous as a mechanical inventor, an' I can testify frae experience that his greatness as an inventor . . . extends also into the regions o' chemistry; for oot o' some four or five kinds o' licker placed before him by the *garçon,* he manufactured— I am not prepared to specify preceesely how many different kinds o' drinks—but they were something 'pretty consid'ble', as he himsel' wad say . . . Havin' completed his chemical experiments, Mr Twentyman poured aff a gless an' handit it to me, wi' a request that I wad pree it.

'Yes sirr,' quo' Mr Pilkem, addin' his gentle persuasives to those o' his freend an' fellow-countryman, 'Gist yeou try that 'ere drink, Mr Bodkin, an' tell me if it ain' better than that 'ere fizzlin' liquid o' yourn. It will do yeou a world o' good, sirr; that it will, onmistakably, sirr; yes sirr.'

'Hoo d'ye ca' it?' quo' I, 'for I aye like to ken the names o' the things I eat an' drink afore I let them ower my craig, or even within my teeth.'

'That licker, sirr,' quo' Mr Pilkem, 'is a most elegant thirst-quencher as ever was invented, and could have been invented nowhere else in creation, 'cept eout West in our treemendjus country. Yes, sirr! That'ere is what we call a "cocktail".'

'Weel, Mr Pilkem,' quo' I, puttin' the gless to my lips, 'I'se tak' a prievin' o't, juist to please ye, because ye're no ilka body, but I maun tak' the liberty to state that I'm no partial to new-fangled drinks, as a general rule.'

So I tane a wee sirple o' the licker, juist no to hae it to be said that I was nice; but my word, it let me ken whaur it gaed!— scouthered my thrapple, in fack, the haill way doon! A 'Cocktail', yea! 'Od, it wad be mair correck to ca' it a hedgehog. Still an' on, though it was het, it had nae ugesome gou aboot it, an' folk, I daursay, micht come to like it in process o' time . . . My recollection o' the 'cocktail' is veeve eneugh, but I am personally oblivious as to the palatability o' the ither kinds o' graith that I am led to understand, were manufactured an' drunk that afternoon within the precincts o' the Hotel Tout le Monde . . . To mak' a lang story short, I am creditably informed, an' have every rizzen to believe, that the followin' drinks were brewed by Mr Twentyman an' partially consumed by the present writer durin' that afternoon's sederunt in the Tout le Monde, viz: 'Sherry Cobblers', 'brandy smashes', 'eye-openers', 'moustache twisters', 'corpse revivers', 'morning glories', 'tip and tics', an' 'one of them things'. Enough to poison a parish! I really wonder hoo I survived sic a fiery ordeal. An' the best o't is, it was a' done oot o kindness to me; *that* was what Messrs Twentyman an' Pilkem professed to have in view; they wad gi'e Mr Bodkin 'a treat' they said. Truly it was killin' kindness. I fervently houp sic anither treat will never be offered for my acceptance. Tibbie saw hoo the bools were rowin', and wisely resolved to hae me transported to the Hotel de la Grenouille Couchant afore a crisis sid occur . . . [22]

Subsequent essays in the series contain much memorable writing, including a hilarious set-piece dinner with all the traditional trimmings—

frogs' legs, snails, bits of dogs and things, consumed in perfect innocence of their true nature and discovered shudderingly afterwards: 'What a revelation! To think there was actually a horse in the *carte!*' There is nothing else quite like this in Scottish letters.

Correspondence in the vernacular had been a feature of the Scottish press before the *People's Journal* entered the arena, and no doubt would have continued at a certain level whether Latto had written or not. But its centrality to popular newspaper enterprise stems from his demonstration of its potential and the readership he built up for it throughout Scotland. The success of the column created an extensive literature in its wake, and the pseudonymous vernacular correspondent became a regular feature of the Scottish press during the second half of the nineteenth century, including such figures as 'Geordie Short' of the *Hamilton Advertiser*, probably created by the paper's editor Alexander Whamond, 'Jeems Sim' of the *Northern Figaro*, hailed as the most authentic exponent of the dialect of Aberdeen during the period, and 'Airchie Tait' of the *Peterhead Sentinel*, alter-ego of its editor James Leatham, of whom more presently.[23]

All of them reflected in varying measure Latto's interest in regional dialect variations within Scotland itself. He introduced people from Glasgow and Edinburgh, Fife, Forfarshire and Angus, Aberdeenshire and the Highlands, and took pains to represent their speech orthographically, so that the way words were spelled reflected the way they actually sounded. While his followers were seldom so eclectic, they treated the nuances of local sound-pattern and idiom with equal fidelity. There arose in Scotland during these years a number of distinct local prose traditions based upon the speech idioms of specific communities whose distinguishing features were represented orthographically. The movement was intimately bound up with the development of the local press. Papers tended to sell within homogeneous speech communities where vernacular usage was the central feature of local identity and they often adopted the local form of Scots in their role as representatives of the people. The commercial organisation of the press reinforced this. Except for the big city papers it was locally produced, locally written, and locally financed. Ultimately it did not matter what people twenty miles away thought, or even whether they understood, because they didn't buy the paper.

Another important influence was the changing nature of journalism, especially the skills deemed necessary for entry to the profession. Recruitment was a rough and ready business at first, as the diverse backgrounds and attainments of early Victorian newspapermen testify, and nowhere was this more evident than in that basic technique of reporting—the mastery of some form of shorthand. Most of the older school of Scottish journalists were self-taught, using *ad hoc* methods derived from the basically visual systems which prevailed during the early decades of the century. The political reforms of the early Victorian period, however, gave a new prominence to the platform, the public meeting, and the spoken word. As the move towards verbatim reporting grew, pressmen found themselves in need of a system of shorthand based not upon how the language looked, but on how it sounded; and in 1837, Isaac Pitman published his *Stenographic Sound Hand*, the first version of the phonographic system that was to dominate journalism for the remainder of the century. It went through eight editions and sold upwards of 200,000 copies in a decade. Not only journalists used it, it permeated the newspaper world; many compositors could set directly from phonetic shorthand manuscript fom the early 1840s onwards.[24]

But Pitman was not content merely to develop his new system; he proceeded to explore its implications for the printed word more generally. He pointed out how much the spoken and written language diverged. Many of the words he read in books as an adolescent were not used in speech by anybody he knew, so although he recognised them and understood their meaning, the irregularities of standard orthography meant that he was uncertain how they should be pronounced. With his friend Alexander John Ellis, he began a vigorous campaign for a rational system of orthography in which the same combination of sounds would under similar circumstances always be represented by the same combinations of symbols.[25] Pitman and Ellis quickly realised that in a speech-based system, in order to spell 'correctly' one had first to be able to pronounce 'correctly', and one of their goals was a reduction in the varieties of spoken English in favour of a more uniform pronunciation based upon an orthographically logical written language. They recognised that this might create difficulties for the Scots whose vernacular was not a divergent variety of standard English, and who possessed a separate phonoglogical and orthographic tradition, but they urged the adoption of their system north of the border because, they claimed, it would widen the market for Scottish writers by making the vernacular more intelligible to English readers; they went on to demonstrate their point by translating 'Tam O'Shanter' into the new orthography.[26]

The Scots responded positively, but not in favour of uniformity with England, and still less in favour of standardisation of the vernacular within Scotland. They began instead to experiment with the orthography of written Scots, making it more responsive to the regional diversity of contemporary speech, with the result that a whole new popular prose sprang into being. The basic medium for this was already at hand, in the newspaper press, with its ample column space, its local control, and its unrivalled penetration of the popular market, as was the personnel, in the shape of a large and growing corps of journalists moving freely between the newspaper and popular literary markets and, thanks to their training, thoroughly abreast of the phonographic and spelling reform movements.[27]

One of the earliest examples dates from 1838, just a year after Pitman published, and it appears in the columns of the *Orkney and Shetland Journal*. This, despite its title, was compiled and published in London, and its editor was Arthur Anderson, a distinguished Shetlander who later founded the P & O shipping line and sat in Parliament as Liberal MP for Orkney 1847–52. The paper was evidently popular in outlook judging from the tone of one at least of its correspondents 'Maansie o' Slushiegarth', who looked on all change as a gentry-inspired plot, and bitterly attacked the new mainland steamer on the grounds that it would put up the price of everything and fill the islands with tourists:

Diel hae me in da warld be na just gaen gyte! Da Lurick fock shuttin' wi' cannon, an' lightin' a der collies an' caandles an' dennerin' an' drinkin' an' rejoisin' aboot a fule ting o' a stemmer shipp itt da Queen is sent ta carry da jantry's letters ivery ook to da sooth! Fule moniments itt dey irr! What gude 'ill dis stemmer shipp doe ta wiz poor fock? Will shoe mak meal ony shaper? Truggs! am fear'd shoe'll doe nae gude ava' 'cept helpin' wirr jantry ta gaing awa' ta da sooth wi' less spewin'. Na, na, I aye said itt nae gude wid come o' new fangled tings an it'll shune come to pass itt dis stemmer i'll mak kye an' sheep an' butter an' eggs an' a' kinds o' cyuntry proddick muckle dearer. Forby da scores an' dizzens an' maybe hunders o' idle jaantin' bodies it'll be commin' frae da sooth, just lek da locusts itt cam da Egypt davoorin' da substance o' da laand! An de'll be tellin' wiz itt kens sae muckle better itt wi' shud hae rodds an' packets an' ferry boats an' inns, and muckle mair nonsense, just ta help dem ta rin o'er an' devoor wiz in a shorter time. Deil cut dem aff![28]

Many of the leading features of the Shetland dialect with its intriguing mixture of Scots and Norn elements are represented here, including replacement of the consonant 'th' (absent from Norn) by 'd' or 't', as in 'da/the', 'ting/thing'; various devices to show the modified Shetland 'o' vowel, as in 'Lurick/Lerwick', 'shoe/she', and 'fock/folk'; and the tendency to insert a 'y' sound between an initial consonant and a vowel, as an 'cyuntry/country'.[29]

There was similar correspondence in mainland papers, marked by the same innovatory spirit. Here, for example, is 'Peter Hardie' writing in the *Free Press* on the bells of Aberdeen. From the carefully phonetic spelling something of the actual pronunciation may be inferred:

MAISTER AEDITUR,—Twa weeks syne a corryspondent o' yours ca'd attention to the bells, an', as it is usual wi' a' sic-like, spak some sense, an' a gude dael o' nonsense aboot them. I dinna mean, hooever, to reply to him, nor to nae ither body in parteekler, but jist to express my nain sentiments o' the subject. An' firstly, that we've gotten a set o' gweed bells, I think, is past dispute . . . tho' . . . I wud add that . . . the lug requares some trainin to appresheate it . . . there's been cry—a'maist bairnly, Sir, in its natur—for tunes playit. Noo, Sir, tak ye my word for't playin' teens upo' bells, is something an'alygous . . . to playin' teens upo' the fiddle wi' yer fingers instead o' the bow—a vera awkard means to an unsatisfactory result . . . I thochtna muckle . . . at first, but noo, Sir, fan I've lockit my choppie door, an' am stappin' awa hame at nicht—(gin the weather binna a' the waur)—ye may see me stannin' up in rapt attiteed at ilka ither point to hear the legitimat bell-meesick. An' as my lug, an' the young lads at the ropes, get better trained, so proportionately does my enjoyment grow.[30]

This shows a number of features of mid-northern Scots like the use of 'nain' as a possessive pronominal adjective, the raising and broadening of vowels in various positions as in 'meesick', 'teen/tune', 'attiteed/attitude', and the initial fricative as in 'far/where', 'fat/what', and 'fan/when'.

The next example comes from Fife, and illustrates the tendency for public debate to be conducted in Scots through the columns of newspapers in a quite unostentatious way. In the mid 1870s there was a lengthy dispute in the Anstruther-based *East Fife Record* about the financial obligations of the school board at Crail. As usual, most of the correspondents used pseudonyms but it is clear that one of the contributors was the Provost of Crail himself. Here, however, is 'Ploughman Tam' on 'Crail Skule Boord', and once again his orthography reflects phonological features of his local dialect—that of east Fife:

> SIR—We are gaun tae hae a nu elekshun o' the Skule Boord very shune noo, an' am nae shure wha is gawn to be nominat, altho' I heer clatters on the streets aboot this ane an' the tither ane; but as warrant baith parties'l hae their ain foulk tae bring forrit in gude time, an' wee, the electors, sud be reddy tae vote for them that wee think wull dae best accordin to oor ain noshuns.
>
> Weel, ye see, my noshun is, we sud pit in men that wull giv us the best educashun at the sma'est expenses. Noo, as far as I can oonderstand baith pairties, ane o' them wants tae turn ane o' the skules intae a Infant's Skule, an' the ither ane intae what they ca' a grammer skule. That's what I rakken tae be whaur they can get thir bairns tae learn latin, french, and greek, an' something else that they ca' mathie mattiks, which is verry creditabel, an' I daursay they are nae verry faur rang, but dae ye no see that they can get that gude things at St Aundrus at thir ain expenses; an' nae be wantin us rate-payers tae pay it for them. The twa teachers we hae e'noo can teach the maist o' thae brainches, but then that sunna pleese sum foulk, for they maun send them awa sum ither way tae learn mainers tae the bargin, an' whaur cun they get that better than tae send them awa frae hame tae mix wi' brawer foulks bairns? A' gude eneugh, but as I hae said, let them pay furt themsels. They maun hae the twa skules altert at a grate expense, after that has been dune alreddy at a hevvy ootlay o' siller. But besides a' that, I'm tell't they want tae build a skule up in the Muirs, for the bairns there awa. That wull cost a gude wheen hunder punds, a'm thinkin'. By the time that's a dune, wee'l be taxed tae the tune o' twa or three thoosans maybe. Sae meukle for the skules.[31]

The following west mid Scots example comes from the comic paper *Seestu*, published in Paisley during the 1880s. 'Comic' papers were a distinct sub-genre of the Victorian newspaper press: they were published weekly at 1*d*. with two colums of large type to the page, anything from eight to sixteen quarto pages per issue, and contained an attractive mixture of illustrations, poetry and prose. Their mainstay was satire on local politics and public affairs, often in strongly-marked local forms of vernacular Scots.[32] *Seestu*—*anglice* 'D'you see?', a local shibboleth and, by transference, an alternative name for Paisley itself—was a lively example of the form, and the following set of spoof love letters between a Paisley servant girl 'Jinnet M'Jinnet' and her boyfriend 'Sandy Alexander', a garter weaver, passed in its columns in the spring of 1881. Here the conventions of the written language are ruthlessly undermined and the rhythms of the spoken verna-cular hold absolute and riotous sway:

1 March 1881

Dear Jinnet,—i wis share i wud rite tae ye, i telt ye that i wud rite tae ye before ye left hear, and it's wi' that feelin' that i noo grup ma pen tae sit doon tae skrape ye twa-three strokes tae let ye ken am aye weel, and the same yet. i ken that ye ken am no vera guid at the riten, and a ken that yer no vera guid at the heerin, sin ye got yer lugs bored for the cheena eerins, but al try and rite as big and as lood's a can . . .

15 March 1881

Dear Sandy—i got ye're letter . . . and am gled tae sae it fun me weel . . . Man, Sandy, i kent yer rite before ever i seed it. Sich a han o rite, every yin in the hoose wis sirprised at it, and Maggy Scudd said she beleeved thir wisna anither han o rite like it in a' Scotland . . . Man, i donno hoo ye could dae yon at a', Maggie said it wis the italyan stile wi sae mony bends int, bit i sed it wis the creechian stile, and wis i no right, for when i opened it oot did a no see it wis ritten wi a compatishun of saft saip an blecknin. Its a gran mixture for stilish riten, naething that ever i seed yet cam up tae the creechian stile o artitectural riten. Faith ye soud tak oot an invenshun fort . . .

29 March 1881 [This time Sandy had news]:

Dear Jinnet . . . ye'll be sorry tae hear that poor Peter the gairdner's wife's a widow . . . Ye mind, Jinnet, that she has a pin leg an the puir body has had mony ups and doons in this worl. She wis owre in oor hoos last nicht, she wis in deep murnins wi her pin leg pentit black, an geyan doon in the mooth wi her way ot, bit deed i think shes no caren very much . . . auld Peter was gie hard on her, for whanever he had a big lot of cabbages, an leeks, an diffrent sorts o trees tae plant, he wid mak her wauk stracht up the saft grun an he wid come efter her wi the plants an drap them intae holes she made wi her pin leg. He used tae say, that forby a gran devision o labour, it pit them at fine equal distances frae yin anither, an that, said he, wis the hole secret o growin big cabbages . . .

19 April 1881 [Jinnet's outpourings, however, continued unchecked]

Dear Sandy— . . . I hope . . . ye have made up your mind tae come tae Pasely shin. Ye micht try and come some saturday aboot the middle o next week, whan am no expectin ye and gie me a happy surprise, naething wid please me better than tae see ye come stapping in withoot ever openin the door and staunin in the middle o the flare wi yer back again the wa before ma vera een afore i kent whaur i wis, man it wid be fine, it wid be as guids a sensational scene in a hapney story o blue luv and murder, and I think ye canna dae better than tae dae it. Man, Sandy ye wid enjoy yersel fine here for a day, bit it wid tak ye a month tae see a' the gran sichts that's here. Man, thir some richt braw streets flanked on every side wi gret big blocks of buildins; every yins as bigs a hoos . . .[33]

The device permitted an unusually wide range of phonetically inspired spellings, even to the extent of overriding word boundaries. Later in the letter of 1 March, Sandy twice uses the compound 'nafu/an awful', as in '. . . he was in a nafu state aboot it . . .'; one notes also 'donno' for 'don't know' (15 March), 'guids/goods as', 'bigs/big as' (19 April). There is also a high tolerance for non-standard idioms designed to throw local speech patterns into prominence, as in 'she sed yer niver tae mind the pasely bodies, for thir queer yins, an thir no yin of them the yae kind . . .' Neither of the correspondents uses the characteristic dental plosive 'tu/tat', and the inference would be that by the early 1880s this was a decaying feature. One writer spoke of his mother using it when he was a boy, with the implication that even then it was considered rather archaic: 'Ma mither's auld-fashioned way o' speakin' was a rale trate. She had the Paisley language at her fingers' end . . . and the lasses used tae staun and draw her oot, as she wad say in rale Paisley Scotch: "Weel na, Seestu tat, and what is't tu wants!"'[34]

Latto himself possessed the sublest ear of all. As a final example, perhaps the following may suffice. It is ostensibly a letter to the editor of the *People's Journal* from Tammas Bodkin's sister-in-law, at a period before either of his biographies became fixed—reproaching him for revealing her age (falsely she alleges) in an earlier issue of the paper. Not only is the usage localised geographically and highly specific in terms of social class and sex, but it is also deftly revealing about the outlook and character of the speaker, a prim, aspiring, pseudo-genteel Dundee woman, acutely conscious of language conventions and fatally unable to control them—she, uniquely, uses the deadly initial fricatives 'fin' and 'fat'. The idiom is that of working-class Dundee affected by a consciously acquired petty-bourgeois veneer. This is a recognisable and, perhaps, surviving type:

> MASTER EDITOR,—I cudna think eneuch on Saterday nicht last fin your paper was handed in to me, an' fin I read yon awfu' like stuff aboot me, wrote by that nesty, ill-luken like footer, Tam Bodkin. Losh, I thocht my een wisna marrows, especially fin I think on the way he treated me fin I was ower at Dindee—but it was an aye my thocht that he was a twa-faced sort o' buddie—an' I'll tell you fat it is, I see it noo. But I think it'll be after this an' nearer Yule ere I veesit Tam Bodkin agen. Sic a nesty leein' buddie to say that I cam ower frae Edinbroch no to lat Jamie ken my age. Jamie kens my age better nor Tam Bodkin at ony rate. But I dinna think Jamie'll commit sic a great mistak' as Tam did onyway, to rin awa' wi' Tib Thrumpints, an' her forty-twa, an' him only twenty-twa, because she had about thirty-sax nots. He shun made spooley o' hit after he got it at ony rate, atween a suit o' new clase an' ae thing or anither. An' I assure you, Master Editor, he had muckle need o' them, for you widna seen a tinkler lookener chield in a' the Cooget o' Edinbroch . . .[35]

This interest in a speech-based prose is one of the most intriguing and least explored aspects of the literary scene in Scotland during the second half of the nineteenth century, but it was not an exclusively Scottish concern. Experiments were being conducted along broadly similar lines in various parts of the English-speaking world.[36] The Americans were particularly active. They struggled to evolve a distinctive national style, a reflection of their growing self-confidence as the USA took its place on the world stage as a great military and economic Power.[37] Like the Scots they had little desire for incorporation into the periphery of a monolithic

London-centred English literary culture, and they too turned to the speech of the common people as the basis for a new literary language. The figure most commonly associated with this movement, of course, was Samual Clemens, more famous under his pseudonym 'Mark Twain', but the way had been prepared by a number of writers during the 1850s and 1860s who won considerable acclaim on both sides of the Atlantic. Indeed American vernacular humourists like Josh Billings (Henry Wheeler Shaw, 1818–85) and Artemus Ward (Charles Farrar Browne, 1834–67) were as popular in Britain as they were in America. All the leading members of the school had close ties with the press, and published, at least initially, in its columns; Shaw in the *New Ashford Eagle*; Browne in the *Cleveland Plain Dealer*; Joel Chandler Harris, the creator of 'Uncle Remus' in the *Atlanta Constitution*; Twain in the *Territorial Enterprise* of Virginia City, Nevada.[38]

This is an intriguing parallel. Scottish writers had access to speech-based American prose in considerable quantities from the later 1850s onwards. Chatto and Windus published the first British edition of *Josh Billings his Book of Sayings* in 1858. Artemus Ward was available in book form from 1866, and was immediately pirated by at least one Scottish paper.[39] Two general anthologies were published during the 1860s: *Yankee Drolleries, the Most Celebrated Works of the Best American Humourists* and *More Yankee Drolleries*, which contained extract from Artemus Ward, Major Jack Downing, Orpheus C Kerr, the Biglow Papers, the Nasby Papers, Hans Breitmann, Oliver Wendell Holmes, and Josh Billings.[40] Material of this type would in any case have been available directly from the American papers, extracts from which were regularly reprinted in the Scottish press. There were long-standing and close links between the two countries and in some respects they faced similar problems as the century advanced.[41] It was to one another, for example, that Scotland and America tended to look as they struggled with the implications of England's rise as the dominant world Power, and this parallel popular tradition is continuously present in the background of the Scottish vernacular revival.

Although American characters occur frequently in popular fiction, there is little direct influence at a linguistic level of any real consequence with the exception, possibly, of one writer, Alexander Burgess of Kennoway, who made his living as a fiddler and dancing-master in Fife (1810–1886).[42] Under the pseudonym Poute he published vernacular poems in the *People's Journal* during the 1860s and 1870s whose orthographic freedom was extreme and whose typographical playfulness may owe something to Henry Wheeler Shaw. Shaw's writing was aphoristic in style, rather like a Yankee version of the Book of Proverbs, and he had a penchant for animal studies, amusing little pieces on the habits (usually undesirable) of horses, mules, pigs and so on:

> I hav studdyed cats clusely for years, and hav found them adikted tew a wild state. Tha haint got affek shun, nor vartues ov enny kind, tha will skratch their best friends, and wont ketch mice unless that are hungry. It has bin sed that tha are good to make up into sassages; but this iz a grate mistake, i hav bin told bi a

sassage maker that tha dont kompare with dogs . . . Thare iz anuther thing about them which makes them a good investment for poor folks. A pair ov cats will yield each year, without any outlay, something like eight hundred per cat . . .[43]

The most accessible source for Burgess's work is probably the collection issued by the Leng press in 1875, with the title *The Book of Nettercaps, being Poutery, Poetry, and Prose*, by Poute, of the Leven Saat Pans. Poute is amusing in small doses, but his assumption of zany sub-literacy can be a little tiresome when the pieces are read in succession. He is seldom merely droll, though; his whimsical meditations on domestic and hedgerow animals often have an undercurrent of seriousness, as in the burlesque A DRESS TO KATTS, whose neo-classical facade masks a gleeful deconstruction of the imperial pretensions of high Eng. Lit. by means of a Scots of the most grossly demotic kind:

> Dicend ye 15. hevinly graces and mewsis 9.
> give words that brethe—and Burnin' thocht to Shine,
> Inspire my Mus—ye Anshint Gods o' greese,
> & ayd a sun to Write A Mr Peese
> on Katts . The bease fo'k Keeps in their hooses—
> for the ekspress purpise of catchin' Their moosis
> ye Bruts—sume of you ar Black & sum o' ye White
> But you ar billys awl to skart & Bite
> you like far Best to ett yer Mise livin'
> & prefer a katsht 1. to 1. Given .
> ye like kys milk & can cry—'kurrow'
> & ye nevir Need to wait till ye'r beard grow .
> You are kittl't with beards . When ye see A kur—
> ye stick up yir Baks, & spit & crys—'wurr'
> ye also can ett sparry's—livin an Raw
> Fethirs, neb & feet, ye stap into yer maw .
> you can ett fish guts, in fac—ony thing
> & spit oot naething—when yer grace ye Sing,—
> yer cairles rins awl nicht—& swears & skreeks—
> & skreps up fo'ks ingin beds—& their leeks
> You dont agree—with 'Jon Filps' 'midnicht
> courtships'.—
> You gowl when Struck with a stone on the hips
> yer wors Than Afrikens—or hethen saaviges—
> For ye destroy both peepils karrits & kabiges.[44]

The exploratory urge that took the vernacular revival out into the vennels and closes of the new industrial centres was reflected in a number of different ways by the press of the period, and the range of tasks for which Scots was used was steadily extended. There were poems in the vernacular, novels with vernacular dialogue, editorial or near-editorial comment in the vernacular, vernacular advertisements, and quite enormous quantities of antiquarian, historical, folkloristic and musicological feature writing which dealt with every aspect of Scottish popular life and culture in which the vernacular also, and inevitably, figured largely.

There was a growing awareness of the complexity of the language situation in Scotland which showed itself in a tendency to report Scots speakers verbatim without silently translating what they said into standard English. One of the best examples is a series of interviews by William Alexander with various local people during the 1870s, including Alexander Henderson the Warlock of Wartle, one of the last of the 'canny men', and George Webster, Sheriff-Officer of Oldmeldrum, the leading thief-taker in the North-East. This was in the vernacular throughout. How much of it was straight reporting of an obviously colourful character, and how much was contributed by Alexander himself it is impossible now to say, although the introduction points to a fairly major role for the latter:

> I am no man of the pen, and never was, nor pretend to be; whereupon I had ill gotten a beginning when it occurred to me that, in these days when mere literary people are so very abundant, I ought to command the services of an Editor, rather than undergo the fatigue of writing. Accordingly, the public and myself have his services by way of scrivener. I'll keep him correct on the real particulars; and if he diverge a little now and then for the sake of what a respected friend of mine calls 'Gran'mither gossip', just blame him and no me . . .
> Anither point—an' I see I'm jist at it by naitral gravitation. My tongue runs freest i' the native Doric. An' so in place o' fine English, which was spoken by none but the gentry in my youth—though ye'll get it in ilka ane's mou now-a-days—we'se leave the Editor to dicht it up as weel's he can in the rael vernacular o' the Coonty.

The result is a minor masterpiece, a racy and vivid account of the North-East underworld at a time when hanging and transportation turned many routine encounters between police and criminals into life or death struggles. It was privately printed with the title *A Criminal Officer of the Old School* (Aberdeen, 1880), and had it reached a wider audience it would certainly have been recognised as a classic of Victorian crime literature.[45]

Crime, indeed, formed a prominent part of the staple fare in the Scottish press. As George Webster told Alexander: 'There's naething fowk likes better to read, Sir, I can tell you, nor a gweed criminal case.' There was detailed reporting of the more shocking offences, and lengthy testimony from all the notable trials. Few things commanded so much column space as a first rate murder. Police court affairs were faithfully chronicled as well, and often in Scots. The lively 'Side Lights on City Life' column which ran in the *Glasgow Weekly Mail* in the 1890s illustrates this well. It revelled in the unrespectable side of lower working-class life in a city of mixed Highland, Lowland and Irish stock, each with its own rich and vigorous patois:

> Mary McFarlane or Law was as Oirish as Conn the Shaughraunn's mother. Mary had 'baptised' her husband in bed, the little ceremony taking place in a house in William Street.

Mary He strook me foirst, yer honour, ind Oi strook him back.

Bailie MITCHELL It's not often that we get this side of the question. (Laughter) It's generally the other way.

Mary Well, he called me a lot av names.

John Law This is my woife. On Saturday noight Oi was in bed, ind she wakened me, ind streek me tew or three toimes. She flang watther about me ind the little lassie. A neighboor woman wint for the polis. Oi didn't know. The tew polises came. Oi didn't charge her, ind they didn't take her, but whin the polisis wint away she became woorse.

Mary He's nat sober the now, yer honour. (Laughter)

John On Saturday Oi only tashted wan schooner ov beer, ind . . .

Bailie M Was she drunk?

John Whin was she sober? (Laughter) She's drunk every toime she can get it. (Laughter).

Mary Me native fut was never insoide ov a public house en Saturday. (Laughter)

Policeman The woman was the worse of drink. Then the girl said that her mother had struck her father.

Bailie M (addressing the prisoner) I don't think I would live long with you. I would be for running away. (Laughter) The case is not proven, unfortunately. Keep your hands to yourself.[46]

Sandy Fletcher was a Hielandman who spoke ta Gaelic petter than he could spoke ta Saxon. Sandy was up for the ninth time for begging.

Sandy I'm ta ole poatman from Tanoon.

Bailie McKELLAR How long since waas you'll pe here before? (Laughter)

Sandy Four mons. I'll go avay pack to Tanoon if sool let me avay.

FISCAL The last time Sandy was here he got thirty days. He has a brother in a good position in Dunoon.

Sandy I waas on ta spree.

Bailie McK You just broke away and came to Glasgow. Do you belong to the Fletchers o' Glenlane?

Sandy If she'll get a shance . . .

Bailie McK You're a lonely man in Glasgow! Man, you should be helping them at Dunoon, where they are busy. You're lazy, Sandy. I send you thirty days to prison.

Sandy Hoo mich?

FISCAL Only thirty days, Sandy! (Laughter)

Sandy It's too mich, P'ilie! (Laughter)[47]

There are many persons in Glasgow who never heard the cuckoo who have heard the Arab Band. Four members of the 'Cowcaddens Gutter Orchestra' were charged at the Northern Police Court with having a stone for their pillow. Their names were Jamie McKinley, Jamie Shaw, Hughie McGuire, and Erchie Bowers.

Bailie McK Are they making it a practice staying out at night and sleeping on stairs?

McKinley's Stepmother No *my* man's boy, onyway! (Laughter)

FISCAL   Jamie, can you write?

Jamie   Naw. My mit's too shaky! (Laughter)

Policeman   This boy was brought here two months ago for sleeping on a stair. He sleeps in 'dunnies' sometimes.

FISCAL   Jamie is the drum-major of the 'Coocaddens Gutter Baun'. (Laughter)

McKinley's Stepmother   Well, he fetches hame nae money.

Bailie McK   Was he ever in a situation?

McKinley's Stepmother   No, but he was in a coal cairt. (Laughter)

Bailie McK   Well, he could earn as honest a penny wi' gaun wi' a coal cairt as doing onything else. (Laughter) I see you've the whole baun' here. Jamie Shaw whit instrument do you play? (Laughter)

Jamie Shaw (looking down)   The penny whussle. (Laughter)

Bailie McK   Mr Fiscal, have they their whussles and drum wi' them? (Laughter)

Policeman   No, they hid them, but I found them.

Bailie McK   And did each yin claim his own? (Laughter)

Jamie Shaw   Naw, we wur feart. (Laughter)

Jamie's Father   His mother, sir, is in the infirmary.

FISCAL   My impression is that you don't pay very much attention to him.

Bailie McK   And these others are—

FISCAL   Hughie McGuire and Erchie Bowers.

An old woman, with no sparkle in her eyes, leant on one of the boys and said—This yin is sma' for his age, 'cause he was sent oot to wark ower sune.

Bailie McK   And you were a' sleeping on stairs? Do you play in the ban' for pleasure or do ye mak' it a profession? Weel, do you play for money: tell me?

Jamie Shaw   W-we play for pennies and ha'pneys. (Laughter)

Bailie McK (leaning back on his chair)   Weel, you've as much right to play on the streets as thae German ban's. (He! He!) Aye have you, as long as the people are entertained. (He! He!) I would rather see and hear you playing than thae German ban's, although you might try and get a wee better instruments; and then, getting money, you could go home to your mothers wi't. (Laughter) But in the first place you must go to the school and be able to write your names. It seems, however, that you boys are going to the bad, and that with you music is not having the elevating tendency that it should have. I suppose you think it's fine fun? (Laughter) Did you say it was for amusement or money that you play?

The Orchestra, simultaneously and *fortissimo*   For money!

Bailie McK   There's some truth left in you yet! (Laughter) I think you would be far better to go back to your work, and give up the big tin can and the penny whussles—(laughter)—the public consider you are becoming a nuisance. By the by, how would it do to give them the birch? Have you, Mr Fiscal, the birch ready? (Laughter)

FISCAL   Yes: we've a few of them.

Bailie McK   Fegs, I believe it would tell smartly! (Laughter) But, I'm sorry to punish you boys.

The Orchestra, simultaneously and *pianissimo*   Aw, don't d'it man! (Laughter)

FISCAL   It's their first offence. Thirty days they would get the next time they came up.

Bailie McK   Any of you wha can write, write 'thirty days' doon, and look at it every morning! (Laughter) But what you should read rather is the good Auld Book. Read a verse out o't every morning, and then you'll be good boys! You are

a' admonished. Now, I've gien you a long address. See and turn it into a wise course; and you mothers, try and look after them better, for if you don't your boys will go to the bad. Take them away.
The Orchestra simultaneously and *fortissimo*   Thenk ye, sir![48]

The last of the important vernacular correspondents during the period, and in some respects the most interesting of all, was 'Airchie Tait', who featured in the early years of the new century in the columns of the *Peterhead Sentinel*. His creator, James Leatham, took over the paper in 1897 as editor-manager in succession to David Scott, the nephew of the ballad-collector Peter Buchan.[49] The *Sentinel* started in 1856 as a popular twopenny weekly. It changed hands several times before it was bought by David Scott in 1866, and it remained in his control until near the century's end.[50] It was Liberal in politics, and served the flourishing fishing town of Peterhead and the surrounding hinterland of northern Aberdeenshire. For many years it was one of the brightest and most attractive papers in the North of Scotland, ably edited, wide in its views, technically well-produced, and full of interesting local literary and historical material. From 1864 it had to meet the challenge of a rival Liberal paper, the *Buchan Observer*, also published in Peterhead, as well as fend off increasing competition from the Aberdeen and Dundee papers. When Leatham took it over it was entering the final stage of its existence.[51]

The new editor was an Aberdonian, born in 1865 in humble circum-stances. His father, a soldier, died abroad and his mother brought up her five children in her native city, earning her living at the family trade as a hand-loom weaver. The boy had a secure and stimulating childhood amongst the still proud remnants of a radical occupation-group which had once formed the artistocracy of labour. He was surrounded by acute and knowledgeable adults who read widely, argued keenly, and could muster amongst them a wide range of interests and experiences; singers and storytellers, richly steeped in popular culture. His house was full of newspapers, magazines and books, the *Illustrated London News*, five Scottish weekly papers, the novels of Dickens and Scott. He used to watch the *Aberdeen Journal* go to press, and haunt the shop of a printer in Schoolhill who specialised in song-slips and ballads and between whose wares, hung temptingly in his window, could be glimpsed a hand press, reams of paper, and racks of type cases. After several years of schooling Leatham was apprenticed into the printing trade. His employers were affable, indolent men, and before many years had passed he was acting as manager. He read voraciously in the field of social theory, politics, and political economy, and became involved with several radical groups in the city, like the Socialist League, the Social Democratic Federation, and the Scottish Land and Labour League. His employers looked on their young foreman's activities with a fairly benign eye; after all, many fellow activists brought him their printing work, and he was good for business. But when he became involved in trade-union agitation and started addressing open air meetings, they dismissed him.

With the backing of a like-minded group, he set up a small press in the city and continued his propaganda work, writing, speaking, and publishing pamphlets like *An Eight Hours Day with Ten Hours Pay: How to Get it and How to Keep it* (Aberdeen 1890), *Was Jesus Christ a Socialist* (Aberdeen 1891), and *The Class War* (Aberdeen 1892). Things began to go wrong when he was persuaded to start up a newspaper. On the 12 December 1891 the *Workers' Herald—A Socialist Weekly* priced at a penny, made its first appearance, and ran for several weeks. The problem was that Leatham did not have the capital to make the venture work. After a little the advertisers withdrew, sales declined, and the burden of running the paper virtually single-handed took its toll. In January 1892 his health broke down. By the time he was fit again, the paper had stopped, and the business was on the verge of liquidation.

In the following months he worked as a compositor on the *Northern Daily News*. When it collapsed in turn in 1893 he got a job as a compositor on the Heywood press in Manchester through the good offices of Robert Blatchford of the *Clarion*. There, he continued with political work, becoming a leading member of the Social Democratic Federation and campaigning for its chairman H M Hyndman in the Burnley election of 1895. He was active also on the trade-union front, being instrumental in forcing a reduction in hours at Heywoods in line with the current agitation for a 48 hour week. He was dismissed again, and in the spring of 1896 became full-time organiser for the SDF with responsibility for the Midlands, the North of England and Scotland. He was plunged into a heavy schedule of writing, travelling, speaking, organising and attending meetings; he was homesick, overworked, and finding it difficult to make ends meet on his modest salary.

In the summer of 1897 an opening presented itself in Aberdeen, and he was quick to seize it. A local bookselling and publishing firm was planning to extend the printing side of its business and needed an experienced manager. There was a hiatus of some months before things got going and Leatham was hanging around the Trades Council Hall one day looking for prospective hands, when he met David Scott proprietor of the *Peterhead Sentinel* in urgent need of a skilled compositor for some weeks' temporary work. Taking an instant liking to the old man and having little better to do in the meantime, Leatham took the job. Scott was a shrewd judge of men and quickly discovered what his temporary compositor was made of; he struck a deal with Leatham's principals in which instead of starting a new plant in the city, they took over the *Sentinel* printing-works in Peterhead, and continued the newspaper with Leatham as editor-manager.

To a master printer of wide experience, the technical side of the business presented few problems; the Peterhead press was in any case relatively modern and well-equipped.[52] Moreover he responded at once to the town itself, thrust out on its promontory into the gray North Sea and the land of Buchan which lay behind it came to hold a high place in his affections especially after the grime of the Lancashire cotton towns. Yet his situation was not an easy one. The circulation of the paper had sunk to a critical point and it would clearly take great energy and patience to rebuild it. These Leatham possessed, and applied, and slowly began to pull the paper back towards the black. But editorial policy was deeply problematic. Here, after all, was a leading Socialist propagandist in charge of a Liberal-Unionist paper owned by a Tory, and circulating amongst a population in which, as the new editor was keenly aware, most forms of genuine radicalism sank like a stone.

He began cautiously, introducing his ideas gradually, building up a network of contacts, taking an active part in social life, and generally becoming an established member of the community. Sooner or later, however, an issue was certain to arise which would seriously divide the editor from the great majority of his readers. In 1899 the Boer War broke out. Leatham made his opposition to it public, and watched his circulation disappear overnight. His house was mobbed, his windows broken, his affairs plunged into crisis.

Ultimately, he weathered the storm, raised money to buy out the business, and soldiered on. He had miscalculated the willingness of the Liberal North-East to tolerate his views or to be influenced by them—at least in English. But what about Scots? He had used the medium before, in a pamphlet issued from his city press in 1891, called *The Ancient Hind: a Monologue in the Aberdeenshire Dialect.*[53] in which he had an old man advise a Glasgow shipyard worker tramping to Aberdeen to look for work about the pitfalls of the local job-market and the activities of the Aberdeen Socialists. Years later, in different and difficult circumstances, he revived the device. In the summer of 1903 he unveiled 'Airchie Tait'. He was conceived to all appearances on highly conservative lines: a prosperous tenant farmer, married, childless, embodying the essence of traditional good sense, moderation and worth. For several months, he was widely assumed to be real.

As time went on, however, his range extended—there was descriptive writing and evocative 'mood' pieces (rare in vernacular prose, or poetry,) and a growing number of subjects fell within his compass: politics and politicians, industrialisation and its social consequences, rural depopulation and the pull of the cities, currency matters and the distribution of wealth, scientific progress and its effects upon attitudes and beliefs, books and reading, temperance and prohibition, manners and social pretension, education, the shortcomings of the popular press. He had a number of pieces on social welfare which drew pointed attention to the condition of the poor and the plight of the working man. These were prompted by a meeting with an aged stonebreaker eking out his closing years in solitude and poverty:

> Says I tull 'im: 'Wiz ye ivver mairriet?'
> 'Fie, ay,' says he, knappin a steen.
> 'Bit the wife's awa, is she?'

'Ay,' says he, 'a curn year syne.'

'Ony faimly?'

'Ay, fowre sins an' a dother.'

'An' fat aboot them, than? Coudna ony o' them gie ye a bit seat bi the fire, an' haud ye ohn come oot ti this kin' o't?'

'Tie,' says he, 'they're a' groun up an' deein moderate weel. Naething ti braig aboot. Bit they a' hae aneuch adee wi' themsels. Foo sid I be a burden upon ony o' them as lang's Aw'm able ti dee mi ain turn?'

'Bit bleed's thicker than watter,' says I. 'Surely it's the duty o' wir ain flesh an' bleed ti dee something for's. Honour thy father an' thy mother's aul' advice. Fa's an aul' fail't man ti leuk tull gin it's nae his groun-up sins an' dothers?'

'Ti the Boord!' says he, wi' the quickness o' a man that's been thinkin't oot, an' hiz his answer ready.

'Tats, min! there's nae a Boord nooadays,' says I. 'It's the Pairish Coonicl 'at tak's aboot peer fowk.'

'Weel, weel, than, the parish coonicl be't. It's them Aw'll look tull. Aw pey't taxes money a 'ear an' day, an' I've a gweed richt ti get back some o't noo. As for mi faimly, they've a' aneuch adee wi' themsels. I dinna consider Aw've ony claim upo' them. I brocht them up—I hid ti dee that—an' I gied them some squeelin—I hid ti dee that tee wi' the last twa, ony wye. But they war a' shankit awa ti wark as seen as they war fit for't an' could get onything ti dee. Na, na, they're nae due me onything. If ye're airt an' pairt in bringin bits o' craturs in aboot, it's only bit yer duty ti gie them maet an' claes an' a curn raiths o' the squeel.'

'Bit gin ye dee yer duty ti them they sid surely dee their duty ti you,' says I.

The mannie turn't owre a steen an' gied twa knaps at it—a little een an' a big een—afore he gied me an answer. In fact he wiz knapping a' the time he wiz spikkin; bit of coorse I canna pit in the knaps.

Says he: 'Dinna fash yersel, gweed man. There's naething comin owre me. I tell ye again 'at a' my young fowk hiz aneuch adee wi' themsels. Aw'll be wearin awa in my bed some o' this nichts, Aw'm thinkin; an' Aw wid like that ony wye. Aw dinna want ti be a hanfi ti onybody. Bit if Aw should grou nae able ti dee mi ain turn, they'll verra lickly sen' me ti Maud. An' gin I gyang there, mi young fowk'll maybe hae ti pey a shullin or auchteenpince i' the wikk the piece for me. So my boord'll by pey't, like; an' that'll be better than sitting up at the fireside o' ony o' mi sins, an' gettin, maybe, a begrudg't bite an' sup, an' bein i' the rodd.'

'Divin ye believe in aul'age pensions?' says I.

'Ay,' says he, knappin anither steen; 'bit fat diz't maitter? Futher they gie ye siller ootside the hoose or maet an' claes inside, it's the same thing, like—it wid a' come aff the taxes.'

'Ay, bit,' says I, 'gin ye wiz ootside wi a pension ye wid hae yer leeberty.'

'Leeberty!' says he. 'Aw'm nae sikkin leeberty. Aw've hid leeberty a' mi days. Aw hid the leeberty ti traivel oot here the day—fowre mile o' grun. Aw hae the leeberty ti bide here as lang as it's daylicht. An' syne Aw'll hae the leeberty ti traivel back again ti the Broch. I hae the leeberty ti brak a' this steens. An' takin't a' thegither it's a lot mair leeberty than I want at my time of life. I could tak a rist fine. A lang rist wid dee me nae hairm. The sunny side o' the dyke on a fine day, the ingleneuk in coorse wither, a full o' tibacca fin Aw'm needin't, an' the bed ti crawl intull at nicht, an' the fient a flee I wid care aboot leeberty.'

'Weel, ye hinna muckle ambeeshin onywye, an' Aw'm thinkin ye've nivver hid muckle.'

The mannie rakit amo' the steens wi' his haimmer, an' aifter he hid pickit oot a shootable steen an' broken't, says he: 'Na, Aw'm nae ambeeshis. An' fat's mair, Aw'm thinkin it widna be a gweed job for you an' the like o' ye gin the like o' me *wiz* ambeeshis. Ambeeshin an' steenbrakkin dizna gyang thegither. An' there wid aye need ti be fowk ti dee the roch wark.'

There wiz plenty ti say, like; bit I cam awa . . .[54]

Some weeks later, Leatham, stung by short sighted and patronising comments in the Southern press returned to a passionate and reasoned defence of the working man and an attack upon what he saw as the gross inequality of the British social system:

Dear Editir,—The workin man's comin in for a heap o' attinshin ayenoo. Yon man Cawml, the Londin minnyster, gyau 'im's kail throu the rikk . . . in a half-croon magazeen 'at the workin man dizna see . . . Well-aff fowk's rael wullin ti believe 'at the workin man's a bleck ony wye, an' fin they wid read Cawml's harangue they wid say: 'There ye are. We aye thocht 'at the workin man wiz a lazy, drucken, orra, fool-moo't, sklyte-for-dawd slung, an noo here's a minnyster sayin't in print; so it maun be true . . .'

An' noo comes Lord Rosebery upon a different pairt o' the same job, like, ti tell the workin man sic a dandy time as he hiz.

Rosebery, openin a Warkmin's Club at Reidhull on Tiesdy, objeckit ti the han' workers bein regairdit as the only workin men. He thocht 'at a Minnyster o' the Croon or a Bishop vrocht far harder than the workin man.

I dinna ken for sure; I hae nae bishops upo' mi veesitin list. I min 'at Gladstone ees't ti gyang linkin awa in Donal Currie's ships ti Denmark an' up the Rhine, an' got into the hat for't eence wi' the aul' Queen. Bit the wark didna seem ti fa' ahin, fin his back wiz turn't. An' I notice't 'at in the verra heid-heicht o' the bather wi' Rooshia Aithur Balfoor took his gowff-sticks awa ti Soothamptin wi' 'im for the Setterday-ti-Mondy sport; an' noo he's laid up wi' a sair leg, an' twa doctirs atten'in 'im. Bit his pey's rinnin on' a' the same—he hizna hid ti 'declare on sick' wi' his Oddfellows lodge. Gin he wiz a workin man, ilky quarter he tint wid be keepit aff o' im'. An' I see 'at the Archibishop o' Kunterbery's awa linkin tull Amerika wi' Peerpont Morgin. So ye may say 'at here's Cawml ringin doon Lazarus at hame, an' Kunterbery chummin wi' Dives abroad. An' Kunterbery's toll's rinin on tee.

A Minnyster o' the Croon *may* work hard; bit he's nae obleeg't ti dee't, espeeshly gin he be a lan'lord, like Aithur or Rosebery. Bit gin the workin man's heowin neeps or coal, shearin a hairst, humph'n saicks o' flooer or guana, he maun keep up wi' the lave. Gin he disna, he aither loses his job or than keeps doon his pey.

Again, yer Bishop's or Primier's wark is interaistin'; bit sheilin muck's nae. An' that maks a' the differ atween pleesint wark an' avin'doon tig-tire.

The Primier gets a pinshin futher he's needin't or no. The warkman gets nae pinshin, nae maitter foo sair he may be needin't.

The Bishop an' the Primier dee their wark in fine rooms, cosy halls, or bonnie kirks. The warkman freezes in the Arctic, sneezes amo' the bone-dust, smores in the stock-hole or gets bar-bil't on the heid o' a hoose in the simmer or numb't on the dicky o' a cab in the winter. The miner an' the diver tak their lives in their han' ilky day, an' their wark's coorse at the best.

The fac' o' the maitter is, the warkman, as af'en as nae, wid need gweed siller for jist stanin or sittin in the place faur he his ti dee his wark.

A Primier may be at it at aichty; bit mony a warkman's owre aul' at forty.

The Bishop an' the Primier can get a lang hoaliday at ony time. The warkman gets a day at the trips, half-a-croon's worth o' a hurl or a sail, an' a bottle o' raivel't ale in the toon he gyangs tull. There's nae up the Rhine, across the Atlantic, or throu the Mediterranean for him. Fin he's nae weel, he dizna get tull a hydropathic. It's a dose o' salts, a mustard pultice, an' a twa'r three days in the kitchen bed, an' awa ye wag back ti yer wark.

The en' o't a' ull be the poorhouse as lickly as nae—that is, gin the warkmin lives as lang. Bit usually he dees at aboot half the age 'at the rich man lives tull.

For fowk at lives upo' rents and breweree shares ti tell the workin man at he hiz a raffy time o't wi' a big wife an' a sma' faimly ti keep aff o' 25s. in the wikk is jist aivin-doon mockery . . .[55]

Airchie Tait was designed, ultimately, to trouble his readers' assumptions, right down to his language.

As a working-class boy from Aberdeen, Leatham had first-hand knowledge of spoken mid-Northern Scots, the more so as the city, which had grown by in-migration from surrounding districts, did not then possess a distinctive urban dialect and so differed little in speech from its rural hinterland. His awareness of language was heightened by the variety of talk which surrounded him. His grandmother was an important influence. As a man he recollected several examples of her powerfully metaphorical Scots, while his mother's usage was highly cosmopolitan, a result of wide travel with her soldier husband.

Most important of all, however, was David Scott, perhaps the greatest single influence in Leatham's adult life, a man of beguiling personality, and a living master of spoken Scots. The older man stayed on at the *Sentinel* for several months while the new editor settled in, and they spent a lot of time in each other's company. Scott was a wit and bon-viveur, a superb raconteur and a man of wide general culture; he was a connoisseur, too, of painting and had one of the finest small collections in the North of Scotland. He had married late, had no family, and although an Episcopalian and Tory, regarded the young radical with an almost fatherly eye. Leatham was the potential saviour of the *Sentinel* (Scott's life's work), and on to his youthful shoulders the mantle was clearly intended to fall. It began to dawn on Leatham, without it ever being made explicit, that Scott wanted him to be his biographer, and he began to record the old master's aphorisms and bon mots, at the editorial table, in convivial gatherings in local hotels and pubs, and in his own special eyrie in the town's library and museum, where, Peterhead being a notable whaling port, he held court amongst the harpoons, kayaks, and stuffed polar bears.

The resulting study was published two years after Scott's death, in 1912, in Leatham's new monthly, the *Gateway*, and later issued in book form, with the title *Daavit*.[56] There can be little doubt that Scott re-awakened Leatham's interest in the vernacular as a more than pastoral medium. Indeed 'Airchie Tait' was at first widely attributed to David Scott, but his attitude towards the language was deeply conservative, and while the Scots of the column was impressively vivid and fluent, it was couched in an orthography unique, almost, in the degree of its departure from the standard, and which, however grateful to the ears of readers, must have struck their eyes as very odd indeed. Leatham more than once felt obliged to defend his usage, and each time he advanced the primacy of the local spoken vernacular, and urged typographical conformity with it as the ultimate test of authenticity:

> Fat ither wid Aw rite bit Scoatch? Aw've spoakn naething else sin iver Aw spoak ava. Scoatch! Of coorse Aw rot Scoatch! Aw *am* Scoatch! Aw rot wi' a pen last wik, an' it turn't oot Scoatch. Aw'm ritin' wi' a pinsl this wik . . . an' Aw'm sair chaitit gin *it* disna rite Scoatch tee. Can the leppirt cheenge 'e's spoats? Should the leppirt try? . . .
>
> The fowk's been compleenin' that they canna read my Scoatch. Aw canna bit think that queer; for gin I dinna rite the wye fowk spikk aboot this gate-en', Aw'm nae judge. There wiz a Frazsherbora chielie sayin' ti me the ither nicht 'at he wiz sure Aw wiz a droll cock; bit that the jokies wiz some lost upon 'im. He said I didna rite Scoatch the wye at Tammas Bodkin or Wattie Scott rote it. Aw wiz some nittle't at that, an' Aw tried ti see gin he *kent* Scoatch. I tried 'im wi' the words 'parrymyack', an' 'kibble', an' 'nabal', an 'pivvle', an' 'pappit', an' 'yaup', an' 'broolyie', an' 'pilgit', an' 'rippet', an' the sayin', 'the sibber ti yersel'. That wiz a' the len'th Aw got; for the Deil een o' them did he ken the meanin' o'. So says I: 'That'll dee for you, mi yalla customer. It's verra plain ye ken naething aboot the speech o' Rottra-Heid. An' noo, are ye sure ye ken the English lang'ige? Fat wye wid ye pronounce "f-e-r-o-c-i-o-u-s?"' "'Verowshis" it be sure,' says he. 'Noo,' says I—spellin' oot the word he hid jist pronounce't—'fat wye di ye pronounce this ither wordie?' An' Aw spell't oot "V-e-r-o-w-s-h-i-s" tull 'im. 'Aw nivver saw sic a word,' says he. 'Ye surely mean "v-o-r-a-c-i-o-u-s"?'—'Gae wa hame an' sup pottach,' says I, 'an' loaf saps,' says I, 'till yer muckle taes is swallin,' says I, 'an' syne ye'll maybe be half as gweed a Scoatsmin as yer grannie wiz.' Of coorse the ablach didna like it; bit fat wid ye hae said yersel?[57]

James Leatham was a prolific writer most of whose output was, perhaps inevitably, in standard English: but he could achieve something like his full stature only in Scots, a dichotomy by no means uncommon in the nineteenth (or indeed the twentieth) century. Whether this sprang from working in a language familiar from infancy or by the liberating effects of assuming a persona can hardly be unravelled here. The point is that the main burden of moral consciousness, social awareness and intellectual honesty in the newspaper is here carried not by English, but by vernacular Scots. 'Airchie Tait' is one of the most abrasive and radical voices in the Scotland of his time, and he marks that fusion of political radicalism with popular vernacular culture which is one of the most notable achievements of the Victorian press.

According to the conventional view, the later nineteenth century is a time of decline, underachievement, and sentimental self-indulgence in Scottish letters. If we look beyond the narrow confines of bourgeois book-culture, however, we can see that with regard to language at least, that is vernacular Scots as a medium of written communication, the second half of the nineteenth century is not a period of decay, but of resurgence, renewal, and growth almost without precedent.

THREE

To Instruct as well as to Amuse

Didactic Fiction in the Scottish Press

There had always been a certain overlap between news and literary functions in the Scottish press; after all one of the greatest of Scots poems, 'Tam o' Shanter' probably first saw the light of day in a newspaper, the *Edinburgh Herald* on 18 March 1791—but the publication of original literary material in newspapers had long been hampered by various pieces of legislation designed to control the press. The Stamp Act of 1819, however, restricted taxable content to news and political comment and cleared the way for Scots papers to carry fiction in the form of short stories and serialised reprints of longer texts. The *Elgin Courier* ran a series called 'Tales of the North', the *Berwick Advertiser* featured 'Tales of the Borders' from the pen of its editor John Mackay Wilson, while the *Edinburgh Weekly Journal* which had Walter Scott as part-proprietor, carried instalments from the Waverley novels.[1]

Indeed Scott's publishing practice is central to the status and availability of fiction at this time. His career marked the climax of several decades of marketing the novel during which it came increasingly to be defined as a luxury item, as publishers sought to increase profits by means of wide margins on low print-runs, perhaps no more than several hundred copies. By 1821 the price of a three-decker Waverley novel had risen to one-and-a-half guineas, which remained the standard price of first-edition fiction for many years to come. This placed it beyond the reach even of most middle-class readers who tended to rent their novels from subscription libraries rather than buy them outright, while working-class readers were at a still greater disadvantage, as the library services available to them through Mechanics Institutes and so on, often tried to exclude fiction altogether on the grounds that it was frivolous or immoral.[2]

One way round the problem for the impecunious book-buyer and publisher alike was number publication. A copyright-expired text could be issued weekly or fortnightly in 1*d.* or 2*d.* numbers, convenient for the small publisher who could thus produce a sizeable text using the most simple technical means and recoup his outlay from issue to issue, and for the reader who could expend his income as it came to him—in weekly instalments.[3] Even costly and prestigious books might have serialisation thrust upon them as the demand for fiction grew. During the 1830s in Edinburgh the needs of the popular audience were met by enterprising middle-men who broke up best-selling novels and re-stitched them into small portions rented out at 2*d.* a night.[4]

In the periodical market, however, the short story was the dominant form at least during the early years, and some idea of its range and preoccupations can be gathered from a typical popular miscellany like the *Buchan Clown*, one of the new wave of magazines launched in the wake of the self-improvement and useful knowledge movements. It described itself as a 'Periodical of an Amusing and General Literary and Moral Character', and it printed at least one short story in each issue. Most of them seem to have been locally written. According to the *Clown*, indeed, the local community provided as authentic an arena for imaginative literature as any metropolitan centre:

> The greater cities of the south have much in and about them to attract attention, of which we of the 'north countrie' cannot boast. Where such multitudes of human beings are collected together, there must always be something curious in themselves or in their works to observe and to reflect upon. Only think of the numberless houses—some gorgeous mansions, others miserable huts—the splendid temples devoted to the worship of God, the public buildings, the charitable retreats, the well-aired, well-cleaned, well-protected streets, the conveniences without number which can be bought with money, all belonging to a great city, and then turn to a small country town, its few and scattered houses, its dull and empty streets—if it has more than one—its old and solitary kirk, with perhaps a dissenting meeting-house, perhaps a town-house. Reader, couldst thou conceive a contrast more complete?
>
> In the progress of our national literature, writers have arisen who have not failed to take advantage of some of these circumstances, in pointing out all that seemed curious or interesting among the busy haunts of large cities. Indeed the 'Great Metropolis' has been ransacked over and over again from its parliament to its pickpockets, in all its characters and capacities, to afford amusement to the reading public in a vacant hour . . .
>
> But the characteristics of our small towns, though sufficiently numerous and marked, have hitherto failed to attract the notice of our . . . writers. Human nature, however, is much the same in all conditions and though it exhibits different phases in different circumstances, its study will always be found to gratify and instruct . . .[5]

And in a remark whigh might be the watchword for the whole subsequent progress of popular fiction in the Scottish press, it went on: 'Shall Cocklane have its *ghost*, Catto Street its conspiracy, and shall the Longate of Peterhead sink into oblivion unheeded and unchronicled?' The writing was animated by fierce local pride, an urge to contribute to a national tradition from a uniquely local, and therefore uniquely valuable perspective. This was coupled with a developed sense of Buchan as a bastion of traditional culture which became a prominent feature of the intellectual life of the region as the century progressed:

> We love thee, O! home of our fathers, we love thy craggy cliffs, gloomy caverns; and we love thy brown heaths, mouldering towers, and silvery streams, and shall every other land boast of its ancient lore, shall every little speck and division of our country issue forth their recorded legends, whilst Buchan alone raises not one monumental pillar to tell of former times, nor gives the world a single *memento* of her past history. No! there is a vast mass of traditionary lore, connected with these localities, storied up in the recollections of those who

have survived 'the olden time', and from this source we intend to select some records of the past . . .[6]

There was an ardent desire to confer upon the locality the dignity of literature, not just in a contemporary sense, but as the numerous mediaeval and gothic tales attest, to equip it with a literary-historical tradition manufactured, if need be, on the spot.

The first of the stories is entitled 'The Brothers' and it is set in the Abbey of Deer on the eve of the Reformation.[7] The monks are at vespers on a wild November night, when in rushes a blood-stained man seeking sanctuary. For several days he raves in delirium and it emerges that he murdered his younger brother years before and has since been tortured by guilt and remorse. Of course the brother is not dead at all, but the very monk who is trying to nurse him back to health—a typical Victorian denouement turning upon a covert kinship-link (common enough in real life, perhaps, in an age of large families and much movement of population).

'The Wild Tower' likewise occurs in a specific setting, the so-called Wine Tower of Fraserburgh, a part of Kinnaird Castle which crowns the rocky headland of the same name and which has long been associated with bloody and tragic events.[8] Here it appears as a place of confinement, complete with a torture-chamber in which the evil Lord Saltoun has entrapped the hero, young William Forbes, gently-born but poor, a suitor for the hand of his daughter Lady Catherine. Saltoun wants her to marry the old and wealthy Laird of Inverallochy, and starves William Forbes to death, so Catherine decks herself in bridal array and flings herself into the sea. The details are, no doubt, mere commonplaces of contemporary gothic fiction, but the kernel of the story springs from a genuine oral tradition still current in the district.[9] It also reflects a common ballad-motif, the idea captured in lines like 'My true love died for me the day/I'll dee for him the morn . . .' that echo through classic folk-songs like 'Bonny Babby Allan' and 'Mill o' Tiftie's Annie'.

The Victorian preoccupation with marriage as the central social convention features largely in the fiction of the time, especially as reflected in relations between parents and children and the extent of their mutual obligations; that is, how far the child was bound to honour the parent's wishes in respect of a marriage partner, and how far a parent might be entitled to exact compliance with an imposed choice. The dilemma had important symbolic dimensions and it formed the pivotal point of the moral system of many stories. One such tale in the *Clown*, 'The Absent Bridegroom' shows most of the features of this interesting genre: a wealthy and indulgent, but also obstinate and materialistic father; a beautiful, ingenuous, marriageable daughter; a handsome, penniless, orphan suitor; and an elderly, rich, and unattractive rival whose claim, of course, is favoured by the father. It is set during the seventeenth century, and George Keith, factor to the Earl Marischal, intends to bestow the hand of his daughter Euphemia on his friend Dr Ferguson, a local physician. Euphemia has different ideas, and fixes her choice upon her cousin William Keith. The

Doctor boasts that if he is late for the wedding he will give up his claim. William Keith arranges for this to happen, and the Doctor is paired off with a convenient maiden aunt. The story ends in reconciliation, avoiding the more usual tactic of killing off the offending parent.[10]

The idea of inheritance forms the dominant theme of contemporary popular fiction, and it is reflected in two stories from the *Clown*, 'The Lost Will', and 'The Doom of Forvie'.[11] The heroine of the 'Doom', Mary Cheyne, is heiress of Forvie on the Aberdeenshire coast. The lands are coveted by her wicked uncle and she is abducted and drowned at sea. She craves vengeance from heaven and the estate is buried by sand in a cataclysmic storm. Once again, there is an external basis for some of this. Sand dunes did indeed encroach on what was once good arable land on the northern banks of the Ythan estuary where Forvie lies, and traces have been found of a mediaeval hamlet beneath them; but the process seems to have been a slow and undramatic one. The story sheds light on the ambiguous position of the supernatural in the popular fiction of the period and its role as the ultimate sanction for all kinds of traditional values. The story's credentials as a specimen of authentic tradition are ostentatiously presented—there is even a ballad fragment in pleasantly bogus antique orthography:

> Yf evyr maidenis malysone
> Dyd licht upon drie lande,
> Let nocht be funde on Forvye's riggs
> But thistl, bente, and sande.

The heroine's invocation of divine vengeance is basically a traditional curse under a thin evangelical veneer. And it works. By virtue of being the true heir, Mary Cheyne possesses spiritual power. We are not very far here from the world of the *Golden Bough*, a further reminder of the folkish quality of so much of this fiction. The lost heir is a representative of all the positive values of society as traditionally conceived—his restoration a sign that they continue to possess validity, that continuity is unbroken, that the present has a proper relationship with the past. The larger implications of the idea of inheritance are shown in many stories where various calamities threaten while the rightful heir is lost, including here, where the community suffers physical destruction in the most horrifying circumstances.

In 'The Lost Will', a young laird is disinherited at the death of his uncle because no will can be found. He learns that the document has been hidden in the coffin by the rascally cousin who now possesses the estate. The hero has to disinter the corpse by night in order to recover his rights; but the resurrectionists get there first, and the will falls into their hands. Restitution is effected, but at the cost of a handsome donation to medical science. The story is typical in its blending of contemporary with more traditional elements, and the uneasy naturalism of its tone: belief in ghosts and a primitive terror of the dead are central to the mechanism of the story, but the supernatural is largely absent from it in any real sense; neither dreams nor apparitions possess real significance; the dead do walk—quite literally—but only because they have been tampered with by waggish medical students experimenting with galvanism. The story thus in its rather crude way attempts to accommodate the implications of science and technology to the value system of an older, basically agrarian order.

Graves and graveyards are very much part of the stock furniture of the popular fiction of the period due in part to the activities of grave-robbers or 'resurrectionists' as they were popularly known. This was an age of great public interest in medicine and in the improved anatomy training provided for students, either in the Universities or in the numerous private anatomical schools. Legitimate sources of bodies—executed felons and so on—could hardly keep up with demand, and the plundering of graves to supply the anatomical table became a widespread practice. Resurrectionism took such an extraordinary hold on the popular imagination and occasioned so many stories even after it had long fallen into disuse, that it clearly possessed important symbolic overtones for contemporaries. During a period of rapid social change the plundering of the kirkyard, that obvious source of inherited value, might well imply, amongst other things, the violation of culture, the severing of links between past and present, the cancellation of traditional obligations.

In a piece called 'Catheld' published in the *Clown* in June 1838, the past is linked to the present through the grave in the most explicit manner. The people of Peterhead are preparing the site of a memorial to the great Reform Act and uncover an ancient Pictish tomb. A spectral presence reveals that the remains are those of a patriotic warrior who has fallen defending his country against the Romans. A contemporary political triumph is thus joined to an ancient military one to mark the presence of heroic virtue in the community across a large tract of time.[12]

This debt to an earlier tradition of tale-telling is also evident in the short stories published in early issues of the *People's Journal*, prize-winning entries in fiction competitions written by working people. Many of them had strongly-marked folk characteristics, in some cases being a simple translation into print of orally circulating material. One reader wrote to complain about this shortly after the series began:

> Sir,—Not very long ago it was the custom in the straths and glens of the Highlands of Perthshire, and likely in Forfarshire, for the young men and old to meet together in the long winter evenings for the purpose of entertaining each other in relating stories and talking about their common affairs. At those cheerful gatherings someone was called to relate some tale, and each in his turn was called upon for a song or a story for the amusement or instruction of the company. At the time I speak of books were not so plentiful as they are now, and the Gaelic was the language best understood in those glens. Some of the men were particularly gifted in inventing and minutely relating tales. The *People's Journal*, I find, has got hold of some of these tales, and published them in a new garb. No doubt they will appear original to many of your readers, and their new dress will make them pass tolerably well. 'The Rival Tailors' [a tailor tries to outwit a colleague but becomes the victim of his own disingenuousness] 'The Minister and the Pat' [about a clergyman obsessed by crockery], and 'The Tempter Tempted' [a minister adopts a stratagem to stop his beadle drinking],

&c., I heard my father relate many a time for the amusement of the youth. When a prize is awarded by the Editor of the *Journal*, I think originality should be a consideration.[13]

One of the authors replied the following week from an east coast address denying any knowledge of Gaelic, but admitting that he had got his stories orally from his father.

The Scottish press continued to print short fiction in large quantities, and in papers like the *People's Journal*, readers contributed significant propor- tion of it. Before long they were tackling book-length fiction as well, and, as we have seen earlier, by the 1890s the *Journal* was paying £100 for a prize- winning 60–80,000 word manuscript suitable for serial publication.

The serialisation of original fiction in newspapers started in France during the 1830s, and appears to have been introduced into Scotland some twenty years later during the 1850s.[14] There was general agreement that it was good for circulation, particularly so in papers with a predominantly working-class readership. As the new popular press came into being after the repeal of the Stamp, many weekly papers began to carry it as a regular feature. One of the earliest examples was a novel called 'Jessie Melville', or, 'the Double Sacrifice', written by a young theatre critic called David Pae which ran in the columns of an Edinburgh paper, the *North Briton*, during the second half of 1855 and caused a considerable stir. Pae went on to become a hugely prolific professional novelist who carried all before him in the popular fiction market for upwards of a generation; but since he almost invariably published anonymously, wrote almost exclusively for newspapers and magazines, and hardly ever appeared in book form, his identity was known only to a handful of insiders. When he died in 1884, his obituarist, a close friend and colleague, Andrew Stewart, had to start by explaining who he was:

> Being naturally of a quiet and retiring turn of mind, Mr Pae did not mingle much in society, and took no part whatever in public affairs. He lived in his study, and had few enjoyments outside his own happy domestic circle. For this reason he was not personally or even by name very widely known in the literary world, and still less was he known to the world at large. Many persons, therefore, whose eyes may alight on the heading to this notice of his death may be excused if they inquire, 'Who was Mr David Pae?' . . . By his writings he is known to many thousands—we might, indeed, say millions—of readers, not only in Scotland, but also in England and Ireland, who, now that he is dead, will learn for the first time the name of him who has for so many years amused and instructed them by his busy pen; for, with a modesty that is rare among literary men, Mr Pae shrank from putting his name to any of his works, although had he done so he might have won for it a very high place amongst those of the literary celebrities of the time . . .[15]

Little known in his own lifetime, and utterly forgotten today, he is still probably the most widely read author of fiction in Victorian Scotland.

David Pae was born at Buchanty in Perthshire in 1828. When he was only

David Pae. Reproduced by courtesy of the *People's Journal*.

a few weeks old, his father, a miller, was killed and his mother brought him up among her own people at Coldingham in Berwickshire. He received an excellent education and was apprenticed to the bookseller and publisher Thomas Grant of Edinburgh where he began to acquire that knowledge of the business world which marks so much of his later fiction. It was in Edinburgh too that he discovered the theatre. He was utterly captivated and before long was reviewing for local papers and trying his hand at original scripts. He wrote a historical play called 'Drumclog', an entertainment 'The Next of Kin',[16] and a piece called, 'Mrs McGregor's Levee' which was acquired by the comedian Gourlay who toured the world with it. It brought its author the princely sum of £5 and since appears to have been lost. On the strength of this work, however, he became editor of an Edinburgh stage periodical called *The Theatre*.

But drama did not monopolise his attention during these years in the capital. He was caught up in the leading currents of contemporary evangelicalism and published extensively in this field as well. The 1850s marked an important turning-point in the religious development of Scotland. After centuries of doctrinal stability during which the Calvinistic tenets enshrined in the Westminister Confession held virtually absolute sway, there was a growing reluctance to accept the narrow concept of redemption which lay at the centre of it, and the negative vision of the Deity which it implied. The notion of unlimited atonement, the idea that Christ died for everybody not just a handful of the Elect, began to be propagated by liberal evangelicals like Edward Irving, James Morison, and John McLeod Campbell. Pae was strongly influenced by them and was one of a number of writers using the popular press to campaign for the new theology.[17]

He published several pamphlets in the 1850s and 1860s on the problem of evil, the nature of the atonement and the interpretation of the prophetic books. Taken together they give some indication of the moral vision from which his novels sprang and to which they all more or less directly related. Like many new wave evangelicals Pae was strongly attracted by millenarianism and wrote extensively upon this subject also.

The problem of prophecy in his view, was that you had to have all of it, or none; and it was clear from various passages in Jeremiah, Daniel, Isaiah, Ezekiel, parts of the Gospels, and above all, the Book of Revelation, that the events foretold in some of the grandest and most alarming passages of biblical prophecy had not yet taken place. Like many other Victorian millenarians he believed the events of latter-day prophecy to be on the eve of fulfilment and looked for the long-predicted day of glory:

> Assuredly, the great leading events in the world's future are indicated in Scripture prophecy,—the overthrow of evil—the restoration of all things—the establishment of the Redeemer's kingdom—the resurrection of the saints—the thousand years of rest and peace—the little season of evil's final outbreak—the final resurrection and universal judgement—the utter destruction of Satan and all the hosts of iniquity—and the new heavens and the new earth which shall

never pass away, but which shall become the eternal habitation of the Lamb and His countless multitude of redeemed.[18]

Sitting in Bank Street in 1863 in a senior position in the Leng organisation, one of the most bustling and go-ahead newspaper businesses in the country, was a man who quite genuinely believed that the world was going to end in just under three years time, and had said so in print.

His programme for the latter days was set out in *The Coming Struggle among the Nations of the Earth* (London 1853), and in a more extended form in *Two Years After and Onwards; or, The Approaching War amongst the Powers of Europe* (London 1864).[19] And it spelled out clearly what was going to happen. If one assumed that the seventh and last vial mentioned by St John had been opened about the year 1830, then a series of complicated calculations gave the duration of the Beast and a target date for 'the indignation' spoken of by Isaiah, the 'great day' of Jeremiah, the 'great tribulation' predicted by Christ in the twenty-fourth chapter of St Matthew of some time in 1866. Armageddon would be triggered off by an Anglo-American attempt to restore the Jewish state opposed by the forces of Czarist Russia and its satellites:

> The autocrat with his legions on one side, and the British power with its supporters on the other, are drawn up in battle array in the valley of Jehoshaphat, and are about to engage in the decisive combat, when, to their intense and indescribable consternation, the trump of the archangel reverberates through the sky, and with the voice of ten thousand thunders shakes the mountains, and smites every soul with awe and terror. The anti-christian legions, the British host, the Jewish company, shall in dread amazement look up, and behold the Son of Man coming in the clouds of heaven, with power and great glory.[20]

Although because he wrote, as he always did, anonymously, he acquired little personal fame, David Pae was one of the most zealous millenarians in mid-Victorian Britain. To be one at all was, *ipso facto*, to be a radical. All millenarians were committed to social change in some form or other, from violent revolutionary upheaval at one end of the spectrum to a gradualist utopianism at the other. Pae shows signs of both positions during the 1850s, but it is the latter view which informs his novels.[21]

His early fiction is placed within an explicitly millenarian framework, and all his writing is suffused by the liberal evangelicalism which ultimately underpinned it, showing itself in an intense moral earnestness, a serene confidence in the possibility of human goodness, a certainty that good must ultimately overcome evil. He may well at some point have considered the Kirk as a career: he certainly composed sermons and knew at least some Hebrew. He could have been a teacher, or perhaps a missionary. But he chose quite coolly and deliberately to become a novelist as the most effective way of expressing his ideas, just as he chose newspaper rather than book publication as the most effective means of spreading them.[22]

His earliest tale, *George Sandford; or, the Draper's Assistant*, was published in Edinburgh in 1853, and dealt with some of the pitfalls lying in wait for upwardly mobile lads whose destination was not the surgery, the schoolhouse or the manse. The hero is a widow's son reared in a thoroughly evangelical atmosphere in the south of Scotland who completes his apprenticeship and goes to London to get a job. There he makes a number of highly unpleasant discoveries about the business world and its mores:

> as George Sandford became better acquainted with the details of commercial life in London, his disgust and abhorrence increased. He observed in its every vein a stream of immorality and deception, which was utterly opposed to the opinions he entertained of justice, equity, and honesty. All recognition of human responsibility seemed to be lost, and a widespread system of dissimulation and deceit pervaded all its parts.[23]

A detailed account of sharp practice in the retail trade follows. His employers accept that George won't take part, and get him to serve their best customers, the ones they can't afford to cheat. He works in London for a number of years, but eventually, thanks to poor working conditions, contracts consumption and dies.

Considered from a technical point of view, *George Sandford* is not a very sophisticated novel. There is not much plot. The main character never changes as a result of his experiences, nor could he, because he is perfect from the start; he is just a convenient pair of eyes enabling the author to project himself into different settings for a little investigative journalism. It might strike the reader as a novel struggling to grow out of a tract and not quite managing. In a certain sense, indeed, it *is* a tract, and quite an important one too. A distinct line of fiction grew out of the tractarian movement in nineteenth century Scotland and *George Sandford* is a significant example.[24]

The movement began towards the end of the eighteenth century with the idea that the morals of the common people could be improved if they were weaned away from licentious chapbooks by cheap uplifting reading matter. It was spearheaded by the Religious Tract and Book Society of Scotland founded in 1793, which later became the Scottish Colportage Society, and employed hundreds of book-hawkers to distribute religious and improving literature throughout the country.[25] The same agencies of supply and distribution tended to serve both secular and religious literature as appears from the career of Peter Drummond of Stirling whose Stirling Tract Enterprise grew from small beginnings in 1848 into an enormous worldwide concern. Most of his printing was done by the *Stirling Observer* press which had itself grown out of the famous chapbook businesses of William Macnie and Ebenezer Johnston.[26]

The Scots tractarians quickly grasped that to hold their own against the popular literature of the day, they had to meet three basic conditions. Tracts had to be as cheap as or cheaper than rival publications; they had to be distributed more efficiently; and they had to bear an at least superficial resemblance to popular secular material which meant decoration with racy wood-cuts and a pseudo-fictional approach to content.[27]

Fiction was at the centre of the struggle for control of the popular imagination in nineteenth century Scotland, but the evangelicals' use of it was always uneasy. One wing of the movement mounted a sustained attack upon the very idea of popular fiction for upwards of half a century, and the controversy broke out anew during the 1850s and 1860s when the problem assumed vastly greater proportions with the advent of a large-scale popular press. One anxious reader of the Edinburgh *Christian Advocate* wrote to enquire whether a Christian could buy, sell, or read popular fiction without hazard to the soul. He received a disconcerting reply:

FICTITIOUS READING—QUERY AND REPLY

We are not sufficiently acquainted with these publications to pronounce judgement upon them so fully as our correspondent may desire; but we can say this much, that such numbers of them as we have seen we could not with a good conscience read. Apart from the time wasted in their perusal, we believe the tendency of such exciting stories as form their principal attraction will be exceedingly vicious. They are mental narcotics which intoxicate the mind to as deadly an issue as man can reach. Who knows the habitual reader of such love and murder fictions, to be also a hearer and doer of the word of God? Who that knows God will say they are fit reading for either saint or sinner? We know not.[28]

But the problem could not just be swept under the carpet. The role of the press in promoting materialistic values was all too evident, and some feared that unless this influence was checked the supremacy of Christian principles might be seriously weakened. On the other hand, the press presented the evangelical reformer with a glorious opportunity if he could control it and turn it to his purpose. This was the theme of a series of articles on 'The "Working Classes" and their Literature: What it is, and What it Ought to Be', which ran in the *Edinburgh Christian Magazine* in the spring and summer of 1856:

There was a time, even within the memory of some still living, when there was no literature for the poor. That time has passed away, and the working man now sits down at his own fireside, when the toils of the drudging day are over, and learns the history of the past, and the events of the present. The press has brought round this mighty change. It is to that press we owe many of our choicest national, social, and individual blessings; but it is still true . . . that to it also we are indebted for many of our direct evils . . . In the first place, the press is importing among us, in large numbers, those vicious and vitiating French novels, which, popular in that country which gave them birth, are also becoming alarmingly so in this favoured land . . . In the second place, we have our own large and increasing home produce, in the shape of licentious romances, and infidel serials, and diurnal newspapers . . . One fact in regard to Edinburgh and Glasgow, and we leave the practical inference to be drawn. Of infidel, immoral, and latitudinarian periodicals, no less than 10,000 copies are sold every week. Allowing *four* readers to each—a very small proportion—no less than 40,000 of the citizens . . . are readers and supporters of these atrocious publications. And let us not forget, that most of these are . . . adapted for Sunday reading, to that large mass of the population which never enters within the door of a church. . . . The Christian public ought to lay hold on the penny press, and it would become a mighty engine for good in their hands.[29]

During the 1850s a new wave of didactic fiction appeared in the Scottish press. It was chiefly distinguished by two things: the first was an absence of any sense that fiction might be valuable in its own right—a feeling, rather, that it required an extrinsic moral purpose, that fictive elements were merely a screen behind which the author worked his real purpose upon the reader.[30] The second thing was its scale. The yawning column space provided by the new press freed authors as never before from restrictions of space. Genuine novel-length—that is 80–120,000 word—fiction now became normal in newspapers, and the very nature of the form began to change. In order to sustain the reader through the marathon experience of reading a serial novel in perhaps three dozen separate instalments spread over a period of more than six months, the plot had to be managed with unprecedented resourcefulness and ingenuity, and grew in importance relative to character and setting. Both these features can be seen in 'Jessie Melville; or, the Double Sacrifice' which gave David Pae, writing his first full-length serial novel, his first considerable success as an author of fiction.

The story is set in Edinburgh, the time the historical present. On a wild winter night the aristocratic William Ainslie discovers young and attractive Jessie Melville huddled in the snow in St Andrew's Square, overcome in her search for a doctor to attend her widowed mother. Ainslie escorts Jessie home to the Canongate, and revives the old lady who starts and seems to recognise him. Next day he learns something of her story. She and her husband had been in service with a Scots landed family and then become shopkeepers in Edinburgh. Her husband had died of cholera, but Mrs Melville managed to give Jessie a proper education, although her savings are now exhausted and the girl works as a bookfolder at Chambers the publishers. William reveals quite casually that he is the son of Sir William Ainslie of Broomfield Park, whereupon the old woman shrieks and faints.

William falls in love with Jessie and supposes, rather naively, that his father will consent to their union. Sir William, in fact, violently opposes it, and Jessie's mother confesses to her daughter on her death-bed that years before in return for a bribe from the doctor (who had in turn been offered £500 by Sir William if his heir proved male) she had given up her new-born son to the laird's wife who had in turn given up *her* new-born daughter to Mrs Melville. And she can prove it, because the physician signed a deposition to the fact and she has still got it. So Jessie is actually a lady, the wealthy heiress of Broomfield, while William Ainslie is a penniless orphan.[31]

Jessie decides to keep this a secret until after she and William are married, in order to spare his feelings and prove her altruism. But at this point there is another snag. She is gazing fondly at her parents in their box at the theatre one evening when neighbours identify the frail but lovely girl sitting beside them as Grace Ferguson, who is apparently dying for love of her cousin William Ainslie. Jessie decides that she must give William up, which means that she cannot reveal her birth because it would disinherit him—hence the double sacrifice of the title.

She persuades William to renounce her and marry his cousin. But the young bride's constitution is so weakened that she does not long survive. Grace has a relative, a rake and gambler called Robert Ferguson who stands to inherit her estate, The Grange, if she dies intestate and without issue. She has left a will bequeathing everything to her husband, but it is still in the possession of Sir William's lawyer Daniel Hooker, and only he knows of its existence. Hooker quickly comes to an understanding with the rake and the latter is served heir to The Grange; meanwhile he retains the original will so that he can blackmail him at his leisure.

Because of her continuing influence on his son Sir William has Jessie abducted, but her gaoler, a henchman of Hooker, succumbs to her superior moral nature, steals the will and returns it to Jessie, giving her complete power over all her enemies. She is heiress of Broomfield Park and can prove it; William Ainslie is heir of The Grange and she can prove that too. They are now equals in fortune and can marry. There is a grand revelation, Sir William repents, and the novel ends happily. Then comes the Moral:

> Our whole and only aim, dear reader, has not been to amuse you. We had a much higher object in view, and fondly trust it will not be altogether unattained.
>
> Our design was to inculcate the great and noble duty of self-sacrifice—to show it adhered to in perhaps the most difficult of all circumstances; and to show that, when faithfully maintained, it brings sooner or later an abundant reward.
>
> Every one of us is called upon in our different spheres to exercise this duty to a greater or less degree, but, alas! many of us shun and shrink from it. What is the cause of much of the social disorder which exists around us but our neglect of self-sacrifice?
>
> Let this spirit be generally cherished, and its practice extended to the great and minute things of life, and the many strings of the large sounding harp of humanity will send forth far more harmonious strains.
>
> Selfishness and heartlessness will then give place to generosity and benevolence, and, under the kindly influence of these, the broad field of human hearts will send forth fruits of the richest flavours, and flowers of the most fragrant perfume.
>
> We all believe in, and hope for, 'a good time coming'; but can we expect it to have an unnatural advent? Is it possible that the golden age, which has been looked for and longed for by the world for many a day, can come while men continue to practise those sins and crimes, shortcomings and unkindnesses, which render society so corrupted, and individuals so unhappy? If we look for this, our expectation will be vain.
>
> Peace, love, and harmony, and the other elements which are to constitute the grace and glory of 'the good time coming', must first exist in the heart of man, and be practised in his every-day life. In no other way, and by no other means, can we hope for its arrival. Let us then resolve to do our utmost to hasten it on.[32]

The dismissal of the art of fiction as an end in itself could hardly be more explicit. Yet at every step the novel subverts Pae's attempt to transform it into a vehicle of popular morality. If one overlooks the implausibility of the plot at various points (the child-swapping device upon which most of it turns; the likelihood of a corrupt physician attesting a document which could later incriminate him; the business of the Ferguson will and so on), and it is clear that contemporary readers did, then 'Jessie Melville' is a most exciting story which unfolds at a spanking pace, full of incident and variety, kidnaps, burglaries, plots and assorted skulduggeries, all appealing to the lowest instincts of the reader. Despite the author's sincere desire to make evil serve the ends of good, he lands in the classic reformist dilemma: vice cannot be treated successfully in fiction without it at the same time becoming interesting; the more deeply the tractarian enters the imaginative domain, especially if he possesses narrative skill, then the more the fictive elements come to predominate. In engaging with fiction at all he endorses the very things he wishes to destroy.[33]

When it first appeared, 'Jessie Melville' caused great excitement. William Norrie, writing about the *North Briton* says:

> It was noteworthy as having been among the first newspapers to introduce a serial tale as part of its contents. The earliest effort in this direction was the publication of a thrilling tale, 'Jessie Melville, or the Double Sacrifice,' by the late Mr Pae, an author at that time unknown to fame, but who subsequently made his mark as a highly popular writer of fiction. The success of the story was prodigious and the field thus opened up has since been largely cultivated by the weekly newspaper press.[34]

Andrew Stewart, the deputy-editor of the *People's Friend*, added:

> In every family circle the fortunes of the heroic and self-sacrificing book-folder were followed with tears and breathless interest till the close, when the demand was imperative and universal that the story should be reprinted in book form . . . few could resist the charms of the style and the beauty of the narration. Everything was forgotten for the time, and daylight often crept in on the fascinated reader turning over the last page with a sigh over a delight that was gone . . .[35]

When it was published in book-form it was rapturously received. The *Middlesborough News* said:

> It is a work emphatically invaluable to all classes of readers, being one of the most beautiful narratives we ever read . . . We are certain the book will force its way into thousands of homes, and be beloved and wonderfully popular.

While the *North Briton* declared, with pardonable warmth,

> We hesitate not to affirm that 'Jessie Melville' is one of the very best tales which has appeared in our day . . . Beauty of writing we have in abundance—strokes

of genuine humour are not unfrequent—while bursts of unmistakable eloquence are to be found on every page . . . Its extreme fascination is the inevitable result of its style and tone. We are intimately acquainted with a literary gentleman who was so riveted with it, that he read no less than two hundred and thirty pages at one sitting. He told us afterwards, that no volume of the kind had so attracted his attention, and so *forced him to read*, since the issue of 'Uncle Tom's Cabin'.[36]

We know in some detail how serial novels were read, especially if they were popular. The paper would come in, perhaps an early edition on Friday evening, and people would grab it and turn to the serial page. It was an age of large families when people even in quite modest circumstances might keep domestic staff, so that the basic readership unit was the household in all its varying shapes and sizes, through which the paper would percolate during the weekend and much of the following week, until every-body—including the children—had read it. The serial then became a topic for shared enthusiasm, speculation and discussion; people would even write to one another about it. But there was no way of finding out what happened next because the next stage of the story had not yet appeared, perhaps even been written, so that every week thousands of readers were delivered to the same point of the narrative collectively conscious of one another in a way unattainable in modern fiction. This presented the author with a number of problems. All over the paper's territory clever people were trying to work out what he or she was going to do next and he had to outguess them, every time, or as nearly so as possible—hence the devious complexity of many of the plots.[37]

Despite the proliferation of incident in 'Jessie Melville' the novel can be reduced to a few basically simple elements. The idea of inheritance is central to it. Unless the heroine can inherit, there is no story. To do this, she has to discover her true father and be acknowledged by him. Both of the main characters are also in some sense orphans: they do not know at various stages who or what they are. Reduced to its most abstract form, therefore, the novel is about the discovery of happiness through the shedding of a formerly-held idea of self, made possible by discovering the true father and being acknowledged his heir. In short, it adapts the central motifs of contemporary popular fiction in order to produce a modern parable of grace and redemption, of a highly deliberate and conscious kind.

This is a story about contemporary city life. The action takes place in various parts of the Old and New Towns of Edinburgh, ranging from shabby closes to high-toned terraces, and introduces a wide cross-section of its inhabitants. The heroine works in a factory, a well-known and actual one, and for most of the novel goes on doing so, even when she could escape. She moves unselfconsciously amongst her workmates, with whom she is popular, and although wooed by a baron's heir, he has to wait for her at the factory gate the same as everybody else. In other words, the novel is considerably at variance with the idea that fiction in Victorian Scotland concerned itself exclusively with an idealised rural past.

This curious notion can be found in one form or another in most accounts of the subject. One thinks, for example, of William Power in *Literature and Oatmeal*:

> Scots people were vigorous industrialists and slum builders, but they never reconciled themselves spiritually to their own urban creations . . . It was better to help to keep alive the native faith and virtues and idyllic memories of the people than to remind them of the scorching fires of Moloch through which they were passing.[38]

Or George Blake in *Barrie and the Kailyard School*:

> The bulk of the Scottish people were . . . condemned to a purely urban . . . and mainly ugly sort of life during the nineteenth century. A really dramatic, often beastly, revolution was taking place. And what had the Scottish novelists to say about it? The answer is—nothing . . . The Scots storyteller either followed Scott and Stevenson through the heather with a claymore at his belt, or he lingered round the bonnie brier bush, telling sweet, amusing little stories of bucolic intrigue as seen through the windows of the Presbyterian manse.[39]

Or, more recently, Francis Russell Hart in *The Scottish Novel*:

> The dominant mode of Victorian fiction in Scotland was pastoral idyll . . . It was a fiction parochial in setting, elegiac in time sense, traditional in communality . . .[40]

But this view cannot be sustained. It is based solely on an interpretation of bourgeois book-culture which assumes the Kailyard to be typical and considers further enquiry unneccessary, while even middle-class fiction during the period is largely unexplored and the real popular literature of Victorian Scotland is practically *terra incognita*. Even in the fairly modest sample taken for the present study, there are cities and slums, factories, workers, capitalists, crime, poverty, disease, in short the whole urban gamut almost wherever one cares to look. The point is an important one. A number of conclusions have been drawn from this apparent failure to deal with the fact of urbanisation highly unfavourable to the Scots as a civilised and culture-producing people. If it is not true—and it is not—then our ignorance of the real range and complexity of the imaginative experience in Victorian Scotland has led to serious subsequent misjudgements not merely in criticism or creative writing, but in the whole contemporary intellectual and cultural milieu.

Further evidence of the willingness of Scottish writers to engage imaginatively with the city will be presented during the course of this study, both in other writings by David Pae, which will be discussed immediately, and also later in assessing the full range of those of William Alexander the subjects of whose fiction go far beyond the rural Scotland with which it is generally if not entirely associated. But, first of all, let us follow further David Pae's career.

In 1859 he became editor of the *Dunfermline Press*.[41] But the arrangement was inconvenient. He was newly married, and his home was in Edinburgh. His job meant being away for much of the week, and commuting across the Forth by ferry which he found irksome. In 1863 John Leng offered him a contract to write novels exclusively for the *Dundee Advertiser* group and he quickly seized it. It was the first such arrangement, so far as I am aware, in the Scottish press, and Pae celebrated his arrival with a story which many of his contemporaries regarded as his best and was remembered with affection until well into the present century—'The Factory Girl; or, The Dark Places of Glasgow'.[42]

It opens on a bleak November afternoon in the office of Daniel Dexter, a commission agent in Glasgow. He has before him a letter from a firm of Irish solicitors instructing him that under the terms of her father's will, he is to become the guardian of his orphan niece, Lucy Livingston aged six, and curator of her property amounting to some twenty thousand pounds. The letter further states that Lucy's brother Walter, aged eight, is to be sent to a relative abroad, and that she will arrive on the Belfast steamer on a certain date. Dexter realises that fortune has at long last placed his life's ambition—a cotton factory—within his grasp and he decides to do away with Lucy and appropriate her fortune.

He is just about to burn the letter at a flaring street-lamp when he becomes aware of a haggard figure studying him closely: this is Sarah Gordon his former sweetheart long ago seduced and abandoned and living a life of crime. It occurs to him that she would be the ideal person to dispose of Lucy and they repair to a nearby ale-house to clinch the deal. Sarah is determined to ruin Dexter if she can, so she drugs him and gets the letter copied by Shuffle and Sleek, a law-firm well-known in the Glasgow underworld. She keeps the original and plants the copy on Dexter. He destroys it and thinks himself safe; but the lawyers, unknown to Sarah, have also made a copy and when she collects Lucy at the Broomielaw, the scene is witnessed by Shuffle, heavily disguised.

Sarah decides to rear the child, produce her when she is twenty-one, and destroy her former lover. The lawyer meantime repairs to a subterranean thieves' den in the Tontine Close; he is agent to the inmates and their mysterious Captain, and he tries to persuade Sarah to join him in blackmailing Dexter. She refuses and flees with Lucy into the night.

A year passes. Dexter builds his mill, and Sarah and Lucy are living under assumed names with a brave and trustworthy friend Hugh the knife-grinder. But Shuffle and Sleek want possession of the child and the Captain and his gang are scouring Glasgow for them. Sarah has just arranged a fresh hiding-place for herself and the child when a snatch-squad from the Tontine arrives. They carry Hugh off to their den and subject him to dreadful tortures on a rack—called 'Govan Bess'—in order to make him talk. He is rescued by one of the band, a little consumptive boy called Willie who has been kidnapped in infancy and forgotten who he is. While Sarah earns some money by playing Meg Merrilies in a production of *Guy Mannering* at the Adelphi Theatre on Glasgow Green, Hugh nurses the child through his final illness assisted by a slum missionary called Clanworth. The boy possesses an anatomical peculiarity which makes him desirable as a specimen and his physician, a Dr Knox, arranges with Shuffle and Sleek to steal his body from the Necropolis. The job is given to the Captain and his gang. Mr Clanworth meanwhile examines a locket belonging to the dead child and discovers that Willie is his long-lost nephew. It appears that his brother, a landed gentleman on Clydeside, had two sons; one, a fiery and impetuous boy who had left home years before and not been heard of since, and Willie, who had disappeared in Glasgow and been given up for dead. When the coffin is exhumed for re-interment at Wellfield, the family home, it is discovered to be empty. At that very moment Willie is lying on Doctor Knox's dissecting table. The Captain calls on Knox to collect his fee, recognises the child, and realises he holds the key to Sarah and Lucy's whereabouts. When one of the cast of *Guy Mannering* falls ill the Captain takes his place as the smuggler Dirk Hatteraick, intending to assassinate Sarah on stage. When he confronts her in the sea cave scene, he shoots her at point blank range. She escapes with a flesh wound, and in the confusion the Captain disappears.

As they are no longer safe in the city, the friends find sanctuary in Wellfield House. Shortly afterwards, however, the Captain and his band try to burgle it. Most of the robbers are trapped in the strongroom, and in the ensuing fracas the Captain shoots himself. As he lies mortally wounded he makes a number of interesting discoveries: firstly that orphan Willie was his brother, and secondly that the man who has just turned the tables on him and caused his suicide is none other than his long-estranged father George Clanworth. The Captain dies in agony and the rest of the gang are transported. Sarah and Lucy stay on at Wellfield until the estate passes into other hands. They are turned adrift again and the last section of the story sees them back in Glasgow.

Twelve years pass. Dexter's firm flourishes, and he becomes one of the leading businessmen in the city. But this is not enough. He wants to join the inner circle of merchant dynasties, and his hopes centre upon his son Henry, a noble youth, just entering manhood. It is essential that Henry make a suitable marriage, but he has already given his heart to one of his father's mill-hands, a girl called Lucy Blair (actually Lucy Livingston), which creates a problem when the lawyer Sleek proposes a match between Henry and his niece Mary Hamilton, and threatens to ruin Dexter if he fails to comply. But Mary loves a young businessman called Walter Lynne who is actually Lucy's brother working for Dexter under an assumed name to see if he can find out what happened to her. Henry has a blazing row with his father, gets a job as a manager in another mill and goes ahead with his plans to marry Lucy. In the meantime Sarah discovers who Walter is, and tells him of their adventures during the intervening years. They agree not to reveal Lucy's identity until after she and Henry are married in case, as now a relatively poor man, his pride may prevent him accepting the hand of a merchant princess. Sarah sends Dexter a carefully-timed message so he arrives just too late to prevent the wedding and she personally witnesses his humiliation. He is unmasked, and confesses all. Henry recovers his inheritance through his wife who immediately interposes to save her father-in-law from public disgrace. He evinces sincere repentance, there is a general tidying up of loose ends, and the novel closes with reflections on the duties of the novelist and the nature and scope of a truly moral fiction.

The story was an enormous success and confirmed David Pae as the leading serial novelist in Scotland—a position he held until his death in 1884. One of the novel's most obvious features is its characteristic blending of fantasy and realism. Real people, like the manager of the Adelphi Theatre, D P Miller, appear in it in speaking parts, and it contains many named streets, wynds, closes, factories, warehouses, and places of popular entertainment in Victorian Glasgow by a man who obviously knew it well at first hand. Pae could handle the visual panorama of the city quite impressively; he had a sharp, almost painterly eye, and a penchant for rich polysyllabic diction that lent itself to set-piece descriptive writing. Here, for example, is a view of the river and the city at six o' clock on a spring evening as the mills and factories reach the end of their working day:

> The slanting beams of the descending sun fell brightly on the Clyde, as it skirted the southern boundary of Glasgow Green, and the golden light they shed abroad gilded all things with mellow radiance. . . . To the north and west lay the city in dense compactness—houses, chimneys, and pointed gables standing in thick array against the clear western sky which was already taking on the deep golden hues of sunset. Above the houses hung the sun, with chastened and broadening disc, and round about him were a few fleecy clouds, whose edges he was gilding, and whom he would, ere long, cover with the most effulgent glory. Between the tops of the houses and the sun and the clouds lay a haze produced by the smoke which was ascending from thousands of dwellings, and thickening and increasing as the evening fires were lighted to effect the preparation of the evening meal.
>
> Across, on the south side of the river, and far down by its eastern bank, and away verging to the north, were tall chimneys and long blocks of high square buildings, with many rows of windows which flashed back the beams of the sinking orb of day. From those many buildings came puffing jets of smoke—and the rush, rush of the engine, like great heart-beats, and the clanking noise of machinery, which uttered its voice in its iron-labour-song, harsh and uncouth as its own hard self. From every one of the buildings came these various noises, and they hit upon the ear of a wanderer on the Green with individual distinctness, for the distance was not great enough to cause them to blend together; but only to mingle in quick confusion, and give a strong idea of bustle and earnest activity . . .
>
> Encircled by these noisy factories was the Green and the river—the former dotted in one direction with trees, and covered every where by groups of laughing, romping ramblers, and the latter bearing on its clear bosom pleasure boats with their happy occupants, who sang and played on musical instruments as the rowers took them up or down the stream.
>
> But while the pleasure-seekers thus sported on the grass and river, the sun sunk lower and lower—till at length he hovered close to the house tops, and cast the shadow of Nelson's Monument far down to the east. In pomp and splendour he lay, encircled by the golden clouds which floated near him in gorgeous brightness. The noise from the factories had, ere this, ceased. At six

o'clock was heard the ringing of many bells, and presently the workers poured out, and the beatings of the engines were silenced, and the light steam jets blurted out no longer from the small pipes. The day's toil was done, and the released operatives walked out rejoicing to refresh themselves with food and rest, and so prepare for the labour of the coming day.[43]

The Tontine itself was one of the black-spots of old Glasgow, a mass of filthy vennels in the very heart of the city, and a well-known haunt of beggary and crime, but the characters who people it owe little to the setting. Pae worked within the basically realistic Scots tradition as a rule, but when it suited his purpose he drew upon a variety of other conventions. The Captain, for example, is a typical Claude Duval figure lifted straight from the popular gallows fiction of the time. The fact that he is supposed to be a Scots gentleman of good family creates few problems, indeed Pae outdoes his sources in fantastic elaboration. The Captain is a master of disguise, but for everyday wear, he sports a brigand costume, with a silk cap, a tight velvet jacket, and a richly ornamented girdle from which depend a brace of pistols and a dagger studded with precious stones. Pae seems to have had little first-hand knowledge of the Scottish underworld, or its language. Scottish thieves cant was widely used by vagrants and had obtained a foothold in certain sections of the manu-facturing population,[44] but Pae imported his criminal slang from the Newgate novels of Bulwyer-Lytton and W H Ainsworth, which were overwhelmingly London-centred in outlook, language and style.[45] The Captain's followers have names like Bushy Bill, Little Tip, Heavy Ben and the Swaggerer, and they are given to remarks like 'Now, old covey, you must be quiet. I say, Bob, shall I take the mitten from his cheese-trap . . . An old cove, Captain . . . we grabbed and mittened him near the Green but we don't know what chink he has got in his thigh bank.'[46] Pae seems to have improvised the stuff as he went along without being indebted to a specific source. He even does it with a certain dash; but he created a most unfortunate precedent. Other writers began to make Scottish criminals talk this outlandish gabble too. Arguably it set back the development of a plausible crime fiction in Scotland by at least a generation.[47]

'The Factory Girl' includes a substantial element of fantasy and wish-fulfillment. In some ways it is an urban fairy-tale with echoes of Cinderella and Ali Baba, but as usual with David Pae, the main intention is deadly earnest.[48] The novel delivers an unrelenting attack on the commercial ethos, the devouring materialism which the author saw as threatening to engulf Scotland in the first great wave of capitalist expansion. The cotton mill is presented as the archetypal industrial symbol and Dexter as the chief representative of the values of the new commercial civilisation; many of the rural gentry at the time were deeply opposed to the new order and advocated a compassionate and paternalistic approach to the social problems of industrialisation. This is the position represented by the Clanworth brothers, whose country house provides a temporary refuge for Sarah and Lucy at a key stage in the story. So that at a structural level the novel reflects important ideological divisions within contemporary society.[49]

Pae did not believe that industrial capitalism was bad in itself, but thought it had been wrenched out of its proper relationship with individual needs, the requirements of society, and with the divine order. The theme runs through all his books. Machines, he urged, should serve men; not the other way round:

> Beneath the strong, whirling, bubbling, seething, foaming river of city experience there is an undercurrent continually flowing. Busy as men are buying and selling and getting gain, they must, perforce, endure the experience of their human natures. The storm of trade and commerce rushing above cannot enable them to get quit of the hopes and fears, the passions and feelings of the heart. These were meant to be ministered to by commerce; and though unfortunately men have reversed the order, and made the heart the minister of commerce, crushing, or trying to crush, its warm and true impulses into the cold, narrow, selfish views which the mere commercial spirit engenders, yet it will not be so tutored and trained. It will assert its true instincts. It will indignantly deny the right and power to set aside its yearnings and aspirations, and between the two—between the selfishness and cruelty of Mammon and the heaven-directed desires of the heart—there is a bitter contest, in which the heart generally comes off at the worst. Hence misery and agony the most poignant are the result. It is as if those hearts which would be true to themselves were crushed between the wheels of iron which now whirl ceaselessly in our factories and were by them torn and lacerated.[50]

His emphasis upon the 'heart' as the ultimate moral arbiter has obvious links with Owen's 'religion of charity' and the attempt to transform the social order not by altering the environment but by inducing through education or evangelisation an internal moral change—literally a 'change of heart'—in large numbers of people.[51] It is in the light of this doctrine that the Glasgow business-classes are pilloried as mercenary and corrupt, especially when they do or induce others to do for money and power things that ought to be done for different, especially moral, reasons. The marriage convention appears again, with forced marriage as a metaphor for the attempted violation of free will; orphans, likewise, and possessing a similar reference to those in 'Jessie Melville': beings who are incomplete until they establish their true identity by discovering and relating properly to an appropriate parent-figure. The idea of inheritance informs the whole work, although perhaps in a less focused way than in the earlier novel. Here, there is no really acceptable patriarchal figure in the older generation of characters: Dexter does acknowledge Lucy as a daughter-in-law, but he remains a complete rascal until almost the end. His disgrace is so complete, however, that he surrenders his role as the moral head of the household to his upright and generous wife, who receives Lucy as a daughter joyously and at once. By this means the dual focus between earthly/heavenly father and orphan/exiled human spirit is preserved along with an additional motif, the will, a ubiquitous symbol in popular Victorian fiction, here used as an image of Providence, so that in repudiating the terms of Lucy's father's will, Dexter violates not merely a human sanction, but also the Divine will.[52]

There are still further Owenite echoes in Pae's general treatment of the family. Owen considered it to be a divisive force (much more so, for example, than social class) and regarded it as the ultimate cause of all acquisitiveness and social competition.[53] There are undercurrents in Pae's treatment of the family which suggest that he may also have viewed it basically as a self-perpetuating, selfish and coercive institution, the removal of its constraints (i.e. by becoming an orphan) being the first step in many of his heroes' and heroines' adventures. The cooperative, communitarian relations enjoyed by Lucy, Sarah, Hugh the knife-grinder and their friends is certainly suggestive in this context.

The extent to which doctrine influenced the scope and nature of the story can be seen in the treatment of the two main characters, Sarah and the Captain. At first glance they appear to be quite conventional: Sarah is one of those wild and mysterious gypsies modelled on Meg Merrilies with which this kind of fiction abounds, while the Captain reflects the popular English notion of the daring and attractive highwayman. In other respects, however, they depart dramatically from conventional typology. To all intents and purposes Sarah is the heroine of the novel. She is the dominant female character; from her actions most of the plot springs; yet she is introduced in the very first chapter as the archetypal fallen woman.

Chastity dominated the contemporary ideal of womanhood. It was equated with virtue itself, and seen as the foundation upon which all other good qualities were based. To lose it was quite literally to suffer 'a fate worse than death', and it is uniformly presented in this way in English popular fiction.[54] But that is not the case here. Sarah works her way towards social and spiritual rehabilitation by a whole series of virtuous actions. She cancels out her fall, and we are intended to acknowledge this and to be aware of its theological implications. The possibility is established at an early stage, when Hugh the knife-grinder, the touchstone of moral authority in the novel, a man wholly unspotted, patient and true, never rash, unjust or wrong, even momentarily, proposes marriage to Sarah in the full knowledge of what she is. Sarah protests:

> 'Now, Hugh, you understand me—you understand why I cannot be your wife. You now know both me and my purpose, and knowing, you must despise me.'
> 'Despise ye!' echoed Hugh, as his fine speaking face worked with strong excitement . . . 'I admire ye and pity ye, but I admire as muckle as I pity. Yer first fa' was a faut, but ye was tempted, and yer tempter will bear the greatest pairt o' the sin; but for what took place after he's responsible—the black cursed rascal. Forgie me for swearin' . . . It's seldom I dae it, but in this case I consider it a virtue; at a' events, I can nae mair haud frae cursin' him than I can frae drawin' breath. Despise ye, sae ye? I admire ye mair than ever, and let what ye hae just telt me be forgotten. I'll forget it, and dae ye forget it tae. Yer heart is as pure as ever, and that is the grand thing . . .'[55]

Pae's treatment of Sarah is a forceable reminder of the universal availability of grace, the more so as he was prepared to demonstrate the point using one of the most debased examples of humanity available to him.

But not even the Captain is beyond redemption. His nature is not wholly evil: indeed he shows a loyalty to his own code which would be admirable if it were not so perverted: he daringly frees one of his comrades from prison and frequently risks life and liberty for others. The Captain's greatest mistake is a doctrinal one. He represents Calvinist man. Regarding himself as unregenerate he despairs of his condition and throws himself into desperate enterprises with a kind of brooding antinomian abandon. But the author carefully modifies this view: his moral nature springs in part from an adverse environment, and although he does not clearly repent at the end, he is forgiven by the other characters and departs into the afterworld in a condition which is to say the least ambiguous. The reader is allowed to feel that even here there may be hope.

This extraordinary tale is brought to a close by a series of reflections on the role of the novelist and the moral implications of the narrative:

> We cannot say farewell to the reader without penning a few moral reflections upon the story now brought to a close. It is the province of the novelist to instruct as well as to amuse; and, when he neglects to aim at the fulfilment of his twofold duty, he fails to accomplish that good which the sphere and character of his labour are intended to effect. Should he strive only to amuse and excite, he may enlist the sympathy and fascinate the imagination of his readers, but he will teach them no new lesson, he will furnish them with no moral or intellectual nourishment. Nay, the great probability is, that his production will exert an unhealthy influence on the heart and mind. We deeply feel our own responsibility in this respect, and during the course of the story have endeavoured to cast in the seeds of instruction and moral truth as occasion offered; but it remains for us to state somewhat definitely our designed purposes in the tale.
>
> Our purpose, and that a prominent if not a central one, has been to show crime in its various modes, characters, and consequences. We have it in its lowest and grossest form in the Tontine Close, where it is followed as a profession—where it is made the great purpose of life—where all the powers of body and mind are bent and concentrated on its commission—where men and women live who have bid farewell to honesty, sobriety, and virtue, whose industry is exerted in the direction of theft, robbery, and even murder . . . But we have also shown the phases of higher class crime, where it is yielded to rather than deliberately adopted, and where it is associated with outward honesty and respectability. We have brought upon the stage men who, tempted by the prospect of gain, have been induced to commit grievous wrongs on the weak, the helpless, and the unsuspecting, to defraud them, and even to consent to their death . . . We have seen, too, the development of the dark passion of revenge—the wronged one bitterly nursing a desire for the ruin of the wrong doer, and working secretly and ruthlessly for its accomplishment. This, too, is a distortion of life, a wasting of high God-given powers and faculties, for the use of which there will assuredly be an account demanded . . . Our tale has likewise presented characters which the reader instinctively loves and admires. If the portraiture leads also to imitation the story will have served a very high and satisfying purpose . . .
>
> Such is life; not as it should be, not as God meant it to be, but as it is—struggling against its sin-produced disorders, and striving here and there, in

various ways, to get into harmony with the Divine purpose. The very sins of evil men produce suffering and sorrow which compel resistance, and herein lies the hope of the world's purification and regeneration. Were the arena of sin to be a garden of pleasure, producing only an easy corruption and death, men would not wrestle against it, but would, in a mass, wander carelessly amid its decaying bowers, till they reached the Lethe river, flowing along its sides, and there lay themselves down to indulge a painless death. But thank God that sin produces suffering, for suffering drives us to war against sin, and seek towards the source and centre of Holiness . . .

Life, then . . . is in a fever at present, but the fever is not unto death. Its scenes are often dark, repulsive, loathsome, but their very intensity of action is a proof of their working for health—for the higher and truer establishment of life, which, when it becomes what the Creator intended, shall be but the true operation of human faculty and power—man working according to his nature, not, as now, doing constant violence to his feelings and necessities. Great and glorious shall human life be then—worthy of that mighty Being who created and redeemed it.

Such is life, its scenes and its lessons. May we all learn them, and grow wiser and better for the instruction!'[56]

During the next twenty years, David Pae completed on average two substantial serial novels annually which were initially published either in the *People's Journal* or in the *People's Friend* whose editor he became in 1870, holding the post until his death in 1884. His total output remains uncertain. His deputy, Andrew Stewart, prepared a list of more than forty titles in order, of publication, but acknowledged that even so it was probably incomplete.[57] The situation is complicated by the practice of syndication, which meant that Pae novels might appear in several newspapers simultaneously but not necessarily under the same title.

Syndication was one of the basic facts of newspaper life during the second half of the nineteenth century. Anything from whole pages of standardised newsprint to individual columns of news, features, or fiction could be supplied to hard-pressed editors by agencies or individuals servicing a number of papers simultaneously. News was the first thing to be packaged in this way through bodies like Reuters and the Central Press Agency; in due course advertising following suit.[58] Before long the idea was extended to fiction, copy reaching subscribers in the form of proof-sheets or flimsy from which the house printers then set up the text.[59] The real breakthrough came when stereotyping was introduced which enabled the customer to print from pre-fabricated plates avoiding costly re-setting by his own compositors. The original text would be set by hand or machine and from this a large number of impressions could then be taken on specially treated heat-resistant matrices. At the receiving end a plate could be quickly cast from the matrix by a hot metal process and fitted to the press along with other plates similarly produced and arranged so as to make up a page.[60] Various fiction agencies came into being as distributive middlemen between novelists and editors. John Leng's brother William ran one as an offshoot of his paper the *Sheffield Telegraph*; there was another in London controlled by the publishing firm Cassells; best known of all was the Tillotson Fiction Bureau based in Bolton, a subsidiary of the Tillotson newspaper group's Lancashire Journals series whose main title was the *Bolton Journal and Guardian*.[61]

Marketing the novel became an increasingly complicated business as the century advanced and the literary market diversified. As a crude generalisation, one would expect the art-novel at some stage of its publication history to appear in book form, middlebrow fiction to find one of its main outlets serially in magazines, while the weekly newspaper press would provide the main vehicle for mass fiction. A novel might appear in all or any of these forms. Serial rights and book rights were carefully distinguished and it was to the author's advantage, other things being equal, to exploit all sections of the market.[62] Although it was not uncommon for a novel to start life as a serial before being issued later in the conventional three volume form, the book trade in Scottish fiction remained at a low level, producing a handful of novels of Scottish interest in any year, while original fiction written for the Scottish press might run to hundreds of titles annually.

By about 1880, most Scots papers publishing fiction were carrying a mixture of locally-produced and nationally syndicated material supplied either by agencies or by individual authors dealing with outlets directly. The records of the Aberdeen and North of Scotland Newspaper and Printing Co show in some detail the day to day workings of the system and the level of expenditure on fiction incurred by one Scots newspaper group during the last quarter of the century. On 15 March 1878 the Business Committee noted that 'It was agreed to arrange with Messrs Tillotson & Son Bolton for permission to publish a serial tale Miss Russell's novel *The Vicar's Governess* at a price not exceeding £15, and Mrs Burnett's forthcoming tale at a price not exceeding £25.' Later Tillotsons asked, and got, £30 for the Burnett novel.[63] That same year an honorarium of £20 was recorded for a local author, the Rev W M Philip, for a serial novel of twenty-seven columns length (about 60,000 words) for the *Weekly Journal*.[64] An offer of a story from the poet and novelist Robert Buchanan provides an example of an author of reputation dealing directly with a paper. It was declined; the obstacle was probably the price.[65]

The wisest heads in the newspaper world reckoned that it was best to carry exclusively original fiction if it could be got but agency syndication was cheap and it could deliver big names.[66] The Tillotsons and their like could pay enormous sums for serial rights—over £1,000 in some cases—because of the sheer scale of their operations. This brought leading contemporary authors like Wilkie Collins and Mary Elizabeth Braddon into direct competition with local writers catering for the local market.[67] By the late 1870s even the *People's Journal* was turning on occasion to agency fiction—a tendency that was to increase with the passage of time.

Although under contract to Leng and Co, David Pae obviously controlled his own syndication rights and he continued to deal with other newspaper outlets after joining the group. Pae stories crop up frequently in the

Scottish press, particularly in the industrial west Lowlands where the *People's Journal* was slower to establish itself.[68] Papers like the *Hamilton Advertiser* and the *Paisley & Renfrewshire Gazette* carried practically everything he wrote, and the experience of several papers serialising his novels illustrates just how dramatically popular fiction could affect sales. Frederic Tillotson started running fiction when he wanted to push the *Bolton Journal* against stiff local competition and one can see the pattern repeated again and again. Return copies of the *Aberdeen Weekly Journal* used to be distributed free to farm servants for two or three weeks whenever a new serial began, and if it 'took', the circulation would increase by several hundred copies a week as the readers began to pay for the paper to find out what happened next.[69] But this was fairly modest in comparison to the gains claimed by some papers as a result of printing fiction, especially by David Pae. The *Fife Free Press* reported unprecedented demand when it started 'Frederick the Foundling' which it printed in massive chunks in the spring of 1871. So great was the excitement that it had to reprint the first several chapters in a special free supplement for readers who had missed them.[70] There can be little doubt that its fiction programme did much to transform the *People's Journal* from an obscure local paper to the huge national weekly it had become by the time of Pae's death; the paper itself certainly thought so.[71] How well he did out of all this is difficult to say. Literary earnings varied so much in the serial market that it is probably pointless to speculate, but he appears to have been fairly comfortable, with a pleasant house on the southern shores of the firth of Tay and Lengs were a firm who knew how to look after their senior staff.

In the Autumn of 1881 David Pae was in his early fifties, securely established as the leading popular novelist in Scotland, and one of the most popular of his later stories, 'The Lost Heir of Glencorran', was about to begin its run in the *People's Journal*.[72] It concerns Conrade Leslie, a young civil engineer assisting Thomas Telford with the Caledonian Canal, and as the story opens he is about to leave his Edinburgh office for a final check of measurements on site in the Loch Linnhe area. It transpires that he is an orphan, left in a basket along with a mysterious package on the doorstep of an Edinburgh solicitor who has taken him in and brought him up. The package is directed to the lawyer with instructions that it be placed in Conrade's hands when he comes of age. Unfortunately it is stolen by a clerk called Edward Raikes who subsequently disappears so that the only clue Conrade has to his identity is a deer's head tattoo on his arm, and a strong sense that he is of Highland descent. He takes with him letters of introduction to the Chisholm family at Glencorran House, and after a while he duly pays a call. He discovers that the mark on his arm is in fact the crest of Chisholm of Glencorran and there is good reason to suppose that he is the lost heir. It appears that the Chisholms had been 'out' in the 'Forty-five and after the Rebellion the laird and his wife had gone into hiding in the slums of Glasgow. There a child had been born, but the parents died and the child disappeared. The estate had meantime been progressively engrossed by the treacherous factor, so that only the house and its surrounding property remains, and even these must go shortly unless the true heir can be found. The situation is aggravated by the fact that the factor is clearing the tenants from his part of the glen to make it into a sheep-run, and intends to do the same with the rest when it comes into his possession. It is vital for Conrade to establish his title to the property, therefore, not just for his own sake, but to protect the people who are left. He resigns from his job, and assisted by Lauchie the piper, an old and resourceful family retainer, he begins the quest to prove who he is and to make good his claim to the estate.

Painstaking enquiries in Glasgow show that he is indeed the son of Malcolm Chisholm, last laird of Glencorran and his wife Edarnoc (Conrade backwards), but without the missing package which contains his legal title, he cannot recover his rights. He must therefore find Edward Raikes. Bearing in mind that Raike's last known address was in Virginia, and that he feels a strong obligation to look after his people, he takes personal charge of their emigration to Canada. When they are properly established, he hunts for Raikes through a wide tract of the eastern United States and southern Canada and he and Lauchie have many adventures. Eventually Raikes is found, the documents recovered and the factor duly foiled.

The atmosphere of this story is noticeably different from the earlier examples. Although the traditional motifs of inheritance and alienation are still present, their symbolic force is distinctly weaker. They are used not so much because they form a satisfying pattern with reference to an external set of ideas, but because they make a good story. To an extent hardly conceivable in the later 1850s, the novel has shed its utilitarian props and become an end in itself. The tone is palpably less religiously moralistic, and the lengthy conclusion which contains a fierce attack upon the Clearances and the soulless materialism which Pae saw lying behind them, has a thoroughly secular air compared with similar utterances a decade or so before. In this case we may feel the moral really is 'tacked on to the end'.[73]

David Pae's career as a novelist spans that period during which a genuinely popular fiction came into being in Scotland free from external religious constraints. He had begun using fiction merely to subvert reader resistance to the message he wished to convey, but by the end of his career, fictional values predominated. The novel had become its own justification and fiction was seen to possess intrinsic value which made the reading or writing of it a legitimate activity not just for the bourgeoisie but for every social class. Although precipitated, ironically, by evangelical liberals struggling to perpetuate a basically theocentric world-view, this marked a decisive step in the secularisation of Scottish society.[74]

Pae's novels help us understand the symbolic codes that lie at the centre of so much contemporary popular fiction, the obsessive reworking of a few powerful motifs: wills, orphans, inheritance, marriage and so on, and to see that they form the lingua franca of a theological revolution, the triumph of the liberal theology that transformed the religious climate of Scotland during the second half of the nineteenth century and was to have such far reaching implications for the later creative and cultural life of the country.

His career reminds us, too, how complex and extensive the Victorian literary market was. As the century advanced the newspaper displaced the book as the main source of popular fiction and serialisation became the dominant mode of publication for the novel in Scotland. At the same time as the Scottish bookmarket declined as a proportion of the total Anglo-American market, and the Scottish bourgeoisie became increasingly absorbed in an all-UK London-centred middlebrow culture, there arose in Scotland a new publishing medium, controlled in Scotland, written in Scotland and selling in Scotland, and with it a whole new wave of popular novelists writing for a specifically Scottish audience, some in an entirely local context using real communities familiar to their readers, others, like Pae, writing for a national audience but still locating his fiction within recognisable and usually contemporary settings. He ignored neither industrialisation nor the social evils it implied, and was throughout his career an outspoken critic of the materialism and self-interest which he saw as their cause. His output is extensive, and from time to time he enters historical or agrarian subject-areas usually considered *de rigueur* for the nineteenth century novel in Scotland. It is clear, however, that a significant proportion of his work lies entirely outside them. Many of his stories have an urban setting and in the rest the city is a legitimate part of the imaginative terrain and may be entered at will. His fiction alone, even if it were not supported again and again by the practice of other popular novelists writing for the press must cast serious doubt—to say the least—upon the long-cherished idea that Scottish fiction ignored the cities and what was going on in them in favour of a nostalgic, sentimental vision of the rural past. Hard-cover or book fiction is not, even remotely, in itself a sufficient basis on which to judge Scottish writing and its subject-matter in the second half of the nineteenth century.

In *Lippincott's Monthly Magazine* in 1890, the novelist William Westall published a lengthy article on serial fiction in the newspaper press. It dealt mainly with England, but he had known Frederic Tillotson and William Leng, and had himself published fiction in the papers. While compiling the piece, he had corresponded with a number of editors in the north of England about popular reading habits, and he quoted their responses at length.

> Nobody, probably, has had more experience in providing fiction for the masses, or studied their idiosyncrasies more closely and intelligently than the conductors of the *Northern Daily Telegraph* (Blackburn) and the *North-Eastern Gazette* (Middlesborough),—papers which . . . give their readers daily doses of fiction . . . these gentlemen . . . have found that the most fetching story (other things being equal) is one possessing local interest. This conclusion I am able to confirm from my own experience. A novel of mine (The Old Factory'), dealing with Lancashire and first published in the *Manchester Times* and the *Glasgow Herald*, has since been reproduced in the country palatine again and again, but

so far as I know, nowhere else; and it was not a success in the Scottish paper.

   . . . the conductors of the two papers in question . . . do not care whether a story be new or second-hand; it is none the worse for their purpose even though it has been previously published by another paper in the same neighbourhood,—always provided that it is of the right sort. Favourable press notices, so highly prized by authors, are of no account. 'Our experience has been', writes Mr Quail, editor of the *Northern Daily Telegraph*, 'that tales which have been very popular and highly spoken of when published in volume form fall the flattest as newspaper serials.' They are tales to be avoided by wise purveyors and discreet editors. Another proof of the truth of the old adage that one man's meat is another man's poison.

   As for eminent names, thus (in another letter) writes Mr Quail: 'William Black, James Payn, Walter Besant, and even Miss Braddon (whom we find fairly popular), cannot hold up a candle to David Pae . . .'[75]

FOUR

A Prophet . . . and from Galilee
The Novels of William Alexander

William Alexander was the author of a famous book of which most people even if they have only a passing interest in literature will have heard, although they may not, because of the uncompromising density of its language, actually have read—*Johnny Gibb of Gushetneuk*. Its reputation has tended to grow rather than diminish with the passage of time, so much so that it has recently been hailed as 'the masterpiece of Scottish Victorian fiction'.[1] Its publication history certainly bears witness to enduring popularity; it has gone through more than twenty editions and been almost continuously in print since it was first published in Aberdeen in 1871. The novel was originally serialised in the *Free Press* from 28 September 1869, to 20 December 1870, with a break of a fortnight in May when the editor William McCombie died, and intermittent gaps in the Autumn of 1870 as the Germans laid siege to Paris during the Franco-Prussian War.

In the *Weekly Free Press* too, appeared most of the short stories later published as *Sketches of Life Among My Ain Folk* (Edinburgh 1875; 2nd edn, 1882) which, although their quality was recognised by contemporaries and by some later commentators, have been out of print for more than a century and are not at all widely known. Alexander also enjoys a secure, if minor, reputation as a writer of non-fiction works, chiefly agricultural, most notably his lively and readable social history *Notes and Sketches Illustrative of Northern Rural Life in the Eighteenth Century* (Aberdeen 1877) which has recently been re-published with an introduction by Ian Carter.[2] From a literary point of view, however, he is very much a one-book man whose fame rests on his classic account of North-East rural society at the time of the Disruption, *Johnny Gibb of Gushetneuk*.

Alexander was a modest retiring man who, although spending most of his adult life in the hurly-burly of newspaper work and public affairs in a burgeoning Victorian city, shunned self-publicity to an almost neurotic degree. He left few materials to assist the biographer; there are gaps in his life which have to be filled by inference from secondary sources, and perhaps most important of all, his family (possibly in accordance with his own wish) did little to further his reputation or to increase our understanding of his life and work after his death in 1894 at the age of sixty-eight.

Indeed the present writer had to hunt for Alexander's obituary in his own paper. It turned out to be an unremarkable column or so—about average for a prominent local businessman—and there was no picture. Perhaps this was not entirely surprising. For years there had been serious political divisions amongst the proprietors. Alexander's younger brother

Henry, by this time editor of the *Daily Free Press* took a Liberal-Unionist line on the Irish Question, while William himself was an ardent Home-Ruler. The two were bitterly estranged.[3]

In 1878, he published a characteristically self-effacing history of the *Free Press*, discussing everybody's role in the paper except his own. Of his contribution he simply noted 'Under the shadow of the names that ought ever to be associated with the foundation and establishment of the *Free Pres*, as a living . . . institution, it was the lot of the writer to labour in a diversified way, from writing newspaper addresses to executing the combined function of Reporter, Sub-editor, and a few odds and ends in addition . . .'[4] Amongst the odds and ends are at least five other novels. They are completely unknown; they appear in no bibliography; not one has been formally attributed to him before.[5]

They are, in chronological order, 'Sketches of Rural Life in Aberdeenshire', which appeared under the pseudonym 'Rusticus' in the *North of Scotland Gazette* transferring to the *Free Press*, 31 December, 1852–2 December 1853; 'The Authentic History of Peter Grundie' published in the *Penny Free Press* between 26 June 1855 and 18 December 1855; 'The Laird of Drammochdyle and his Contemporaries: or Random Sketches done in outline with a Burnt Stick', published in the 'Free Press, 15 August 1865 to 17 April 1866; 'Ravenshowe and the Residenters Therein—Sketches of a Hamlet of the Olden Time' which appeared in two series, 5 February 1867 to 21 May 1867, and 31 December 1867 to 28 April 1868; and 'My Uncle the Baillie' in the *Weekly Free Press*, 2 December 1876 to 5 May 1877. The last of these was described as being 'By the Author of *Johnny Gibb of Gushetneuk* when it was published in the *Weekly Free Press*; 'Peter Grundie' was identified as Alexander's in the *Daily Free Press*, whilst the remainder are attributable on internal grounds.[6] In the light of this new evidence, we are able, indeed compelled, to re-assess his career and his significance for Scottish letters more generally.

Alexander was an enthusiastic genealogist, declaring 'The more essential facts concerning one's immediate ancestors must be a matter of more than merely sentimental interest to every man and woman of sense,'[7] and he traced his descent from a long line of tenant farmers in the Garioch stretching back into the seventeenth century. Three generations of William Alexanders tenanted the farm of Westerhouses in the parish of Bourtie a few miles from Rescivet near Pitcaple where the author, the fifth of the name, was born on 12 June 1826. Following a family quarrel his grandfather gave up farming to become a country blacksmith. His son followed in his footsteps, but after a while he took up the lease of a small-holding called Damhead and it was here that the author spent much of his childhood and adolescence.

His father returned to farming at the height of the 'rage for improvement' in Aberdeenshire. Much of the county was waste ground: a featureless expanse of moss and moor pitted with stones and boulders, and farms were being let on advantageous terms to the tenants willing to tackle the daunting task of reclamation. It was a heroic age in a way, a triumph of human drive and ingenuity, as acre by acre the little farms advanced across the moorlands and up the brae sides. Despite its naturally indifferent soil, ungenerous climate, and remoteness from southern markets, Aberdeen-shire was slowly transformed into one of the most advanced and efficient agricultural areas in Europe.[8]

It was this which underlay Alexander's lifelong interest in the shaping power of heredity and the environment on human character, and gave him the central imaginative apparatus of his later fiction. Give or take a mile or two, his family had lived for centuries in the Garioch, the 'girnal of Aberdeenshire', a pleasant rolling valley formed by the river Urie winding round the northern slopes of the hill of Benachie, and people like the Alexanders had made it practically with their own hands. Their lives were woven into its history. The local laird had been 'out' in the Jacobite Rising of 1745. A near relative witnessed the battle of Inverurie during the same campaign. At a little distance lay the field of Harlaw, one of the most famous and bloody battles in Scottish history in which the North-East folk held off a great Highland army and prevented the sack of Aberdeen. From his later writing it is clear, too, that he grew up within a vigorous folk-culture, rich in witch-belief, fairy-lore, folk-tale and song.[9]

Dr William Alexander. *Source: Transactions of the Buchan Field Club, Vol. XIII.* Reproduced by courtesy of University of Aberdeen, Special Collections.

His world was a place of violent, even revolutionary, change, involving
the introduction of steam-power, railways, electric telegraphy, mass
communication, and he himself played a leading role in the transformation.
An old world vanished and a new one came into being, and conflicting
themes of change and continuity inform nearly everything he wrote. The
most obvious break of all took place in his own life when a serious injury
prevented him pursuing his career in agriculture. The nature of the
accident is not clear; perhaps he was scythed or something fell on him—in
any case his leg was amputated and Alexander had to find another job.

This happened in 1846 or perhaps 1847, when he was about twenty, and
what he did during the next five years or so is not clear. His parents had
nine other children and only two of the boys were old enough to contribute
to the labour force of the farm; the family could not afford a passenger. We
know he used the long recuperation period to study and reflect; he learned
to sketch and draw and retained a lifelong interest in painting; he read
voraciously, studied shorthand, taught himself some Latin, and began to
write stories, essays and poems, and to have them published in local
periodicals.[10] His formal education had been of the normal, fairly scanty,
pattern for a country boy of his class. He had been sent for a few 'raiths' to
the parish school at Daviot with little edification or profit, judging from the
many slighting references to parochial schools and schoolmasters scattered
throughout his works.[11] But these were not the only schools to be found in
rural areas. As the arable area extended and the population grew, people
often found it inconvenient to send their children to the parish school, and
a whole network of informal schools sprang up. These 'venture-schools'
were staffed by a heterogeneous teaching force ranging from elderly
women eking out a slender subsistence by instilling basic literacy into
young children, to bright but 'fusionless' men unable for various reasons to
discharge their normal role in the rural economy. Such people may have
lacked the formal academic training of the regular parochial schoolmasters,
but they were sometimes better teachers, and were often more finely
attuned to the particular parish community they served. Alexander may
have received the early stages of his own education in such a school and he
shows the non-parochial system in a uniformly favourable light. One thinks
of Sandy Peterkin's school in *Johnny Gibb*, for instance, or Isaac Ronald the
dominie's school in the story of the same name. In the latter especially,
Alexander's detailed acquaintance with the minutiae of teaching strongly
suggests that he had once actually done it. Keeping a private or adventure
school was about the only thing a clever young man with a physical
handicap could do in a country district anyway, unless, perhaps a little
clerking or book-keeping. This was probably how he supported himself
between the end of his farming days and his entrance into the professional
world of letters as reporter, chief clerk, and general factotum on the *North
of Scotland Gazette* in 1852.[12] His early career is similar, then, to William
Latto except that Alexander enjoyed advantages that his colleague in Fife
did not. He became involved in one of the most interesting educational

movements in Victorian Scotland, the Aberdeenshire and Banffshire Mutual Instruction Union, and through it, he won the friendship and patronage of the remarkable William McCombie.[13]

When Alexander came within his orbit, McCombie was in his late thirties and already enjoyed a considerable reputation as a speculative thinker. Alexander had read his books *Hours of Thought* and the anti-Calvinist essays entitled *Moral Agency*,[14] and in any case the name itself was one to conjure with in farming circles. The philosopher had helped his father create the family farm of Cairnballoch in the Howe of Alford, and was an authority on agriculture in his own right, as well as being a cousin of William McCombie of Tillyfour, probably the greatest cattle breeder of the age. He had little formal education and was virtually self-taught: indeed contemporaries regarded him as the most impressive autodidact of his generation with the possible exception of Hugh Miller.[15] By the mid eighteen-forties, the farmhouse at Cairnballoch had become the centre of a literary and philosophical coterie whose sphere of influence extended throughout the North-East. McCombie was a genial and expansive man with a fine sardonic wit and brilliant conversational powers. Philosophical theory, abstruse theology, social and political speculation poured from him in an unceasing torrent: he was a walking liberal education, and Alexander was an apt pupil. His attitudes towards land-ownership, for instance, his dislike of the landlord class, his interest in advanced Liberal politics, were all coloured by McCombie's thinking, and from him it seems likely that he also received a thorough if informal grounding in contemporary philosophy. He could have gained a fair insight into mechanistic and positivist theories, for example, just by listening to McCombie—a devout Christian—savaging them.[16]

The two met probably in 1849 when McCombie became President of the Aberdeenshire and Banffshire Mutual Instruction Union. The movement had started at Rhynie in the western uplands of Aberdeenshire in 1846, and it spread throughout much of the rural North-East during the following decade, as a loose federation of affiliated classes presided over by the Rhynie group and linked by district correspondents attached to each branch.[17] The most vigorous of these, apart from Rhynie itself, was at Lentush near Old Rayne a mile or two from Alexander's home. Although he modestly disclaimed any direct role in the movement, the most exact and well-informed of his biographers, Alexander Mackilligan, who interviewed many friends and surviving members of the family in the early years of the present century, states him to have been a district correspondent.[18] The point is of more than antiquarian interest for it was here that the magazine of the Union, the *Rural Echo* was produced. It was compiled entirely by members of the Lentush club and may well contain some of Alexander's earliest published writings.[19] In some ways the *Echo* was an extreme product of the self-improvement movement; it aimed at 'the popularising of scientific truths' and its view of the world was strongly coloured by contemporary utilitarian and materialistic theory. A paper in the second issue, for example, on a 'New Theory of Vision' typically traced how external physical reality could create and condition ideas, extolling Thomas Reid and the Scottish 'Common Sense' school of philosophy.[20] Its temper was highly abstract and speculative, and although there were essays on more mundane subjects like agriculture, phrenology, education and spelling reform, poems in Scots and English, and even a little fiction and drama, it was a dauntingly cerebral publication.[21]

Society meetings must have been something of an ordeal too, especially for speakers. Each member had to read an essay of his or her own composition and then submit it to public discussion by all the other members of the branch. They might even be asked to speak extempore on a subject nominated by the chair. It tended to create a distinctive 'house-style' in debate that marked members of the Union whenever they spoke in public. And several of them went on to public careers, particularly in journalism. James Macdonnell of the *Daily Telegraph* and the *Times* was a Union product, as was Alexander Allardyce who eventually became deputy editor of *Blackwood's*.[22] It was here, too, that McCombie found his bright young men to staff the *Gazette* and the *Free Press* when he became editor of the papers in the early 1850s.[23]

Alexander's first substantial contribution was a series entitled 'Sketches of Rural Life in Aberdeenshire' written under the pseudonym Rusticus which began in the *Gazette* on 31 December 1852, and continued in the *Free Press* until December of the following year, ranging widely over contemporary country life. It was framed as a series of dialogues between two representative figures, a worthy tenant farmer called Peter Stark and his friend, a venture-school dominie, named Tammas Gray. To an old Mutual Union hand, the debate was the natural vehicle for handling ideas, and Alexander used it to some effect.[24] It enabled him in addition to present nearly the whole text in the natural idiom of the speakers, that is, vernacular Scots, with little connecting English prose. Various themes were duly aired in dialogue or in extended monologue, things like work and work-discipline, social change and the reasons for it, the growth of the intellect and the provision of education, the relationship between the past and the present. There were a number of descriptive genre-pieces, market and bothy, a ploughing-match, a penny wedding and so on, all providing opportunity for set-piece discourse in the vernacular. The 'Sketches' were intended to be objective in their approach to country life, they adopted Pope's line 'To catch the manners living as they rise' as their motto, and were received by most readers as a faithful account of the subject. Much of the content of Alexander's admired socio-historical study *Northern Rural Life* appeared here in embryo—and in Scots—a generation before. Here is a typical passage, delivered by Peter Stark, when pressed by the dominie to give an account of the old-time farm touns when he was a boy:

> Fan I was a little fite-headed laddie o' ten or eleven year auld, I was sent to herd the farmer o' Gateside's nowt; the auld guidman was livin than, and it's him that I mean to speak o' i' the first place. He was as fine a specimen o' the auld fashiont farmer as ye cud wuss; his family war a' grown up, and even middle-

aged men some o' them at the time I've mentioned, so the farmin affairs war a' managed by them—but it was wonnerfu hoo the auld man contrived to gar himsel think that he had still the charge o' conductin matters. He cud lippen the boys noo to gae to the market wi' a beast or the like o' that; but nane o' the wark at hame cud be deen till he contrived hoo, and he wud shak his head fan his sons spak o' tryin ony new-fangled notion. Weel div I mind hoo he used to come ower to me at my herdin, and we wud bait the kye close to the edge o' the corn for a while, and syne turn them ower to the middle o' the leys, and he wud sit doon upo the auld fail-dyke at the end, and tell me mony a divertin story. He was a man o' auchty years o' age by that time, but as active and lively as ye like; as a proof o' that, I need only say that for a' his great age he aftener than ance defate me in a race ... He had been but a slicht-bigget man originally, and noo that he was worn doon to his second childhood, the close knee breeks and ribbet hose gae his limbs an unco slen'er appearance. He wore aye a braid blue bonnet wi' a red cherry tap upo the croon o't, fan he was in full dress; but, fan the weather was warm, or him nae gaen aboot muckle, he clappit on a red stripet nicht-cap. Auld Gateside declared he had never in his life drunk a haill glass o' whisky—that was an example o' temperance for ye; and he used to cry oot sair against the use o' tea. 'Ah,' he wud say, 'an they wud lat that foreign trash alane, and tak pottage and cauld kail to their breakfast, there wud be less word o' that rheumatisms and ither new-fashiont diseases;' but, for a' that, the auld bodie turnt gey fond o' a cup o' tea i' the evenin o' his days.[25]

The old man goes on to tell a story about the 'Forty-five which reflects a tradition actually current in the author's own family.

A number of things about the passage invite comment: its objectivity, its powers of observation, its use of exact and telling detail. The language is interesting too. Although southern literary influences have not been entirely shaken off—one notices *alane* instead of *aleen*, for example—the Scots reflects the speech patterns of mid-Aberdeenshire with a distinctive orthography and an easy naturalness of style. There is little of the lexical and idiomatic density of the later Alexander: the prose is relaxed, low-key, almost ostentatiously un-rhetorical, and although the underlying grammatical structure still owes something to the written standard, there is a genuine attempt to follow the rhythms of the everyday speaking voice. Alexander became famous in press circles for the speed with which he could transcribe speech, and his ability to capture the personal idiosyncrasies of the speaker. The skill was obviously well developed even at this early stage.[26]

But the 'Sketches' raised a fundamental problem which was to reverberate throughout Alexander's long literary career. They triggered off a correspondence about the nature of realism as a literary method, and the extent of his commitment to it, not just with regard to superficial accuracy, minutiae of language and so on—but with the basic ability of the writer or, for that matter, the technique, to reach the truth about the lifestyle of the agricultural workforce. The 'Condition of the Farm Servant Question' was beginning to cause widespread concern. Housing, education and moral welfare were all felt to be threatened by the exploitative tendencies of the new high capitalist farming. Alexander had won a prize

for an essay on the subject just a year or two before, but the true extent of
the problem revealed by the shattering illegitimacy statistics contained in
the Census of 1851, which seemed to indicate—*prima facie*—that the rural
North-East was the most depraved community in Britain, took even the
gloomiest commentators aback. It was on this ground that Rusticus was
attacked in the summer of 1852 by a correspondent signing himself 'Auld
Ploughman'. According to the Ploughman, Alexander had deliberately
avoided the extremes of rural life, and, above all, had glossed over the
actual grossness of the rural proletariat:

> [Ye] gie us little licht on the disgusting bothy system, so much in vogue at the
> muckle farms . . . the bulk of the news spoken by the inmates a string of cant
> phrases bordering on, if not downright obscenity . . . Among the hay on the
> har'st rig, fillin' the barn, thrashin' or at ony occasion where the sexes mix, they
> are characterized by the same disgraceful obscenity. And, often, the full blown
> farmer o' ane an' twenty, wi' spurs and whip, is more ready to smile than frown
> at these exhibitions o' depravity . . . And how often do obscene stories lead to
> obscene actions, in which the farmer himsel', if a young free man, is ready to
> play his part? . . . I hae seen the lassies fechtin' and tearin' out ilk ither's hair
> about their young master! . . . Ye speak o' 'catching the living manners as they
> rise'; this, I think is wrang. Ye dinna tak them as they come, but jist wyles out
> what you think to get printed, and this way you cheat the folks, by leaving out
> the warst; this is nae very honest after a'.[27]

Various correspondents sprang to his defence, but Rusticus had to
acknowledge that the speech of the majority of the rural working-class
could not be rendered with absolute accuracy because the result would be
unprintable. Although Alexander attained in his mature work a masterly
command of suggestion—the ability to imply all kinds of vices and
shortcomings in his characters by means of non-obscene corruptions in
their spoken idiom—it was here that the outer frontiers of realism were
fixed for at least half a century to come.

The method of 'Sketches of Rural Life in Aberdeenshire' also possesses
interest: a central core of objective *reportage* mediated through fictional
characters representing a typical range of response to what passes before
them. Although applied to a very different subject, it is the same in essence
as Tolstoy was to use in his Sevastopol sketches a year or two later. By a
curious irony, indeed, the siege of Sevastopol provided the occasion for
Alexander's next—and much more ambitious—work, the 40,000 word
novella entitled 'The Authentic History of Peter Grundie', which enjoys the
distinction of being the first novel of any quality specifically written for
serialisation in a newspaper in Scotland.

The excitement caused by the Crimean war led to a great expansion in
newspaper activity in Britain. The *Free Press* went bi-weekly and brought
out a cheap Tuesday edition for the duration of hostilities to catch the
popular market. Alexander's novel appeared there every week from the
end of June to the middle of December in 1855 with occasional interrup-
tions caused by extra news from the front.

Like 'Sketches', 'Peter Grundie' had its roots in a major social problem—the threat to traditional agencies of social control in the mushrooming Scottish cities, where the growing concentration of population in inner urban parishes was putting intolerable pressure upon welfare provision. The publication of the Poor Law Commission report in 1844 and increasing expenditure under the new 1845 Poor Law was occasioning widespread debate about the nature of the state's obligations towards its citizens and the extent of social responsibility of individuals towards one another. 'Peter Grundie' examines the question: what constitutes social disability, and what ought a rational society to do about it?

The hero is a failed house-carpenter in Aberdeen, and when the story opens he and his wife Tibbie run a little backstreet shop in one of the shabbier quarters of the city. Mrs Grundie seems an admirable person, bustling, competent, and kindly, but Peter is a fish of a different flesh: a sleek and outwardly imposing man who is in reality an idle, shiftless, self-opinionated ass, held in contempt by practically everybody who knows him, except his wife. He is incompetent at his trade, and cannot hold down the simplest casual job, yet ambles through life with an easy self-complacency that makes him impervious to all reverses. The only person capable of disturbing the even tenor of Peter's way is a gruff old gentleman called Roderick Graham, who regards him with fierce resentment, firstly for ensnaring his ex-housekeeper Tibby, and secondly for keeping her permanently on the verge of destitution by his fecklessness. It emerges that the Grundies had begun well enough, but Peter's true character soon became apparent.

> Thanks to the energy and activity of his worthy spouse, Peter Grundie's house was got thoroughly cleared out, and a supply of tolerably decent furniture placed therein. Peter, fully aware of the important duties devolving on him as the head of a family, began to act accordingly. He zealously assisted his wife in arranging the various articles of furniture; under her directions, fastened up a window-blind; cut one corner off and attached a leg to an obstinate old basin-stand, which had been made of a peculiar shape to fill a certain position in somebody's house, and refused to accommodate itself to any other, until brought to its senses by the aforesaid process. But Peter went farther than this: he talked in a decided tone of commencing business on quite a grand scale. It was necessary, however, to have some workmen ere he could do that. Peter, in short, resolved to have a journeyman and an apprentice looked out and engaged as a beginning. It was not the season for jobs, however, being the latter end of autumn; and after a deal of theorising, he at last resolved to take Mrs Grundie's advice, and devote himself to such work as he could by himself accomplish during the winter months, attending meanwhile to putting his premises in order, and leaving to spring the development of more extensive schemes. Spring came and found Peter Grundie pretty much where autumn had left him . . . Something must be done. Not without reluctance indeed, though still on the principle of 'what is yours is mine', &c., did Tibby withdraw the bulk of her snug deposit from the savings-bank to procure a stock of deals and set Peter fairly afloat. The apprentice and journeyman scheme was

dropped, or at least it was to be kept in abeyance for a time. Slow but sure was to be the motto now. By-and-by Peter's woodyard 'cuist a bit o' a dash', as Peter himself rather consequentially remarked. Alas for Peter that, instead of converting the contents thereof into useful implements, he should, in no long time, be under the necessity of 'truckling' away part of them at a 'reduced price' to keep matters square if possible in Tibby's eyes! Yet so it was. Peter in his professional capacity being nowise famous for the excellence of his workmanship any more than for the assiduity of his exertions stood rather a poor chance in competition with more industrious and not less efficient brothers in trade. Winter came round again and no change for the better so far as business was concerned. Our hero could not find work enough to keep even himself 'joggin'' as he began now to affirm in a wondering sort of strain. Still Peter was hopeful, nay, more, he was marvellously well contented. Not so his wife. It was with a heavy heart that Tibby saw her own honestly earned savings gradually melting away notwithstanding Peter's affectionate talk and her own efforts to 'mak some industry' by taking in, or at least offering to take in washing and do other little jobs. A second winter saw Peter's hopes in a business way fairly blasted. He was in a bad locality for work. So Peter himself said and no doubt thought. He must 'flit' if the term were come; and so Peter did flit, but not as he had contemplated to a more favourable business locality, for it so happened that the proceeds of Peter's winter labours—these labours consisting mainly of a spasmodic attempt at raising the wind by the manufac-ture of a stock of knick-knacks of which he made a raffle at Christmas—fell considerably short of the amount of liabilities incurred in the shape of rent to the landlord, &c. Peter made a 'displenish', sold off his shop-furnishings, and part of his superfluous furniture and tools, and moved from his house, the faithful but downcast Tibby by his side, a couple of pounds sterling in his pocket, and his whole stock of worldly goods, forming a rickety load a-top of a crazy old cart that went a little in advance.[28]

At this point a contrasting figure is introduced, William Gerard, or 'Willie Jerrit' as he is usually called, a skilful country wheelwright forced to move into the city after being cleared from his croft by an improving landlord anxious to add his few acres to a neighbouring muckle farm. Alexander does not let the behaviour of Gerard's laird pass unremarked, of course, and he has some interesting reflections on the differences between town and country manners as they are perceived by the wheelwright when he arrives in the city. Aberdeen had closer links with its surrounding rural areas than any Scottish city, but even at this date, there was clearly a sizeable difference in social behaviour:

To the town's inhabitants, men and women, each and severally, he was an entire stranger, and no less so to many of the town's habits, wants, and way of life. It was an important and thriving town, and, like other important and thriving towns, the traders and business-men thereof were making haste to be rich. Greyhaired men with sunken cheeks and thoughtful countenances pushed along the streets, with steadfast and unswerving step. Young men, with premature sagacity painted on their countenances, the interiors of their heads arranged, it may be supposed, in something like the form of a stock list, or multiplication table, were to be seen perpetually nodding to other young men of like disposition, or if they were in an unusually talkative mood, saluting their friends with a mechanically uttered 'D'ye do?' not slacking their pace in the least, however, to receive an answer, which was of less consequence, as the customary and understood reply was a repetition of 'd'ye do', uttered with a friendly emphasis.

It is no wonder if Willie Jerrit, who had rarely in his life passed any individual within the distance of a hundred yards, without enunciating, or hearing enunciated, an opinion of the state of the weather, at least, felt himself out of the element in the midst of this city life. He might walk a twelvemonth, without intermision, as it seemed, along its busiest streets, and though hundreds would jostle him daily, not a single individual would feel called upon to cheer him by the assurance that it was 'a fine day'.[29]

Peter asks him for work and gets a few odds and ends to do, although the results are so shabby that they are fit in Gerard's eyes only for kindling. He does his best to help the couple, though, once he discovers their circumstances. He reasons that Peter must be of use for something. Exactly what is not at first clear, until he receives advice from a rather unexpected quarter:

One of Willie's occasional customers was a Mrs Hartshorn, a lady whose charities were widely known. Her Willie had asked to patronise Mrs Grundie, by giving her a little work. Mrs H had complied with the request, in so far as to give some small items of knitting, &c., which were thankfully received, and finished to her entire satisfaction, but as the lady saw no appearance of degradation or haggard poverty about Tibby, she could not see the philosophy of being charitable after so tame a fashion as this. She had, indeed, patronised and instructed the wickedest and most abandoned of human beings, having, among other good deeds, almost brought up from infancy the progeny of a thoroughly blackguard father, and a not very whiteguard mother—the latter of whom told to the lady melancholious stories of the utter 'meesery' of their lot, were it not for the good Mrs Hartshorn and her 'angel daachters', from whom it must be acknowledged (while her worthy husband 'jouket' out of sight) the worthy woman was ever ready to receive a half-cheese or a parcel of tea, with unaffected pleasure, or a religious tract with a whine of hypocritical piety. And, we may add, Mrs H had the satisfaction of seeing every member of this model distressed family grow up and sink as low in vice and immorality as their parents had done, giving promise thereby of affording wide scope for the benevolence of those who might come after. But reverting to Mrs Grundie. Here was a decent looking woman, with no complaint on her lips, and no sign of squalor or filth about her person or dwelling. Where then was the foundation on which to build the fair monument of benevolence? Go down to the lower strata, good reader, if you wish to renovate or elevate society. Excavate till you reach humanity in a bestial state—idleness in everything, but mischief, gross and glaring vice, and every sort of vileness under the sun; then begin the work, and men *must* see what you are about, and will applaud the philanthropic act. But those struggling, careworn creatures, who cling to solvency with a fond though precarious grasp—who plead with their fellow-men for 'leave to toil', and who, it may be, would want a meal every day ere they would let you know their real distress, what can be done with them? We can at least let them alone in their poor pride. If they will neither clamour nor curse, whine, nor beg, they must not be surprised if they and their struggles are passed unheeded by. Whether such thoughts as these, now, or at any other time, had passed through the mind of Mrs H it were hard to say. Perhaps they did perhaps not. One person may come to a given conclusion intuitively as it were while another reaches it by a definite chain of reasoning. Certain it is, the lady, all agog in view of attending a committee meeting of the ladies' cast off clothing, broken victuals, and starving humanity Society, of which she was a leading member, told Willie that, having well considered the case of his protege, she was persuaded the best thing the woman could do was to commence keeping a small shop, or get a clothes-mangle and make her 'lazy worthless husband' drive it.[30]

The mangle is duly installed, but just as things seem to be looking up, the Grundies experience a stroke of genuine misfortune, losing all their possessions in a house fire. But 'the poor feel for the poor' and they are given food and shelter by a neighbour almost as impoverished as they—a pointed contrast to the antics of Mrs Hartshorn.

This is too big a problem for William Gerard to manage on his own, so he turns to his wealthy friend Roderick Graham for help. They have known one another since their Militia days, and after much persuasion, Graham swallows his animosity towards Peter, and provides the necessary funds. Tibbie meanwhile has fallen ill and Peter is drifting from job to job, finally ending up as a dustman, and failing to cope even with that. The couple are brought to the brink of actual destitution, the workhouse and separation looming before them, but Peter maintains a philosophic calm. He is a simple man, the sport of forces beyond his comprehension, insulated by a good-natured insensitivity to things outside his own ego and a copious stock of deterministic proverbs: 'Folk canna aye help themsells—the best 'at is maun submit to fate—' he declares.

But Gerard comes to the rescue in the nick of time, the couple are installed in their modest shop-cum-laundry, and at last Peter experiences success. As odd-job-man in a miscellaneous mangling business he discovers his forte—his gift for superficial conversation, his easy and confiding address with womenfolk old and young, becomes a positive asset. Alexander even suggests that had Peter enjoyed greater advantages in early life, his talent for easy sententiousness would have equipped him admirably for the ministry or the law. He is a loon o' pairts after all, although of a highly ingenious and unorthodox sort. He flagrantly contravenes the most basic moral standards—especially the ferocious North-East work ethic—yet we are invited to consider him in his own way as rather admirable. This is one of the first novels to have a working man as the main character. Are we also to consider it a celebration of idleness? Hardly. The point seems to be that society needs Peter Grundie and he in turn deserves its constructive support. The novel sets out to expose the limitations of self-help and *laissez faire* in the Scottish urban context, substituting for them a kind of Owenite collectivism. For whole sections of the population the notion of self-help is meaningless; the poor are poor because they are forced to be, rather than fated to be because of moral inadequacy or other personal failings; they do not possess the resources to enable them to escape from the vicious circle of deprivation. As for *laissez faire*, it is evident that market forces, if allowed to operate without restraint, crush people like the Grundies. Without William Gerard and others like him who still preserve the essentially 'country' virtues of neighbourliness and concern in an anonymous and atomistic social setting, they are doomed. The gospel of work with its attendant conviction that ability can rise above adversity is thus, with an ingenious irony, both vindicated, and exposed.[31]

At this point in the narrative external factors began to create problems. The denouement, to all appearances, had been reached, the intellectual sub-structure was complete, the characters disposed of satisfactorily; but still Sevastopol held out, and war news continued in an unabated flood. Somehow or other the Tuesday edition had to be furnished with copy, so Alexander soldiered on, and confessed that he was doing so.[32] The narrative was spun out for another half-dozen chapters, and from a technical point of view the result is quite interesting.

In the 'Sketches', Alexander had explored the possibilities of Scots as a discursive medium, maintaining a low authorial presence and letting the characters as far as possible speak for themselves. In 'Peter Grundie' he tried a different approach, a single controlling voice, the narrator's, determining the sequence of events, commenting on the action, controlling access to other characters, and habitually using standard literary English with a sprinkling of Scots. The characters—all of whom speak Scots, including the impeccably bourgeois Roderick Graham—say relatively little, at least not out loud. One of the objectives of the novel seems to have been the conscious cultivation of a sophisticated 'English' manner; perhaps Alexander may have felt at this stage that it was the better vehicle for the generally ironical and sardonic tone he was trying to establish.

In the final chapters, however, the characters often talk, vividly and at length, not in the rather stilted Improvement Union style of the 'Sketches' where they had acted mainly as vehicles for ideas, but in a flexible inter-personal way, revealing themselves as independent people in a more sophisticated fictional setting. Here for example, is a little of the Grundie's slatternly neighbour Mrs Calder; instead of being just a fixed feature on the ideological terrain, she and her children define themselves mainly through spoken idiom, a useful example of Alexander's ability to place people by their speech habits:

> Peter Grundie was most laudably engaged examining the pinions of his mangle when Mrs Calder entered his abode. Incontinently he ceased from his work, and courteously placed a chair for the lady.
>
> 'Na, Peter, I wunna sit doon; I hinna time to bide a minet, though I jist gae a cry in at the door. Ye ken he'll be in till's denner, an' I'll need awa hame an' scrape the taties, an' get them pitten on.'
>
> 'Aye, weel, the like o' thaese things maun be attenit till,' rejoined Peter.
>
> 'A wat that's a trowth, an' ye ken he's *that* ill-natur't an' he be keepit waitin' ae minet.—She's nae in hersell the day?' was the enquiring reference to Mrs Grundie.
>
> 'Na, na; ye see, she's been awa the feck o' this ouk, an' I can assure ye, I've hed my ain a-dees here, wi' ae thing or anither.'
>
> 'Deed a wat I rael weel believ't', answered Mrs Calder ... and with a

lengthened 'pech' she 'jist leant her doon' on Peter's chair, unbandaged the diminutive person at her breast, and, after fondling the creature for a little, and applying to it a number of endearing epithets, which need not be repeated here, proceeded to give it suck. Peter, with his arms folded across his breast, half stood half sat at the front of the mangle; and the 'newse' went on slightly interrupted now and then by the proceedings of the two youngsters on the floor, who at one moment were meddling with Peter's goods and chattels, and the next 'mischievin' themselves with some 'uncanny' thing, and then tormenting their mother by their mutual complaints against each other and their outrageous requests. The worthy woman stormed and scolded vigorously; but Robbie and Tammie knew too well the value to be attached to such utterances as 'Sorra, laddie, I'll ca' aff yer head'n ye fash me', and 'Haud yer peace, ye nickums, or I'll pran ye,' varied occasionally by a threat to 'Cleave' them, or 'Ca' oot their een', to pay very much attention to her. Peter, being in an elevated frame of mind, had not thought fit to recognise formally the presence of the juveniles; and so, while he carried on the current of conversation with the mother, he attempted to remain as far as might be, oblivious to the uproar occasioned by the screaming, grumbling, and 'greeting' of her hopeful offspring. The task was an irksome and difficult one, it must be allowed; yet it was wonderful how Peter, and Mrs Calder too, continued their discourse unobservant of such remarks as 'Come awa hame, mid-al'; 'Fat needs ye bide he-al mid-al?' 'Mid-al, O-i dinna loike 'at man stannin' the-al', uttered in a sour tone by the 'twinnies', when, tired of exploring Peter's premises, they had stood up to tug at their mother's apron.

'Keep's, there 't jist upo' twa o'clock!' exclaimed Mrs Calder, as, after an hour's conversation, she at last started hastily up on observing the steeple clock from Peter's window. She again gathered the shawl about herself and youngest born, and set off, followed by her tail, to prepared dinner for Robert Calder, senior. Peter resumed his inspection of the mangle.[33]

Some of the hallmarks of Alexander's mature style are here: the orthography of his vernacular has become stable in a regionally distinct pattern in which southern forms derived from standard literary Scots are notably infrequent; there are signs, too, of his interest in the varieties of spoken Scots—not in the geographical sense which one sees (intermittently) in writers like Hogg, but in the differentiation of usage as a result of social class, occupation, and age. He is particularly sensitive to the no-man's-land where Scots and English overlap. One's impression is that although he used it with great skill Alexander regarded English with little ultimate relish.[34] He seldom seems to have used it in everyday life, and he was alert to check its invasive tendencies, especially when inspired by vulgarity or social pretension. One of the more unpleasant characters—the 'whiteguard woman'—illustrates this when she speaks gushingly of Mrs Hartshorn's 'angel daachters'. Not only is the phrase itself woefully second-hand, but it is idiomatically corrupt. 'Daachter' is a nonce word, neither 'daughter' nor 'dother' but a shoddy compounding of the two. It is obviously insincere, and Alexander views it and its user with palpable distaste.

The story reaches its final stage when Peter is knocked down by a runaway horse belonging to a philanthropist who liberally stocks his shop in compensation. The Grundies' future is secure at last, and with this derisory gesture—which seems to strike both at the prevalance of money-based values and at the gross misuse of coincidence in contemporary popular fiction, this ironical and pioneeringly realistic novel comes to a close.

Hostilities in the Crimea petered out early in 1856 and the *Penny Free Press* stopped publication, having failed to attract enough advertising to keep it going once the war news ran out.[35] The *Free Press* reverted to being a weekly paper with a single issue priced at 3*d*. and a readership which was solidly middle class. It was another ten years before the proprietors tested the market with a penny edition aimed mainly at proletarian readers, quite possibly to check the inroads of the *People's Journal* whose Aberdeen-based northern editions had begun publication just over a year before. On 20 June 1865, the *Free Press* went bi-weekly again with a four-page penny issue published on Tuesdays and the original edition continuing in an eight-page format published on Fridays at a price of 3*d*. The latter was designed to have a more 'regional' appeal, while the Tuesday edition was specifically a 'city' paper, and in it, from 15 August 1865 to 17 April 1866, ran the next of Alexander's novels, a still more ambitious work of some 80,000 words, entitled 'The Laird of Drammochdyle and his Contemporaries; or, Random Sketches done in Outline with a Burnt Stick'.

The story is set in the North-East of the 1850s in the flourishing sea-port of 'Strathaven' (probably Peterhead) and the surrounding countryside. Local society is dominated by two figures: Edward Boyce, the laird of Drammochdyle, a second-generation landed gentleman whose father made a fortune in the law and used it to buy his way into the county élite; and the still more *arriviste* Patrick Crabbice, Esq, of Vatville, a prosperous brewer and distiller who began life as plain Patrick Craib the carter, and has since risen through a mixture of graft, business acumen and ruthless self-interest to head the commercial element in the district. The most important working-class character is Robert Morris, a journeyman carpenter who loses a leg while working on an extension of the laird's fake-Elizabethan mansion. While recuperating, he begins an extensive programme of self-improvement under the guidance of Dr Graham, the able, but flawed, local minister. The Doctor is another loon o' pairts who has raised himself from humble circumstances to a distinguished position in the church—a powerful preacher, a shrewd adviser, and a man whose natural bonhomie and ease of address make him a favourite with the muckle farmers and town professionals who dominate his congregation. The Doctor's wit and conviviality have proved his downfall, however, and by the start of the narrative he is already alcoholic and deeply in debt to Patrick Crabbice. Meanwhile Robert has completed his recuperation, and the laird induces the brewer to offer him the tenancy of one of his inns. Robert refuses, and the lease is taken up by his friend and former work-mate George Ross, who has married the daughter of a wealthy tradesman and so has money to plenish it. Robert meantime has been befriended by James Monro, an engineer at Strathaven foundry, and anxiously seeks his advice about what he should do next:

'Gae an' offer yersel' as manager o' the new Strathaven Gas Work,' said James. 'The place is advertised vacant in the *Independent!*'

'The joke's rather owre grim, Jamie, for a man that sees actually naething atween 'im an' the status o' legal pauper.'

'But its nae joke—it's sober earnest, Bob.'

'An' dee ye actually mean to say that I sud gang an' pit *my* name to the list o' half a score that we ken to be already seekin' the place?'

'An' why not?'

'Weel I dinna need, ance erran' to make mysel' ridiculous.'

'Listen to me, noo Bob.—Tell me if you can, hoo mony o' the half score candidates are better qualified than yoursel?'

'Weel some o' them are nane better—that's true aneuch.'

'Nane o' them are better. I ken something o' the entire lot—ye only want sufficient impudence to push yer claims, man.'

'I fear there's anither element o' success wantin', an' which canna be so readily picke't up—influence.'

'Deed I daursay ye're no far oot there. That's the curse o' yer bits o' sma' toonies especially. There's never an openin' occurs worth ha'ein', but there's some drucken, blethrin, half broken doon 'local man' needin' the job; wi freen's ready to stap him in neck an' heels; or some brainless young goose whose fader happens to be brither to a bailie, or siclike—he'll gae in, ass that he be, against the best qualified man in the universe.'

'So you think my chance wud be very encouragin' I daursay?'

'Weel, I suppose I've raither upset my ain argument, Bob. But lat me assure you that a good stock of cool impudence, an' some tack—for a man needs to be discreetly impudent—gae far in carryin' a man through the warld. I'm nae an aul' man yet, but I've seen *that* mair than ance successfu' against fat seem'd great odds.'

'Aye, but then it's been impudence against merit only—nae impudence against local "influence"; but fat gars ye denounce sma' toonies in particular—doesna influence operate in the same way in the case of big toons?'

'Scarcely; ye see in the like of Strathaven they're a' linkit thegither in bits o' cliques an' family relationships. An' fan an openin' occurs, an' some gawpus that happens to hae a fader or an uncle o' some standin', casts his ee upon't; or his mither thinks "This wud dee richt weel wi' oor Johnny"—or his daddy is feelin' tiret o' mainteenin' the useless howffin—forthwith the strings begin to be pull't. This man can get the Baillie's lug, an' that the Shirra's—I can sair your business a gweed turn, an' maybe ye cud dee mine a bad ane; so that the hail local circle is secured; or at least a "workin' majority." Noo in big toons it's impossible to get the en's o' a' the strings in your ain han'. An' so merit may hae some chance. In sma' toons it has nane.'[36]

Robert eventually becomes a clerk in a local timber-shipping firm where he works hard and steadily rises in the confidence of his employers. The narrative now focuses on the struggle between the laird and the Crabbice family, including Patrick's wife, daughters, and son Tom, who show different aspects of the social corruption which springs from the father's version of the business ethic. The young laird is a good-natured easy-going fellow, popular with his neighbours and tenants and well-regarded in the district generally. After marrying Dr Graham's beautiful daughter Elsie, he decides to play a more prominent role in the affairs of the county. This is the first step on the slippery slope. His innocence makes him easy prey for the mercantile and professional operators who work the levers of power, and attack him at his weakest point—the traditional lairdly obligation of hospitality. He is systematically debauched by practised local drinkers. As the laird falls the carpenter rises. Robert Morrice is assumed into the partnership of the timber business, and there is an immediate call upon his credit. His former patron Dr Graham, after being abominably although covertly hounded by the Crabbices dies of 'apoplexy'. Robert settles the Doctor's debts incognito, out of his own pocket.

Fortune has hardly smiled upon his old friend George Ross either. The railway has robbed the Mill Inn of its passing trade and its profitability, and George is drinking the balance. He is becoming thoroughly demoralised and deeply indebted to the proprietor Patrick Crabbice who puts in a new tenant and moves to set George up in a little back-street dram-shop in Strathaven, to cash in on rising demand amongst the local labouring classes. In this project, however, he meets with an unexpected check. 'Run, Eliza' and see that the covers are laid—papa's home in bad humour with something or other; and if the dinner's kept waiting he'll be perfect verocious', cries Mrs Crabbice, sensing a storm:

Mr Crabbice, sen., did come home in a bad temper on the day of the licensing court, and he spoke but little, notwithstanding the mollifying presence of Captain Ryrie, until dinner was nearly finished. He then broke out in proper style to the Captain, Tom being also an auditor, upon the pitiful, contracted notions of those petty traders, his brother magistrates in Strathaven, who could be swayed by a parcel of ignorant fanatics, and refuse to industrious well-doing men the means of making an honest livelihood.

'Confounded shabby, say I,' echoed Captain Ryrie . . .

'Ross has been doing no good in the Mill Inn. So we've resolved to displenish him at the ensuing term—in fact the Inn is let already to another, a very substantial man, who was in want of a good opening. Ross made a great ado about it, of course; but I had the thing entirely in my own hand, he wasn't able to square accounts with me, and I could and would have poinded him, if he hadn't given up the lease.'

'Aye, aye—quite right,' said the Captain . . .

'But you know, Captain, I would never treat a man harshly; so as the ground floor of that piece of property of mine in Batter Lane has been without a tenant for a couple of years, I've let it to Ross; and have no doubt he could do a very good business in it among the working classes. It is centrical you see, for a whole lot of them the worst paid kind of labouring and handicraft people—who, let met tell you, are good consumers. Why, we suppply five to eight pounds' value of raw whisky per week to some similar houses; and I mean, even yet, to give Ross some stock on credit for a short term. But here these upstart fellows come forward, and at the cry of a set of teetotallers, refuse a licence. It's really too bad.'

'Confounded shabby,' said the Captain.

'Appeal the case,' said Tom.

'Appeal! Certainly I will—that is, I'll get it appealed.'

'Ap-pealed?' said Captain Ryrie, not very certain apparently what that signified.

'Yes, to the Quarter Sessions you know, Captain—all of us county gentlemen have seats there you know.'

'Oh bless me, yes, Aye, aye, so we have,' said the Captain in great delight', and these poor beggars, who are only burgh baillies, have not—have they?'

'No, Captain, not one of them has the qualification to get on the Commission of the Peace,' said Mr C, stretching himself up in full dignity.

'First rate!' exclaimed Captain Ryrie . . .

'The Sessions sit next week,' said Tom.

'Yes,' replied Mr Crabbice, 'and we must not lose a day in making preparation. Let's see how the Bench can be arranged. There's Sir Joshua—who is sure to be there as preses—a high-minded man, but full of whims sometimes—his vote can't be safely counted upon, though he generally goes against the burgh magistrates. Then there's Heddles of Weetmire—we can reckon upon him—there's Macveerie of Rappoch, he can be managed by a little tackling beforehand, if Sir Joshua don't speak on the wrong side during the sitting; and Topwell of Bibster—we've a large account against him. Then there's yourself, Captain, and poor Boyce—Tom will bring him up—five votes, and my own, in case it should be absolutely required. Well, that would turn't, I'm convinced . . .

And so it proved.

On the day before the meeting of Quarter Sessions . . . sundry . . . Justices of the Peace were all Mr Crabbice's guests at a jolly dinner at Vatville. To-morrow's business was talked over, and a revised forecast of the voting taken . . .

On the day of the Quarter Sessions, 'a full bench of Justices met', there being, as the local organ of public opinion averred, 'a great amount of important business to transact'. Sir Joshua Krustie occupied his usual position of president, and expounded law points with his usual air of authority, freely quoting those scraps of dog latin which lawyers occasionally use, and which he, not being a lawyer, liked all the better to repeat. It were utterly needless to recapitulate the arguments used by the burgh fiscal in support of the judgement of the Strathaven Baillies, refusing licence certificates to 'George Ross, 30, Batter Lane', and four others, seeing the law was laid down from the Bench, that the local judges had no right to deal differently with different applicants—to grant licences to sixty-five and refuse the other five. To Mr Crabbice's infinite delight, the President declared that this would be 'applying the lextalionis to those whose applications were refused' which was intolerable! So in the case of George Ross and his brother appellants, the vote stood seven to four in favour of a reversal of the decision of the local Magistrates—'Mr Crabbice of Vatville declining to vote.'

Directly on this decision being given. Mr Crabbice, senior, and two or three more, his friends, left the Court. They had discharged their public duty for the time, and now went to look after their private interests. Their departure was noticeable, inasmuch as the great part of the business for which the Quarter Sessions had assembled was yet to be done; and inasmuch as, when two or three other exactly similar appeals from country districts came up they were promptly dismissed, because Sir Joshua and others held that the multiplication of public houses in rural districts was a great evil, which ought to be discouraged by all available means; and that therefore the local Justices, who were best able to judge of the circumtances, had acted with great propriety in refusing licences.

Perhaps the persons interested in those cases were not aware of the mode in which that noble institution the Quarter Sessions may be worked for the public behoof; perhaps *they* had not influence to enable them to 'arrange' a bench beforehand.[37]

Meanwhile the female Crabbices have been getting their claws into the more eligible local bachelors, and the eldest daughter, Eliza, has made a very advantageous match—with Captain Ryrie, the corpulent, bibulous, dimwitted proprietor of a stretch of highly desirable nearby real estate. The local countrywomen describe him, very aptly, as an 'aul' debush't slype—a blotch't, drucken, ugsome breet' and he is at least twice Eliza's age. But he has a certain appeal, and it consists in this: he has no next of kin . . . In the event of his death (doubtless at no very distant date given his partiality for brandy and Eliza's domestic management) and failing male heirs, his estate with all its pertinents and adjuncts will pass to his lawful spouse. Alexander makes his own views about such trafficking witheringly explicit:

> It was not in the nature of things that a man of such local position as the proprietor of the Grove should get married without the subject being much and variously discussed. That were indeed an insignificant wedding, which in respect of the covert brutality, the unprincipled heartlessness, and spurious pretensions, the awkward boobyism, the blinded misguided affection of the bridegroom—poor man; and the pert 'forwardness', the trumpery beauty, the undeniable grimness, the finical nicety and desperate extravagance, the slatternly habits, and shrewish temper of the bride, did not furnish topics of engrossing talk to their acquaintances generally . . .
>
> Captain Ryrie, until he was taken in hand by Mrs Crabbice, had really no idea what a frisky young man he was. True, it was now well on to thirty years since he resigned the commission he had the honour to hold from His Majesty in the militia of his native county, so that he could not be altogether so juvenile as a young lady very dear to him who was not then born. Yet when nudged on the elbow by this familiar matron, when pulled up to the serious exertion of dancing at her evening parties, when joked by her on his flirtations which she knew about—ah, didn't she?—it was not easy for the Captain to resist the notion that there must after all, be a fund of gallantry within him which somehow had hitherto lain latent, and unknown to him
>
> And thus was the gallant if unwarlike soldier led—(no, not like an ox to the shambles, because Eliza Crabbice was, as everybody should know, a nice young lady, and the Captain emphatically declared that he had been in love with her to a serious degree for ever so long)—but thus, let us say, was he led on to the hymeneal altar.[38]

The laird's moral disintegration continues apace. He takes to staying out all hours in the company of a drunken pettifogging lawyer called Lillie, frequenting low dram shops, and, ultimately, beating his wife. Patrick Crabbice, on the other hand, seems at the apogee of succeess when he suddenly dies, and is succeeded by his still more despicable son, Tom. In him the Crabbice blood runs true—he has all his father's acquisitiveness and lack of scruple along with some highly developed vices of his own. He is, for example, a consummate hypocrite who enforces his ascendancy in local society by cynically manipulating the machinery of respectability. He is forward in 'philanthropic' movements, an elder of the kirk, and at the end of the story, is still perceived as a pillar of public virtue.

The novel moves towards its climax. The lawyer Lillie is found dead in a ditch and there are suspicions of foul play. As the laird was the last person with whom he was seen alive, and his wounds could have been caused by a knife the laird is known to have possessed, he is accused of murder and arrested. The trial verdict is the equivocal one of 'not proven', but by now the laird is a broken man. His wife, after a long illness largely induced by his mistreatment of her, lies on the point of death. The trial kills her, and the laird enters the last downward spiral of dissipation. His behaviour becomes increasingly bizarre until he is declared insane, and confined in an asylum.

'The Laird of Drammochdyle' is a study of power, and the destructive influence of capitalist values upon all but a few natures not already corrupt. It is a recurring theme in Alexander's fiction, but it appears here in by far its most sustained and explicit form. It would be doing less than justice to his sophistication as a writer to suppose that the business ethic is crudely or unequivocally condemned; the upright Robert Morrice, for example, rises by means of it to a thoroughly deserved affluence. But he alone remains uncontaminated by it. The reader is constantly reminded that someone like Tom Crabbice is a far more typical product of the entrepreneurial ethos. Outwardly he is a benefactor; in reality a pitiless, base, and dishonourable man, a fomenter of suffering and evil, the source from which the corruption of a whole society proceeds, and as long as he has wealth he will never be found out.

And so, the minister and the laird, the twin pillars of traditional agrarian society are swept aside by the representatives of the new capitalist order. There is little nostalgia for their passing. Elsewhere Alexander was unsparing in his condemnation of the landlord class and the established clergy, but the threat they pose to human dignity and well-being is seen here to pale in comparison with the hellish destructiveness of the unrestrained economic individualism which is supplanting them and what they stand for. 'The Laird of Drammochdyle' is a powerful and original novel, and it is sad to think that it should have lain unacknowledged and unpublished—except in a newspaper of which, perhaps, two copies survive—for more than a hundred years.

'Ravenshowe and the Residenters Therein—Sketches of a Hamlet of the Olden Time' appeared in the *Free Press* in two sections, 5 February–21 May 1867, and 30 December 1867–28 April 1868, amounting in all to just over 60,000 words. It was Alexander's first mature attempt at a historical theme which was to exercise him throughout his adult life, the rural society of North-East Scotland as it existed during his own time and for about two generations before. His interest in family history has already been noted, and during the 1860s he built up a formidable knowledge of the 'social economics' (his phrase) of the region, derived in part from the rich oral tradition which had surrounded him from childhood, and still more so, from a painstaking study of primary and secondary historical source material.

Indications of this begin to appear in the *Free Press* in unobtrusive little occasional series like 'Leaves from the Note Book of an Idler', a pot-pourri of personal reminiscence and extracts from parish registers; 'The Garioch Folks in the Olden Times—Extracts from the Burgh Records of Inverurie' which ran briefly during the winter of 1863-4; and a feature entitled 'Illustrations of the Olden Time. Extracts from the Kirk Session Records of Chapel of Garioch', in the summer of 1864.[39] The novel 'Ravenshowe' occupies much the same ground as Alexander's well-known social history *Notes and Sketches Illustrative of Northen Rural Life in the Eighteenth Centure* but it uses fictional rather than discursive techniques and possesses an immediacy and vitality even greater than that notably lively and readable book. In addition, it is narrated in the first person, a relatively rare tactic with this most objective writer, and contains some interesting autobiographical detail, particularly from his early boyhood.

'Ravenshowe' covers the period from the 1780s to the 1830s and it tells the story of Eppie Copland from early womanhood until her death. When it opens she is a crofter's daugther in the Garioch, being courted by her father's ploughman Donald Cameron. The pair of them 'canna 'gree', and Donald goes to be a smuggler at Newburgh on the Aberdeenshire coast, the trade then being rife, owing to war-time restrictions and the unsettled nature of the times. He passes utterly beyond ken for ten years, although at no point is he more than twenty miles away. This is a point Alexander makes again and again during the course of the novel—the way technology and the physical environment shape not only the immediate life-style but the whole mental world of the community. These are the days before turnpike roads and an intricate rail network transformed the internal communications of the North-East: travelling is a laborious, risky, and time-consuming business, and the outside world seems unimaginably remote.[40] The idea of the sea haunts the imagination of this landlocked parish as a mystical and unchancy element, gateway to places with shifting barbaric names and fairly hotching with 'peerats' and other wild characters.

Donald eventually has a serious brush with the Excise and while skulking in the Garioch, renews his acquaintance with Eppie Copland. They marry, and Donald takes over the tack of the croft. They have a son, Andrew, and various episodes are recounted from his boyhood and youth. He is an attractive but unstable character with an eye to the main chance and a notion of loyalty which seldom extends much beyond himself and his own needs. With the help of his mother he sets up in a shop—Andrew calls it an 'Emporium'—in Aberdeen. But he regards money merely, and lacks the finesse to conceal from his customers his basic contempt for them. This is not a good basis for prosperity in the retail trade. The business fails and he is declared bankrupt. He enlists and for some time nothing more is heard from him. Eventually he comes home, altered in garb and speech, a cripple sergeant from the wars with a vulgar trollop of a wife and a son, Jamie, trotting at his heels. But he soon tires of Ravenshowe and takes to the road again leaving the child with Eppie.

The novel is a study of the effects upon human behaviour of heredity and environment over several generations, and a richly elaborate picture unfolds of what it is like to be a child in a community like this: nursery lore and rhymes, the transition from petticoats to trousers, the rough and tumble of the dame school and the first brush with education, daft boyish pranks like hanging cats, meetings with exotic representatives of the outside world like the pack merchant and the travelling writing master, and a growing awareness of the world of adults, with their physical strength and knowledgeability, their political talk gleaned from ageing copies of the *Aberdeen Journal*, their sensitivity to the supernatural, their regard for signs and tokens, their belief in witches and fairies.

In the final instalment, Alexander noted:

> The purpose of these sketches . . . was to trace as clearly as I could the history of her whom I have chosen to rechristen Eppie Copland; and, subordinately, of her husband, her son, and her grandson, and along with them to depict certain features of a style of social life which is now extinct, or fast becoming so. The characters just mentioned, who lived and acted in the precise spheres assigned to them are doubtless drawn imperfectly enough. But I have done the best I could in a hurried way . . . Most of the other people introduced, perhaps not the whole of them, I have seen somewhere or other—several of them, however, it must be admitted dwelt not in Ravenshowe. Eppie Copland and Donald Cameron, with their son Andrew and their grandson Jamie are perfectly recognisable I find to those who knew anything of the originals; and if the sketches have any merit at all it consists in the honest attempt made to reproduce the characters precisely as they were . . .[41]

It is in the arena of language that the modern reader is likely to feel that the realist intention has been most strikingly carried into effect. Alexander believed that the vernacular was losing its distinctiveness and strength under the impact of education and the printed word. This did not relieve him from the obligation to represent it as it actually was in his contemporary stories, but in 'Ravenshowe' he placed the language in a historical perspective and revealed it in the fullness of its expressive strength as it had existed in central Aberdeenshire at the beginning of the nineteenth century. The difference between this and most of the registers used in 'Drammochdyle' (twenty miles to the east and half a century later on) is dramatic. Not only is the vernacular incredibly dense, even more so than in *Johnny Gibb*, but it is quite masterly in its lexical range and idiomatic assurance, as perhaps the following sequence may show. A number of men are gathered in the smiddy, and the conversation gets round to Donald Cameron's days at the smuggling.

> 'Aye', [says Donald] '. . . it was kittle aneuch wark to keep clear o' the gaugers. Ye jist hed to dee the best wi' wiles, or speed o' fit, an' whiles a' wudna dee.'
> 'Wus ye ever fairly into their grips, Donal'?'

'N--o. Weel aw cudna say't a hed. I hed ance a bit o' a sharry wi' a sooperweeser creatur't fesh the haill pack o' them doon aboot my lugs. We hed gotten a nice frauchtie o' Hollan's run in fan some sleumin' hed won oot aboot it; so we gat the keggies buriet amo' the san', an' leet them lie there for sax ouks. The gaugers dakkert ilka hoose roon an roon, and ca'd up the bents an' breem-knowes as weel they micht, for it wus a' fell snug mair nor four fit doon amo' the fair sea san'. Aweel a' this wears ower; the bit luggerie wus awa aff the coast for ouks, an' they hed gi' en't up for a bad job. So ae gloamin jist about Michael day, we wud tak oor Hollan's up to them't they belang't till—we kent brawly faur to tak them.'

'Oh ye hed the gin saul afore han'—hed ye?'

'Ye wud won'er man fa wud be pairtners i' the concern,' said Donald, pursuing his narrative. 'So there's a mannie liv't oot the roadside, he'd newlins gotten a Moray cairtie wi' a timmer aixtree—there wus hardly onything but the creels gaen than-a-days—he wud len's his horsie an's cairtie un'er cover, to ca' the kegs o'er the knowe, but wudna gae 'imsel', upo' nae accoont. I gets the horsie an' the cairtie, and sets oot—it wus gweed meenlicht, but the lift owre cas'en wi' flichterin' bits o' cloods. Aweel, a' gaes on fine till aw'm in the road a gey piece, fan ane o' the wheels o' the cairtie began to skirl at ilka turn like the vera mischief . . . At that time o' day, the aixtree jist ran i' the nave wuntin' ony iron bush, an' bein' baith timmer, fan't began to skirl, it made a heemlin noise. The kegs had been gey wechty maybe for the concern, an' the cairtie wud skraich and skirl i' maugre o' my neck, an' ye wudna hin'er this to play me a bonny pliskie, for fa sud be comin' across the hill but a Sooperweeser creatur', new come to the quarter, an' jist as I turn't the horsie's heid aff to get clear o' a kittle bit, up starts he fae the lythe side o' some heich breem busses. 'I comman' ye i' the name o's Maijestie to stop, Sir!' says he, an wi' that he presents a muckle holster pistol an' thraten't to sheet me deid gin I muv't oot o' that. Says I, 'Ye needna draw soord nor pistol to me; I'm but a peer man sairin' ither fowk; I'm vera muckle at yer service, sir.' 'Come noo, my man,' says he, 'ye'll better clear yer feet o' this scrape as quick's ye can—turn yer beast's heid to the public road, noo, an' go on afore wi' my direction.' 'Jist heely a minit,' says I, ''ll we see gif the lade be lyin' richt—the wheelss been skirlin' till they wud alairm a haill kwintra-side—we better stop that or we'll only be scryin' wur ain flicht to lat the smugglers follow.' 'Ye're quite richt, my man,' says he, 'quite richt,' an' wi' that he pits the pistol intill's belt—he didna luik like bein' gryte deykn at it for a' this—an cam's wa's roon to tak' a luik o' the cairtie. I wus fummlin awa amo' the kegs. 'Ah,' says he, rubbin's han's, 'thats a find worth havin'—hoo mony kegs hae ye?' 'Feint haet o' me kens weel,' says I, 'but there can be nae hairm in coontin' them noo.' I min't that there was a fyow faddoms o' sma' line kinkit up lyin' i' the neuk o' the cairtie—it's a terrible handy thing to hae a bit tow wi' ye at ony time—so at the length I gat a haud o't. 'Seyven or aucht, is't, Sir?' says I, as he glampit awa ower the edge of the box of the cairtie: an' wi' that I grips 'im by baith elbucks, an' layin' my leg afore 'im, plyps 'im doon on's belly on a bit sma' hillock to win'art, and there he lay an' roar't like a vera sticket swine. 'Come, come noo,' says I, 'maister gauger, jist stop yer noise; or I'll cut the tongue fae yer jaws. Time aboot's fair play, ye ken; it's nae five minits syne't ye was thratenin to sheet me deid.' By this time I hed's han's plaitit across ither ahin's back, an' wus wuppin the line tichtly roon's shackle-banes. Oh, an' ye hed but heard fu the wile bodie—he was English spoken—curs't an' bann't fan he cudna better dee. I tiet's han's first, an' strappit's feet thegidder neist, an' syne I flang 'im in at the back o' the breem buss't he hed been makin' a scug o' afore. 'Noo,' says I, 'ye may tak' yer eese o't as lang's ye like, ye'se get it a' to yer leen for me;' an' I joggit on again wi' the cairtie skirlin' as ill's ever . . .

Ye wudna hin'er me aifter gaen back wi' the mannie's horsie neist mornin', to tak a stap roon to luik aifter a coblie that wus lyin' in a sma' cove, fesn't till a stake, wi' only a bit feckless painter line, an' like aneuch to be carriet aff to sea fan the tide rase. Gaun oo't the gate, I meets Rory Breece comin' in wi' an unco breeshile. 'Eh, man,' says Rory, 'I'm fear't there's been a man murder't amo' the knowes the streen, for as I cam' throu that gate afore screek o' day, I heart a maist aihfu granein' an' kin' o' deleerit outcry.' 'Fat wud ye say gin somebody hed brain't a gauger?' says I, takin Rory aff, caus I didna want 'im to be owre quesitive o' the subjeck. 'Deed awat, gin it's naething war there wus greater mishanters at Flodden, nor though the haill set o' them war braint,' says he. An so the thing fare't on, Rory turnin' till ither discoors, an' I never leet licht a word forder o' the subjeck. Ye see I kent gin I mintit to gae an' tak ony fittininment aboot gettin' the sooperweesor lows't, I wud be kent immedantly as the man't knit 'im up there. It wud appear that he hed lyin i' the lythe o' the breem buss mair nor four-an-twenty hoors, for it was the neist mornin' aifter that't a mengyie o's nain kin' o fowk lichtit upon 'im—they hed been oot ca'in up the haill kwintra side for 'im ye ken . . . They gat 'im as I wus sayin', an' pooer't brandy owre's throat till he cam' till 'imself an' begood to bann again. 'Oh yes,' said he, 'I kno the villain by headmark; he woor a gryte scaup o' a sealskin cap on's heid.' . . . Says ane of them 'I'll wad the lugs fae my heid that's been Donal' Cameron—I saw 'im wi that vera caip twa three days sin' syne.' Wi that the hilliebulloo gat up at ance, an' doon by the shoreside they cam in a body. We hed jist come in fae the nets an' beach't oor coble, fan we saw noo ane, an' than ane comin' strollin' throw the bents fae different airts, appearantly, but a' driftin' oor gate. 'I've nae gryte feast o' them' says Sawny Paip, 'there's some mischief or ither't there ettlin at.' 'It'll be that sooperweesor creatur I'll be boon,' says anider—there wus four o's. 'My certy, an' there he is,' says I, as the mannie 'imsel', cam' in o' sicht cleukin into the airm o' anither lang trypal o' a chiel. 'Spread oot lads,' says Peter, 'an' throw ye yer sea beets fae ye Donal'; yer nae the man't I tak' ye to be, gin ye dinna lick them a' throu' speed o' fit—never min' their thrates, they winna sheet at ye.' An' wi' that Peter 'imsel' takes in the san's vera close to the water, makin' as gin he had something hod aneth's kwite. The gaugers wus closin' in by this time; there was half a dizzen o' them forbye the ane wi' the sooperweesor on's airm. Oor brakin' aff's we did, espeeshelly Peter takin' up the san't stowlins wi' sic a scowder amplush't them a bit. Twa three o' them tyeuk aifter him till the mannie roar't oot 'No that yun, the long legg't fallow with the fur kyap.' Throw the bents gaes I, scuddin' o' my bare soles—I hed slippit past jist as they war gowpin' at Peter—an' the yells o' them mitha been heard three mile awa. 'Stop, sir, or I'll shoot ye'—'surren'er, ye villain.' 'Run, my men! run, an' hunt 'im doon, deid or leivin,' and so on. I min'et on Peter's adwise, an luik'sna owre my shooder, but pays doon; an' there like a pack o' beagles wus the haill set o' them at my heels . . . The first gweed rig length beat oot ane or twa—drucken broken win'et houffins't hed been at the trade, gaugin' an' guzzlin' drink o' a' kin kin' for years. Wi' ony glimsh't I cud get, there was only three keepin' up, an' ance twice some o' them was as near's I cud hear their hause pipe whusslin hearse aneuch at my back. We war owre twa mile o' grun', I'm seer, throw feedles, owre banks an' hedder hillocks, fan we came roon the lip o' a bit boggy heigh, faur they keest puckles o' truffs for back divots an' siclike, an' winter't orra beasts amo the foggage o't. Thinks I, I'm as lickly to get my road throu's anider at ony rate. Doon the brae I gae's lair or no lair, an' skelpit throu the mossie mair nor ance hinch deep i' the quakin' bog. Aweel, ane o' the gauger's deen for noo. He's edder birsen or, gengyies to be't, an' flaps doon on's braid back at the near side o' the mossie. The ither twa plash't on aifter's, an' gat throw—ane o' them nae bit a-hin. This was ane Corbet, a sooth kwintra man, a stoot weel knit chiel he wus. I pursues up the brae, an' him nearer nor ever. I thocht it was a' up noo; so I hove my naipkin an' my caip fae me, an' set in my taes, till my vera legs war like to split aneth me. Corbet keeps close tee for maybe three or four minits, but losses grun' raither, gaun throw a bit torry-aten lan' weel up the brae. Jist o' the croon o' the hill there wus a piece o' a faul dyke stan'in richt afore's. I stacher's up to the dyke, an' claps my back foregainst it, an' my face turn't fair roon aboot, an' there I stan's, blawin' maist like your bellows there Robert . . . Weel, Corbet wusna owre a stane-cast back; his neepour hedna come in o' sicht . . . Oot o' that I cudna gaen at that minit though ye hed sticket me faur I steed. An I trow the lang-win'et gauger was little better. Gin me cam' within a dizzen faddom o' me I hed hed time to draw a lang breath fae the boddom o' my stamack ance or twice, an' as he cam' stoitin' up in a halfin' swither, wi's face as red's a coal, an' pooerin' doon o' sweat, I hitches up a wee thing, an' cries—'Come awa'; come awa' Maister Corbet ane o' the twa o's 's be a deid man!' . . . aifter a glint roon for's comrawd, he spread 'imsel' amo' the hedder, fobbin' like a deen oot tyke, an' wi' a broken growl o' something aboot 'a gallant race, an' lost by a set o' leaden' heel't coofs.' But wi' that I starts to my feet, an' says I, 'Maister Corbet, ye'll jist better wear away your nain road, an' lat me gae mine.' . . . he hover't aboot, an' wud mak' a'e sham aifter anither, like a' the kin' o' 'im, to pit aff the time. I kent—an' maybe he kent tee—'t bett oot as I was, I cud'a thrawn's neck till 'im at that vera minit. But I was fear't, gin he hed a pistol aboot 'im he *mith* sheet or try some ither foul play. So I begood to airm mysel' wi' fat aw cud get—a knablich o' a stane or twa, an' a piece o' a broken plew stilt't wus lyin' aboot. So he woor awa' back the road he cam' grum'lin' an' vooin' vegeance, but nae freely ready to fecht appearantly.'

'An' ye gat clear oot o' their grips.'

'Aye; but I'll tell ye fat it is, it wus a gey curn ouks aifter that till I sleepit in a bed,' added Donald.[42]

'Ravenshowe', *Johnny Gibb of Gushetneuk* and the short stories collected under the title *Life Among my ain Folk* form a group on their own in Alexander's fiction, the central expression of his life-long preoccupation with the revolution that transformed the agricultural North-East and its social, cultural, and political consequences. In the vanguard of this movement, as we have seen, were small tenant farmers on improving leases, people like himself, or, as he would like to have been, often sons and daughters of small farmers joining the agricultural workforce and scraping together enough money to buy their way back into the cycle as small farmers in their own right.

The interests of the big landowners and muckle farmers were at odds with this basically democratic tendency and the gaps between the traditional social orders of the older countryside increased as the years went on. Tenants could find years of work appropriated by the laird when the lease ran out, or holdings thrown together into bigger units yielding high returns on the kind of investment only great capitalists could contemplate. The cottar class was disappearing as landlords evaded Poor Law assessment by ejecting potential paupers from their estates. Bothying and chaumering were fostering a rural lumpenproletariat amongst the landless workers. Traditional farm touns and hamlets were being destroyed. Emigration and the drift to the cities was increasing. Steam ships and railways were meshing North-East agriculture more closely into southern markets, promoting a soulless pragmatism of outlook and the spread of narrowly commercial values. All these things were implied by the success of the lairdly ethos.[43]

Alexander saw the decent small tenant farmer, the douce gudeman who held his own plough, the typical Johnny Gibb figure, as the backbone of the old order, and the last defence of traditional decencies and a human scale of values in the rural economy. His non-fiction writings show clearly where the idea for this figure came from. In an essay he wrote towards the end of his life entitled 'Aberdeenshire Character and Characteristics: Old and New' he revealed his prescription for many of the positive values advanced in his agricultural novels:

> I shall content myself with . . . the case of a small old fashioned 'carlie', . . . engaged in the operation of working himself up by sheer industry and thrift from the very slenderest beginnings to the position of a fully established farmer upon what is known as an 'improveable subject'. I have fully in my mind's eye both him and those sixty acres of bleak-looking 'reisk', with only a dozen acres, or so, brought under the plough in an indifferently workmanlike way when he took possession, and a 'steading' the erection of which, including the 'fire-hoose' had not cost over thirty pounds. His money capital at the outset, in addition to a wife and a couple of young bairns . . . a cow, and a few of the more indispensable farm implements, was less than ten pounds sterling. For years—indeed until the bairns grew up to be helpful—he and Bell his wife did every bit of work, out and in, upon the place, summer and winter, springtime and harvest. And it was not merely the bare routine of the farm; for every succeeding year saw several acres of the forbidding reisk 'riven in' by that 'fersell' little man's own unaided efforts, the plough being called in as far as it could be made serviceable through the exertions of his hard worked, though often not too well appointed team; and where the plough would not serve, the pick and spade wielded by his own hands had to accomplish the task . . . It was nothing uncommon for him, when the daylight was long, to be a-field and hard at it by four in the morning; and, with the briefest practicable intervals for the necessary meals to go on till between nine and ten at night . . . And in this wise the reisk in due time became arable land, every acre of it, yielding fairly good crops, as it does to this day; a good slate-roofed new steading had come to supply the place of the old 'rape thackit' one; and the greater part of two 'nineteens' having come and gone, his fairly numerous family were well off his hands, able to do for themselves, and to relieve him of the heavier part of the burden of work. Not without his due share of ambition, when reclamation of the reisk demanded his attention no longer, he would patronise the local cattle markets freely, discuss the 'points' of a cross or polled beast with the best of his

neighbours, and even affect to deal a little on his own account . . . I freely admit that many cases more or less similar to it could be found in Aberdeenshire among the class to which my old friend belonged. But where, out of Aberdeenshire, will you find such examples of continuous, unremitting toil, hard thrift, and steadfast, unflinching endurance? That is my point; and when all the elements of the case are taken into consideration I am inclined to hold that the genuine Aberdeenshire men of the olden type may fairly claim to have had but few equals, and still fewer superiors in respect of the qualities named, and what they succeeded in achieving through their exercise . . . And what has been 'bred in the bone' in connection with the pursuit of that indispensable occupation in the case of the fathers has signalised itself in a hundred other connections in the case of the sons, to whom by the ordinary law of heredity it has been transmitted.[44]

While extolling the virtues of these men as individuals in his non-fiction writings, Alexander charted in his agricultural novels and short stories their decline and fall as a class.

'Ravenshowe' was set during the opening decade of the century before capitalistic farming came to the Garioch, in a community of small farmers and rural craftsmen and crofters living in arcadian simplicity, practising that good-neighbourliness which Alexander saw as the touchstone of the old values, and enjoying supportive and uncompetitive relations with their Scots-speaking laird.[45] Johnny Gibb shows the system in crisis, with the laird become not only an oppressor, but an alien and an absentee locked in conflict with his tenants.[46]

It is a large scale work which takes a panoramic view of North-East rural society during the 1830s and 1840s, but centres on the estate of Sir Simon Frissal of Glensnicker, and two of his tenant farmers, Johnny Gibb of Gushetneuk, a clear-sighted, dogged, incorruptible little man who embodies the very best features of the Aberdeenshire farmer according to Alexander, and his neighbour Peter Birse the farmer of Clinkstyle, who embodies some of the worst, a complete nonentity driven by his termagant wife to aspire to the status of a muckle farmer, and to start the process by absorbing some of Johnny Gibb's farm when the lease expires. For much of the book, this seems a reasonable prospect. Johnny Gibb has led resistance to the laird for years, openly voting against his candidate at elections, setting up a voluntary school in defiance of the incompetent parish schoolmaster, leading the non-intrusionist faction before the Disruption, and becoming the driving force behind the Free Kirk afterwards. He is ageing, childless, and as his tack has little time to run, it is assumed that he will be quitting the estate. It emerges, however, that he has in the past lent money to the laird, and some of the account is still outstanding. At the term, the tables are turned on the Birses, Gushetneuk is enlarged, Clinkstyle reduced, and the lease granted to Johnny's nominee.

As in 'Drammochdyle', Alexander uses a family unit to show the different kinds of corruption that flow from the crudely capitalist outlook. The Birses' greed is matched only by their vulgarity and pretentiousness. Mrs Birse aspires to be a *grande dame* with a housemaid and carriage, but is a mean grasping ignorant woman who cannot even read; her daughter, the 'maiden' of Clinkstyle, is given an expensively genteel education at a finishing school in town which leaves her half-anglified, semi-literate, and wholly absurd; Benjie the petted younger son, destined by his mother for the professions, is a hopeless dunce; while Peter, the elder, who is to be set up as a muckle farmer and confirm the family's arrival among the ranks of the rural haut-bourgeoisie has talent for little but raking, and ends up, to his mother's horror, married to the daughter of a fish-cadger. So in the end, Johnny Gibb wins, although the fact that he is childless, i.e. he has no direct heir, has a certain suggestiveness . . . and his creator seems to have been genuinely uncertain almost to the final paragraphs of the book whether to kill him off or not.

The stories in *Life Among my Ain Folk*, which began to appear in the *Weekly Free Press* from the winter of 1872 onwards, show a later stage in the struggle and a more pessimistic vision of the outcome. The failure of the peasant class to reproduce itself, hinted at in *Johnny Gibb*, becomes explicit in 'Mary Malcolmson's Wee Maggie', the first story in the volume, published in the *Weekly Free Press* 14 June–6 September 1873. It concerns Saunders Malcolmson, tenant of the fifty acre holding of Skellach Brae, and his daughter Maggie. Saunders is a self-made man who has risen by thrift and industry from being a farm labourer to being a successful small farmer, and now, approaching the end of his tack, is looking out for a suitable match for his daughter. Unfortunately for him, she has already given her heart to Willie Fraser, his own ploughman, a farmer's son like himself, and following much the same course in life, capable, intelligent, amiable, and penniless. The last is a fatal disqualification. Saunders banishes Willie from the toun, but eventually is forced to permit the marriage. Maggie leaves, tocherless, and an outcast, to join her husband now working as grieve to a great improver, Patrick Ellison Sgurr, Esq, of Seggieden in a distant part of the county. Only a short period of happiness is granted to them. Willie is killed by a horse and Maggie contracts tuberculosis and dies in the insanitary hovel provided for the grieve on an estate where the livestock are better housed than the workers. They leave little behind them but a few trifling debts and a sickly little baby daughter, also called Maggie. She is brought up by the chastened Saunders, but it is clear by the end of the story that her future will lie in the schoolhouse or the manse rather than in agriculture.

'Francie Herrigerie's Sharger Laddie',[47] shows the plight of the cottar class in the new social and economic order. Francie is a married ploughman compelled to live virtually as a bachelor because the landlords have cleared their estates of labourers' cottages, and his wife and son must lodge in a distant town. He only gets home for the odd evening every three weeks or so and finds a normal family life quite impossible—a great hardship for someone of his simple and affectionate nature. He is even prepared to give up being a skilled horseman to work as a day-labourer nearer his wife and child, but the weather is bad, and work is scarce, and his need for a regular income forces him to take another fee and leave home again. There is a typhus epidemic in the town and his bright, frail little boy succumbs to it, but Francie cannot be present at his death bed because the farmer's skittish prize mare is about to be delivered of a valuable foal and a capable servant can hardly be spared at such a time. He even has to provide a substitute before he can take a day off to bury the child. He is interred near Francie's native village—except there is not a village any more: it has been ploughed under, and there is nothing left but graves. Francie is filled with an overwhelming sense of loss, and the bitter reflection that a six-foot-by-three rectangle of red earth is the only place in the world he can call home.[48]

Some of the more obvious consequences of this systematic degradation of the rural workforce are shown in 'Baubie Huie's Bastard Geet' published in the *Weekly Free Press* between 30 November and 31 December,1872. The story lays repeated stress on the bad moral effects of a poor physical and social environment. Baubie's father Jock is a day labourer forced to bring up a numerous family in a squalid hut. Proper family life, or even adequate parental supervision in these circumstances is, of course, out of the question. In due course, Baubie leaves home and goes into service and before long her parents discover, without enormous surprise, that she has 'gane the auld gate'. The father of the child is found, and shirks his responsibility. Baubie goes back to work and a year or so later marries an older man with children of his own. The Geet is brought up, roughly but affectionately, by Jock and Eppie Huie, and the cycle is prepared, no doubt, to repeat itself in the next generation. There is no condemnation or moral attitudinising. Alexander handles this explosive subject with a tact and compassion which is really quite remarkable and can be seen to good effect in the beautifully handled climax of the story where Baubie reveals her condition to her mother. It is difficult to think of a comparable passage in the whole of nineteenth century Scottish, or for that matter English, fiction.[49]

The author attached a note to the story not reproduced in the book edition, which is both an eloquent summary of intent and an indication of the distance he had come as a realist since the 'Rusticus' days:

> The picture I have attempted to sketch is one sufficiently homely to be in the estimation of some—very probably—repulsive in its rudeness. Of one thing I am certain, the outlines are not put in with a darker shade than the reality justifies. Whether the better service is done by presenting the bare unvarnished truth, and leaving it to tell its own lesson; or, in deference to a not over-healthy moral sensitiveness, glossing over all the 'sair bits' in our social life, is a question which, of course, I do not pretend authoritatively to decide. All I can say is, that I have my own deliberately formed opinion, and have felt bound to act upon it.[50]

The longest—and probably the best—story in the book is 'Couper Sandy', a superb study of the economic forces that Alexander saw as creating and conditioning the social phenomena he depicted in the others. It concerns the rise to wealth and consequence of Sandy Mutch, an absolute clod with a single conspicuously marketable talent. He is a marvellously gifted 'coo-

couper' (cattle dealer) with a rare eye for a beast and an instinct for a deal
that seldom deserts him. In North-East agricultural terms, he represents
'economic man' raised to the highest power. But cattle are the only things
he understands. He has no insight into the financial system of which he
becomes the centre, or into anything else, really; he is just a brilliantly
instinctive operator who rises from youthful hustling at country fairs to
being a prosperous muckle farmer, not through any choice or ambition of
his own, but because his backers, particularly the shrewd banker Tammas
Rorison, want to protect their investment in him. He is rescued from
bankruptcy at one point because it is ultimately cheaper for the moneyed
interest to bail him out than let him go under. The banker controls Sandy:
he threatens to stop his credit when he shows interest in the 'wrong'
woman (her father supports a rival bank); pushes him towards the
economically rational bride, and combines with her equally astute muckle-
farmer father to manage him like a well-run investment portfolio. Seldom
even in Alexander's fiction is the material basis of society exposed with
such splendid irony:

> The farm-house of Mill of Meadaple, it should be known, was of modern
> construction; not the old-fashioned sort with a thatched roof and the minimum
> of window space, but a commodious, well-lighted two-storey house, with
> carefully enclosed and neatly laid out garden in front. Sandy's social estate was
> that of a bachelor, and his previous domestic surroundings, while living in most
> part at the humble cottage of his father and mother, had not been of an
> elaborate sort. In the circumstances, Sandy had thoughts of removing the old
> people to occupy part of his newly-acquired residence, provided the souter
> would agree to come, which was by no means certain: for the souter, who still
> maintained a sort of standing protest against his son's career, had even gone the
> length of denouncing the leasing of the farm as the act of a man fairly 'left to
> 'imsel" for no good end.
>
> 'No; ye'll do nothing o' the sort,' said Tammas Rorison, to whom Sandy had
> mentioned the subject, on calling to arrange some money transactions
> connected with his entry to the farm. 'They're owre aul' to tak reet again
> though ye hed them transplantit the morn. To take yer fader awa' fae his
> birse't-en's an' 's lapstane, nae to speak o' 's cronies, owrehaulin Kirk an' State,
> wud be to kill his comfort, an' maybe add little to yours, for he wud never tak'
> to new haibits an' new company. Hae patience, man; the hoose'll be worth itsel'
> to you yet,' continued Sandy's sagacious adviser.
>
> 'It's sic a muckle jamb,' said Sandy, 'an' mair nor the tae half o''t 'll hae to stan'
> teem.'
>
> 'Nae fear o' that; ye maun get the principal rooms made habitable in a decent
> fashion, an' a fyou raelly gweed things intil't—a sideboord, for example, for the
> best parlour.'
>
> 'Hoot, a side-boord! Is that the name 't the gentles gi'es till a mahogany claise
> press?'
>
> 'No, no; it's a dining-room article.'
>
> 'Oh, but I've aye ta'en my bit maet i' the kitchie, I wud never hae nae eese for
> the like o' that,' pleaded Sandy.
>
> 'Maybe,' said the banker; and he added enigmatically 'but some ither body

will, come time; an' a hantle depen's on appearances in maitters o' that kin'. Hae you gotten a gweed hoosekeeper?'

'She's a vera cawpable servan'.'

'Elderly person?'

'N-o; nae passin' foorty or thereaboot.'

'Well, that'll do. Let her keep the ither servan's weel at the staff en'; but take ye gweed care yersel', Sandy, lat me tell ye, that ye gi'ena 'er owre muckle heid room aboot the place. D'ye un'erstan'?'

'Weel, but a hoosekeeper maun tak a gweed hantle o' chairge aboot a fairm.'

'Ou ay, ou ay; but hoosekeepers o' forty are sometimes unco willin' to tak chairge o' raither mair nor it's canny to lippen to them, Sandy man;' and the banker looked straight at Sandy with a waggish air. 'Hoo-ever, ye maun luik oot for a hoosekeeper o' anither kin' on yer ain account by an' by.'

'Aw dinna ken aboot that,' said Sandy Mutch, with a half sheepish look and a decided shake of the head, 'a bodie's as wise to keep their heid oot o' the mink as lang's they can.'

'It depen's a'thegither upo'fat an' fa ye buckle wi', Sandy,' replied his astute friend. 'Dinna ye think that for a chiel' settin' oot as ye are, a sonsy fairmer's dother wi' a gweed tocher wud be weel worth gettin' a grip o'? Eh?'

Sandy, who had not expected the point to be pressed so closely, and was consequently rather taken aback by the banker's query, stammered out a sort of affirmative reply. The banker was quite in earnest, however, and he went on to point out to Sandy Mutch that 'a wife wi' a tocher' was simply the natural adjunct of a young man in the position he had now attained; not to say the essential factor in a fully satisfactory solution within a reasonable time of the financial and general business problem now before him.

'Ye ken, afore ye pay your inveetors, an' ae thing wi' anither, ye'll be workin' upo' paper again for maist pairt: an' if ye're to keep on your transack amo' beasts it mith be that I could hardly streetch the tether far aneuch for you. Wudna a thoosan' poun' or so come in unco handy, man, sax or nine months aifter this?'

'Weel, aw'm nae sayin' that it wudna—or aiven the half o''t for that maitter.'

'The half o''t! Na, na. Ye ken fat wye yer accoont 'll stan' by the time that yer stockin' an' wark leems are paid for. Na, na; there's little eese o' fowk throwin' awa' their advantages; ye've that muckle to leern yet, Sandy, appearandly.'

In short, Tammas Rorison had calculated on his protégé making a suitable match as a part of the general plan on which he had based his support of him; and he proceeded to give him very practical advice, even condescending on the names of two or three young ladies who he knew very well had the necessary pecuniary qualification; and they were otherwise extremely attractive; so said Tammas.

'Here's the maiden o' the Muirton, noo; a strappin' lass wi' a lady's eddication—can play the piano or sing fae the buik, an' mak' 'er menners wi' the best o' yer toon-bred misses—her fader canna turn'er aff wi' less nor a gweed aucht or nine hunner at onyrate; fat gin she war to come your wye noo?'

What if she were to come his way! Plain, blunt Sandy Mutch, who could buy an ox with any body, and talk in phraseology entirely appropriate to the occasion, or drink the accompanying dram with a natural and becoming gusto, but whose literary accomplishments merely enabled him to sign an accommodation bill occasionally in a rude way, and whose social advantages hitherto had not been such as to permit him to feel perfectly comfortable in drawing-room society of the type that Tammas Rorison had referred to; Sandy was startled into positive uneasiness as he declared his fear that such fine ladies were not 'the kin' for him.' The banker merely laughted at him in his own jocosely confident way.

'Fat! fairmer o' Mill o' Meadaple, wi' a hoose that hisna its marrow for miles roon aboot; an' nae think 't ye may hae the pick an' wile o' the lasses i' the pairt. Oh, fie man!'

'But ye ken the like o' that uppish fowk wudna think me'—

'Tut, tut—ov coorse ye're un'erstood to be weel fit for the place; an' sae ye are,' continued the banker, not heeding the interruption further. 'An' lat ye that be weel kent, man; get yer hoose pitten in order an' hae some o' yer neebours in aboot come time; only ye mauna mak' yersel' owre cheap; an' for ony sake dinna speak to the women fowk—especially wives wi' dothers o' their han'—as gin ye thocht the best o' them sair worth huntin' aifter. Haud ye up yer heid man, an' dinna lat them forget that ye're Mill o' Meadaple. Fan ye come to the point ye winna hae to seek some o' them twice. I can tell ye; tak' ye my word for't, noo.[51]

The penetration of society by money-based values here reaches its highest pitch, when the hero himself turns into a commodity.

These rural novels and tales represent the summit of Alexander's achivement as a literary realist. Realism was, indeed, the only positive quality their modest creator was ever disposed, publicly, to claim for them. As he remarked in the preface to *Life Among my Ain Folk*:

> The Sketches that compose this small volume profess to be nothing more than slight studies, *in situ*, so to speak, of certain phases of local life . . . The characters are, of course, ideal in one sense (or, say typical), and in another as truly realistic and close to the actual life as the writer could succeed in making them. Possibly some will hold the little book to be lacking in loftiness of sentiment, and refinement in the *dramatis personae*; but we must picture life as we know it. And, after all, who is it that has not, oftener than he wished, in his experience found loftiness of general sentiment and a profession of high principles set in the fore front, where the veritable life was guided by considerations as mean and sordid as well might be. Better, at any rate, have things in their real and undisguised forms then; and this merit we claim.[52]

Alexander's fiction has frequently been praised for its realism—particularly so in the case of *Life Among my Ain Folk* which dealt with matters that seldom found their way into other writers' pages.[53] And yet if we examine the criticism on his works more carefully, we find him credited upon the whole with excellence in a fairly narrow range of literary qualities, and these perhaps not of the highest order. He is acknowledged to have had a keen eye, a refreshingly objective stance, a penetrating ear for language and a real gift for female characters.[54] But we sense at the same time a number of implied shortcomings, a feeling that there is a nakedness, a lack of symbolic richness about his prose; that he is deficient in a sense of form and overall artistic intention—that he is basically a naive writer, a purveyor of simple statements about how things were in a particular place at a particular time, a kind of inspired primitivist.[55] This is particularly noticeable in commentary emanating from the North-East, which shows a typical confusion, an urge to extoll him to the heavens on one hand, balanced by a neurotic conviction on the other that, as no good thing can possibly come out of Nazareth, he must somehow have feet of clay.[56]

Alexander's own technique has presented one of the major barriers to his appreciation outside the dialectal area of North-East Scotland. He abandoned standard Scots in favour of a literary language based on the usage of central and southern Aberdeenshire in the period from about 1780 to his own time, and intended it to possess a scientific accuracy and value with regard to vocabulary, grammar, idiom, and orthography.[57] This made it diffcult for other Lowland Scots to read him with ease, and his reputation outside Aberdeenshire grew slowly.[58] J H Millar's *Literary History*, for example, barely mentions him, and it has taken nearly a century for him to be acknowledged as a figure of national importance.

There has been, then, a tendency to parochialise Alexander, and consider him in relation to his specific linguistic and historical situation.[59] And yet, as recent studies have shown, a wider perspective can pay considerable dividends. Ian Carter has reminded us that his social and political outlook is of central importance to his art, and that there is a continuous dialogue between the fictional and the non-fictional writings.[60] There is a large body of such material, not just in books, articles and pamphlets, but distributed widely in the columns of the newspapers to which he contributed over a period of more than forty years.[61]

Now we can look at his development as a writer of fiction. His career did not begin in 1869 with a powerful but unrepeated thrust from the field of history and politics into the neighbouring territory of fiction. He was a diligent and sophisticated creator of fiction for more than thirty years, and some contemporaries at least were fully conscious of his artistry. Discussing *Johnny Gibb* in a review in 1873, a source close to the author declared:

> It is the faithful delineation of life and character that gives value and charm to work; the grouping of the incidents is but secondary and subordinate. The author might, possibly, have awakened and sustained his readers' interest, had he cared to make the attempt, by a cleverly conceived plot, and led them on expectantly to a thrilling denouement. But he has wisely chosen to do something else, and something better. He has done well to leave that much-trodden road, and seek fresher scenes. He knows better what he is about, too, than introduce any such incongruity. For the life he depicts—the rural life of Aberdeenshre—has in it little or nothing of the sensational. It presents no startling contrasts of colouring; its shades are sombre, not to say dull.
>
> In holding the mirror up to this common-place hum-drum life, the author of 'Johnny Gibb' has displayed an extraordinary power or skill in investing his characters with life-like attitudes. This is a 'true story' in an artistically higher sense than as being a narrative of facts or of incidents that have actually occurred. It is true inasmuch as it is an admirably correct representation (indeed, it would not be easy to find a more exact representation in fiction) of a particular phase of life and a particular class of people.[62]

Although his subject matter is local, the context of his art is not confined by the parochial bounds of the North-East of Scotland as narrowly conceived. In the very fullest sense he was a Realist, an heir not merely of the native vernacular tradition with its roots going back deep into the Middle Ages, but a pioneer of that European-wide contemporary movement in philosophy and the arts which was to become the corner stone of the modern consciousness.[63] Nearly all the hallmarks of the sophisticated Realist style are present in his works: his mistrust of the traditional plot tied up by a trite denouement (his best-known work *Johnny Gibb of Gushetneuk* begins *in medias res*—a favourite Realist device, with the famous opening apostrophe 'Heely, heely, Tam, ye glaiket stirk, ye hinna on the hin' shelvin' o' the cairt.'); his interest in the lower orders of society extending even, as in 'Baubie Huie', to their sexual drives; his accuracy in recording observed behaviour down to the subtlest niceties of common speech; his repeated disavowal of authorial omniscience; his interest in social causality; his eagerness to find a rationale for human behaviour in external forces like heredity and environment;[64] his broadly deterministic view of society; his underlying pessimism—all contribute to make him a conspicuous figure in Realist aesthetics, a contemporary in art of Tolstoy, Dostoevsky and Turgenev, a writer whose techniqe in some respects anticipates developments in France where the theory of Realism as a literary aesthetic was to achieve its definitive shape in the novels and critical writings of Emile Zola.

Alexander's last and perhaps most ambitious novel, 'My Uncle the Baillie', was published in the *Weekly Free Press* between 2 December 1876 and 5 May 1877, and marks a return to an urban theme. It is set in the city of 'Greyness' (Aberdeen), in the period *c.*1840 to the historical present, and the narrator is an apprentice clerk in a warehouse belonging to his uncle David Macnicol. There also are to be found John Cockerill, the senior clerk, a flashy insubtantial young man, and Sandy Macnicol, David's younger brother and assistant manager, a quiet, circumspect, deeply human character who forms the main focus of the book. Uncle David has started life just like the narrator, as a raw country boy apprenticed in the town subsequently rising to wealth and position by marrying his employer Baillie Castock's daughter, and then inheriting the business. He is a force to be reckoned with in commercial circles in the city, and has already served on the town council, resigning because his services have not been rewarded with civic office.

The theme of burghal politics runs strongly through the novel. One of the narrator's first actions is to admit a pair of party bosses come to inveigle Uncle David back on to the Council:

> 'We took a luik in to see you, Mr Macnicol—aboot the election, ye ken,' said Baillie Gudgeon, addressing my uncle, David, when salutations had been exchanged, and the two visitors had got seated in my uncle's own room. 'Ye'll need to gie's a hitch this time.'

'I fear there's naething in my poo'er, Baillie,' was my uncle's guarded reply. 'No; I fear there's naething in my poo'er.'

'We're vera anxious to get good men,' suggested Mr Sneevle.

'Men o' expairience,' interposed the Baillie.

'There's so much important business comin' afore the Cooncil that it's a positive duty for men that the electors can hae confidence in, an' men that hae a lairge stake i' the toon, to offer themsel's,' pursued the lawyer.

'True, true,' said my uncle, meditatively, 'an' I've nae doot, though it's a thankless job, that men'll be forthcomin'.'

'Weel,' said Baillie Gudgeon, coming to the point at last, 'there's a vera strong wush to get you back to your aul' ward at the Craftheid; an' in fac' Maister Sneevle an' me, as twa aul' freens, an' him yer nain awgent forby, cam' here to get your consent.'

'I cudna think o' sic a thing!' answered my uncle with a decision that seemed greatly to shock and stagger his friends, who simultaneously exclaimed—

'Hoot! hoot! Maister Macnicol.'

'No—no. It'll be a close fecht—a mere throwin' awa' o' siller to nae purpose. I've naethin to gain by gaein' back to the Cooncil.'

'Oh, but Mr Macnicol ye've aye stood by the pairty ye ken,' urged Mr Sneevle.

'Ay ay; as weel's the pairty's stood by me,' replied my uncle firmly.

Baillie Gudgeon and Mr Sneevle looked at each other with a knowing glance, as the former cautiously said—

'The cast's nae a' thegither sattle't yet, ye ken; there'll be a bit office or twa free, sick like's the Hospital convenership.'

'I dinna want the Hospital convenership. It's a thankless job sairin' the public, I tell ye. Hooever, ye'll get men ready an' willin' to be cooncillors nae doot; an' it seems ye hae plenty luikin' for onything else 't's a-gaein—providin' ye cairry yer men.'

'Oh, we canna but cairry ye ken,' said Baillie Gudgeon. 'The tither side's fairly pitten their fit in't by proposin' a bawbee tax for the drainin' o' the Stinkin Lochie; the public will not stan' mair taxes; an' there's ither things that we a' ken aboot that'll craw i' their craps."

'Weel, weel,' said my uncle, with a touch of dryness in his manner, 'There micht be waur things nor drainin' the Lochie.'

'Eh, but ye cudna speak o' a tax,' said the Baillie earnestly.

'I'm nae sayin't I wud,' was my uncle's reply; 'It's nae lickly I'll hae to express mysel' ae wye or the ither.'

'Weel, we jist cam up to you in a frien'ly wye first, Mr Macnicol, kennin' that the Provost has a vera great regard for you,' said Baillie Gudgeon, after a pause.

'Ye needna lat on that we've been in i' the meantime,' added Mr Sneevle. 'I've nae doot things'll come a' till a proper bearin'. This meetin's quite an informal ane, ye ken. There's nobody committit. But I do think raelly that it's your duty to come forward at this time, whan we've sae mony questions o' public importance comin' up. As the Baillie was jist sayin' afore we cam' in, there's nane mair capable, an' fyou likely to be mair willin to yield private feelin's for the general good than you. Ye'll think fawvourably o't, Maister Macnicol; an' min' the Ward meetin's 'll be upon's in a fyou day's time.'

With this flattering speech, and a sufficiently distinct understanding of how the land lay, my uncle's visitors took their leave and proceeded to call on the next possible candidate for municipal honours.[65]

Uncle David eventually agrees to take the platform at the adoption meeting in the turbulent Crafthead Ward, and the last of the important characters is introduced. This is Ritchie Darrel, a particular friend of Uncle Sandy, a fiery little man who owns a second-hand bookshop specialising mainly in works of theology. He has a jaundiced view of human motives generally, and open contempt for the way the city is run, as the narrator quickly discovers:

'Weel here's your cash,' continued Richie, opening his till—'An' so ye're come down a' the wye fae Strathtocher to be Provost o' oor toon?' he added, suddenly changing the subject and addressing myself in a more directly personal fashion.

'Na, nae to be Provost,' was my slightly sheepish reply to the bantering obervation of the queer little man, whose particular manner seemed to compel a sort of interest, not unmixed with apprehension.

'An' fat for no, lad? We're jist settin' on to hatch a new brodmill o' toon cooncillors. They're the raw material o' baillies and siclike, ye ken—the baillies bein' seleckit wi' due regaird to the size o' a man's painch, an' a' that; though we've aiven seen them win to the bench on the principle o' the scum comin' to the tap. An' fat better stuff hae ye to mak a Provost o' than a weel trackit Baillie? Wudna ye like to be a toon cooncillor than; as something within the limits o' your modesty?'

'No I wudna,' was my answer, blurted out in a state of mind, half of amazement half of amusement, at the dimly understood observations of my interrogator.

'Wow, man, but ye've nae public spirit ava; fat greater object o' ambition can be set afore an aspirin' youth than to busy 'imsel i' the toon's affairs, win into the Cooncil, takin' fat share he can get o' the scran, an' feenally sit doon wi' a baillie's chyne aneth's chowks; or maybe step into the muckle cheir itsel'—Fat wud your schaime o' life be, if it's a fair question?'

'I want to learn business, an syne gyang abroad,' said I, with that air of raw confidence and consequence, which harmonises so well with utter lack of knowledge and experience of the world.

'H—m!' said Richie Darrel, in a changed tone, and with his thoughts apparently half abstracted from the subject in hand 'H—m. I daursay ye're nae the first that has startit wi' ideas o' that kin' at fourteen, an' foun' oot that though the warld's a big place maist ot's inhabitants maun be content to be gey little bookit by the time they're fifty . . . i' the meantime . . Min' to tell the Deacon, [Uncle Sandy] wi' my compliments, that I'll expec' to see 'im at the Craftheid Ward meetin' on Monday nicht. If he winna come forrat 'imsel, it's little aneuch that he sud tak' the trouble o' catecheesin' the candidates that offer themsel's to the suffrages o' the free an' independent electors o' the Ward.'[66]

The meeting takes place in due course, and the electors do ample justice to their reputation for fractiousness. Alexander is good at crowds and he conveys a lively sense of the packed hall, the humorous banter as various local worthies make their entrance, the procedural slickness of the ruling party which insinuates Gudgeon into the chair and Sneevle into the clerkship of the meeting *nem.con*. There follows an address of consummate suavity from Uncle David, and then the cut and thrust of the general question session begins:

When the speeches had ended, and the clerk of the meeting, having written up his minute to that point in the business, had elevated his spectacles to the top of his brow, and lain back on his chair to await the next act in the drama, the chairman tentatively asked—

'Noo, gentlemen, are ye satisfeet wi' the candidates' views; or wud ye like to pit some questions?'

'Satisfeet! nae very lickly,' exclaimed a heavy shouldered man, with a short neck and double chin, who had got himself stuck into an elevated corner seat at the wall, fronting the chair, and commanding a good view of the audience. 'We've had little to be satisfeet wi' yet—lat them be pitten throu' their catechis.'

'Fire awa', than;' and 'Go on wi' yer barrow, Tam,' were the cries that greeted this exclamation, to which Tam replied by a grunt and a choleric 'Time aneuch; hurry nae man's cattle . . .

'I want—to put a question to—,' exlaimed a thin-faced nervous-looking man, rising up in one of the middle seats. 'Haud yer jaw, min, till ither fowk be throu',' interposed the first querist, and the man sat down again suddenly.—'Will ye use your influence wi' the Government than to obtain a grant for the purpose o' levellin' the Castlehill an' gi'en employment to the workin' men o' Greyness at fix't waages?' asked the working man in a tone of increased severity. This safe and sweeping question was promptly and unanimously answered, amid many 'hear, hears' and much cheering, with a 'certainly,' 'certainly,' 'with much pleasure,' and 'delighted—a vera proper proposal.' The querist seemed satisfied and threw himself back in his seat without uttering another word, whereupon the man in the back seat who had spoken first demanded to know—'Fat aboot the drainin o' the Stinkin' Lochie?' 'Hear, hear,' exlaimed the two opposition candidates. 'That's it noo, Tam,' exclaimed the occupants of the rear benches, stamping the floor with their feet emphatically. My uncle looked wise; and the chairman looked perplexed, till, having stooped over and consulted the Clerk, he rose and declared himself at a loss to understand the gentleman—'Come noo baillie, nane o' yer gammon,' exclaimed some anonymous elector. 'A' humbug ye ken'—'Weel, if ye wull hae't plainer,' cried another, 'Fat are the candidates prepar't to dee aboot drainin' the Lochie? pit that to them.' 'Oh, I un'erstan'. But gentlemen, I doot if that's a constitutional question. Oor excellent Clerk, Mr Sneevle, than whom no one knows better, will tell you that that's a question surroun'it wi' vera, vera sairous dif—' 'Buff an' nonsense, Baillie, lat them answer the question!' broke in the man with the double chin. 'Order, order,' cried Mr Sneevle; 'hear, hear, hear,' shouted others, while many laughed uproariously and stamped upon the floor. The chairman, who, in the endeavour to make himself audible, had got red in the face, was heard to utter some disjointed words about 'vestit interests that aiven the Coonci daurna meddle wi',' and 'mair taxation'. He had no choice, however, but put the question which was the crucial one of the time, in a party sense. My uncle made a politic reply . . . He admitted the growing obnoxiousness of the Loch in a sanitary point of view—though it was really wonderful how remarkably healthy residents in its neighbourhood were—but dwelt on the great engineering difficulties attending the draining of a sheet of water an acre and a half in extent and only twenty feet above sea level, and still more the formidable business involved in meddling with those who, as the chairman had reminded them, had vested rights in the Loch. Still it was a question for the inhabitants to consider at the right time. For his own part it was no new question to him; far from it; he had carefully looked at it in all its bearings—antiquarian and social—and if the state of trade were such as to warrant it and other burdens reduced to a proper point, he would consider it—he certainly would consider it carefully . . .

The question of the Loch warmed up the meeting in a wonderful way . . . the nervous man again got on his legs, and rapidly put the queries that burdened his mind, which had relation to the attitude of the candidates toward international disarmament in the first place, and toward a decimal coinage and the metrical system in the second. He had got but the scantiest possible satisfaction in the way of response, when a sallow, sleek-haired man, who affected the role of the social reformer, stood up with a determined air and a long string of written questions in his hand, which he desired to put *seriatim* . . . as the querist went on to explain and sub-divide his questions, the temper of the meeting gave out more and more; and the cry to 'Pit him oot,' became urgent. The sleek-haired man stood his ground resolutely for a time, bearding both the candidates and the audience, and reiterating his opinions in a hoarse shout, but he was finally snuffed out by persistently-continued 'ruffing', amid which somebody moved thanks to Baillie Gudgeon for his able and impartial conduct in the chair, and the meeting of the Crofthead Ward, which was declared to have been an eminently successful and satisfactory one, immediately came to an end.[67]

The scene shifts to a quiet Sunday morning some years before these events. Ritchie Darrel and Sandy are in a little country kirkyard not far from the city, regarding the Darrel family grave; it is well tended and the stone bears several names along with a conspicuous and rather mysterious blank. We discover next something of Sandy's earlier life. He has been a small farmer on an improving lease on a mixed arable and sporting estate, and been eaten out of house and home by the laird's game, initiating a series of events which lead to him losing his farm, his reputation, and his sweetheart, the bright and blooming Elsie Robertson. The cause of these reverses is his scrupulous honesty. He refuses to continue his lease under such conditions, to the astonishment of his brother farmers, some of whom have in the past cursed the laird as heartily as he. They regard him as dangerously principled, feeling that he should do as they do, making up what they lose to the laird by cheating somebody else further down the line. They regard his intention to emigrate as suspicious, and their growing hostility towards him begins to affect Elsie Robertson. Relations between her and Sandy rapidly cool. He becomes seriously ill, watches his capital dribble away, never recovers fully, and has little to fall back upon in the end except the good offices of his brother in the city. He is forced to take a menial post with Castock & Macnicol while Elsie Robertson goes into service as a lady's maid in the south.

After Baillie Castock dies, Sandy plays a more important role in the business and some of his failings, his affability and easy unpretentiousness, begin to come under critical inspection, notably from the Baillie's daughter the aspiring Mrs Macnicol:

'Mithna ye try an' persuad yer brither to gie up some o's countra haibits, my dear, an' keep mair amo' the kin' o' company 't we wud like to see 'im ta'en oot wi?' said my uncle's wife.

'His countra haibits?' answered my uncle David inquiringly. 'I'm nae aware that's haibits are waur nor ither folks.'

'Tut man; what's mair common nor to see 'im stan' up i' the braidest street o' the toon, be wi' 'im fa may, an' speak wi' some roch half heilan' creatur in a grey plaid an' clatterin' tacketie sheen; or some sma' fairmer's wife wi' 'er butter basket on 'er airm. An to see 'im wi' a glove on's han's, Sunday or Saturday, is neist to a ferlie.'

'Folk canna help speakin' to a countra body at a time,' said my uncle, evidently not desirous of pursuing the subject, the truth being that he did not much relish the idea of admonishing the uncircumspect Sandy.

'Weel, ye k-now perfectly that it's not becomin' in his position noo; an' fa wud speak till 'im if his nown brither wudna dee't.'[68]

Mrs Macnicol's deliciously mangled Scots/English sufficiently indicates the author's attitude towards her. But David has too much sense to interfere and Sandy goes on his way incorrigible.

In due course, David becomes first a junior then a senior Baillie and we learn much about the shambles that passes for the administration of justice in the burgh courts. The bench is woefully ignorant of the law and its forms, and the professional advocates behave as they please. The result is undignified, unpredictable, and usually unjust. And yet to be a Baillie is a great thing, shedding an indefinable but very real lustre not only upon the office-bearer himself, but on his friends and relations, his employees, and even, in Uncle David's case, the inhabitants of his native strath, some of whom pop in to consult him on their legal affairs bearing chickens, slabs of butter, and great placatory kebbucks of cheese. The caustic Ritchie Darrel keeps up a continuous verbal assault upon the entire institution, dismissing it merely as a vehicle for cynical self-advancement, insufferable complacency, and vulgar display.

John Cockerill's star has meantime risen along with his master's. He becomes David's 'private secretary', and is admitted to the society of the Macnicol daughters. An arrogant coxcomb in reality, he is able to exploit for his own ends the superficial cultural standards of the mercantile bourgeoisie whose hold upon genuine refinement is about as secure as his own: he can sing in the approved drawing room manner (just about), and hold his end up in the utterance of fashionable inanities, and this is enough. The ease with which this brash impostor is able to gain *entrée* into 'good' society is seen as a natural consequence of the hypocritical and corrupt burghal ethos in which ruthless self-interest runs everything under a cloak of altruism and the public good. After making conquest of the female Macnicols, Cockerill leaves to push his business career in the south, armed with introductions and glowing references. The narrator moves up to chief clerk and a successor must be found to occupy the junior stool. No task is too trivial for the law agents to deal with (itself a comment on the incestuous, parasitic nature of the city) and Sneevle duly advertises for a boy:

As my Uncle Sandy walked down to the office of Mr Peter Sneevle, solicitor, to perform the duty devolving upon him of selecting an apprentice, the absurdity of the lawyer being employed in what seemed so simple an affair came up in his mind once and again, as a fresh illustration of certain weakeness to which the Bailliehood was liable. He was not however, aware, till informed, of the elaborate fashion in which Mr Sneevle had gone about the matter intrusted to him. That gentleman's business was of an omnivorous sort. He liked to style himself an agent; and his agency comprehended much from the compilation of an ordinary roup bill to the drafting of a feu charter, from the sale of a wooden shed to the purchase and bonding of some of the best heritable subjects in Greyness. And he did everything according to the most ponderous legal form, a peculiarity of Mr Sneevle's method, moreover, being that in place of the formality diminishing in proportion as the business was trifling, it seemed rather to increase.

'Of coorse we advertis't,' said Mr Sneevle.

'Indeed!' said my Uncle Sandy.

'There were just thirty-four candidates—the replies are here. Wud ye like to hear them read?' asked Mr Sneevle, lifting a bundle of variously sized sheets of paper, folded and duly tied together and marked.

'Oh, no, no!'

'Well, they're all classified here, I can give you a *précis* of the whole as we go along.'

'I understan' ye've reduc't them to a leet o' three. I'm quite willin' to trust your judgement so far, Mr Sneevle.'

'Ay; vera good; but it'll be mair in form if I report generally. There's a synopsis here; let me see. Good penmanship, you know, is an essential requisite. Well, o' the total number o' thirty-four, twenty-one were below par in the formation o' the letters, wi' mair or less bad spellin'; six passable writers also spelt badly. The reduc't the list to seven. Then a closer scrutiny became necessary. O' the seven, twa that wrote weel had nae feelin' for capitals, an' even spelt the first personal pronoun wi' a single i; a habit nae radically incurable, perhaps, but indicative o' a tendency to looseness in form. The neist twa—perhaps ye wud like to see them;' and the lawyer lifted the bundle and began to pull at it with the intention of drawing out certain of the papers.

'No, no,' said my Uncle, 'go on.'

'Weel, in a sentence; ane was blotch't wi' ink, and the ither tussl't an' torn at ae corner. Here they are. Noo I think that's the substance o' my report almost—No—let me see—'

'Can ye lat me see the three laddies?' said my Uncle a little impatiently.

'Stay, stay, Mr Macnicol, we haena come to that yet. Allooin' that ye pass fae the ithers; we come to a leet o' three a' eligible; but nae equally eligible it may be. Afore we come to questions o' personal appearance, mainner, an' the like, we can mak' a comparative analysis o' the han' writin'—'

'Weel, really, Mr Sneevle, my pooers o' discrimination are nae equal to that. If the boys write decently it's a' that ye can expect, an' I wudna care a button for ane bein' a little better an' the ither a little waur—jist let me see the laddies.'

'Weel, Mr Macnicol, if ye'r satisfiet, though it doesna exhaust my remit in a formal mainner, I'll do as ye wish, only there's a risk o' miscarriage—Will ye tak' them ane an' ane for scrutiny or a' in a bunch?' and Mr Sneevle dabbed down the button of his table bell as a call to his attendant clerk.

'Oh, bring them a' in, an' we'll judge the han' writin' as far as needs be aifter seein' the writers.'

'Simon, sen' in the boys in the waitin' room,' said Mr Sneevle to his oldish and impoverished looking clerk, when that functionary had pushed the door half open and looked in for his order. 'In *cumulo* Simon,' he added, as the clerk seemed to hesitate with an inquiring look: 'in *cumulo*—not *separatim*—but *seriatim*, and in alphabetical order—Anderson, Baxter, Thomson—you have the check list.'[69]

One of the applicants is Jamie Thomson, Elsie Robertson's son. She has married while in the south and is now widowed with a family and keeping a boarding house in a shabby northern suburb of the city. Sandy engages the boy, aware that there can be only one reason for the gifted Jamie giving up his studies and seeking work—his mother must be in financial trouble of some sort. One evening shortly afterwards she calls at Sandy's lodgings to ask for help. She had expected to receive a small inheritance under the will of a relative but another claimant is threatening legal action and she does not know what to do. Sandy gains possession of the will which establishes her claim beyond doubt, and friendly relations are once again resumed.

Meantime one of the keys to Ritchie Darrel's enigmatic personality are discovered. It appears that as a young man he had fallen deeply in love with a cousin. She rejected him and married somebody else who treated her badly. Eventually she had been found dead in circumstances suggesting suicide, and buried at a crossroads in unconsecrated ground. After years of patient enquiry, Ritchie proves she died of natural causes, but none of her immediate kin will do anything about it so, out of his own pocket although it takes half his bank balance, he has her re-interred in the family grave and adds her name to the stone.

Uncle David continues to prosper. He seldom now appears in the warehouse, devoting most of his time to attending board meetings of the many companies of which he is chairman or a director. He has also acquired a small estate on the outskirts of the city and seems poised to become provost. His eldest daughter Amelia Matilda is courted by John Cockerell now partner in a fly-by-night wine firm in Glasgow, but David opposes the union and draws up the marriage settlement so as to give Cockerell no control over his wife's dowry. Unfortunately he must have it to stave off bankruptcy and his company promptly collapses, leaving David to pay a substantial sum in order to save his new son-in-law from his creditors.

The closing section of the novel takes place five years later, and shows David finally declining to seek the Provost's chair, content to be senior Baillie, John Cockerill a pushing commission agent in the city and about to stand for the council, Ritchie Darrel prematurely dead, Sandy and Elsie married, and Jamie Thomson a rising young physician. Everything ends happily.

It will be evident that 'My Uncle the Baillie' represents a significant departure in technique from the pattern established by the rest of Alexander's mature fiction. There are, not unusually, several strands to the narrative: the parts concerning David Macnicol and the burgh politics of Greyness; Ritchie Darrel's struggle to vindicate his lost love; Sandy

Macnicol's recovery of Elsie Robertson; and various other parts involving the narrator, John Cockerill, and Jamie Thomson. Unique among his novels, however, the 'Baillie' possesses a highly developed and complex plot with a 'satisfying' traditional-style denouement. The political sections of the novel are couched in Alexander's usual objective/realist style, but the rest adheres to a different aesthetic, narrator-dominated with lengthy sections of standard English prose, tightly plotted, and peopled with characters whose behaviour is obviously intended to have transcendent meaning.

Ritchie Darrel and Uncle Sandy clearly possess symbolic reference although it is subtle and resistant to simple interpretation. They are the representatives of positive moral value in the novel, upright, decent, independently-minded men, determined to do their duty as they see it to God and man. Most of the other characters are shallow, self-seeking, materialistic and corrupt, and we learn much about their misgovernment of the city. It is noticeable that both Sandy and Ritchie were countrymen originally—but as the latter points out, so are most of the inhabitants of Greyness, 'we were a' strangers ance', and there is no obvious opposition between city and country; that is, the countryside is not represented as a reservoir of moral purity any more than the city is perceived as the source of its own corruption; there are plenty of immoral people in both. The 'Baillie' is not an anti-urban tract.

Sandy and Ritchie have both loved and lost; Ritchie absolutely, Sandy temporarily, and as a result they stand in a certain relation to the past. Sandy recovers something of great value from it; Ritchie goes back into it to alter its shape: by demonstrating his cousin's innocence he changes its relationship with the present. Of course the proper burial of the dead is an imperative Christian duty, but the point here seems to be more than a doctrinal one. We may indeed be in the presence of a variation on the resurrectionist motif of quite unusual sophistication and imaginative reach. If so, then Sandy and Ritchie are probably meant to represent continuity and the need to keep faith with the best of the past in a world of shifting moral and material conditions. There does, however, seem to be a deeper set of ideas at play: a subtle perception of the double interaction of 'history' with the present. Not only may the past condition the present in countless ways, but the present can change the past—Ritchie does it—and so free itself from the deterministic circle. The novel may be an exploration of the ability of morally gifted people to resist the conditioning pressures of an all too mundane environment, an essay on free will and the possibility that the individual may rise, damaged perhaps, but ultimately triumphant above the world of circumstance.

Sandy and Ritchie thus possess a different order of significance from the usual run of Alexander characters who tend to be endowed with the realist virtue of being 'typical' rather than 'ideal' in the sense of embodying transcendent value in conformity with the basic assumptions of high Romantic fiction.[70] It may be that Alexander is attempting to achieve a unified aesthetic by reconciling the two dominant philosophical approaches to the art of fiction. Even if the results are judged only partially successful,

'My Uncle the Baillie' remains one of the most interesting and ambitious novels of its period.

William Alexander is an important writer, and newspaper sources enable us to add very considerably to our knowledge about him. They also help us to place what we already knew in a significant new light. One of the weaknesses perceived in *Johnny Gibb*, for example, is that it is set in the past, about a generation before the time in which it was actually written. This has left it open to the charge of being 'backward-looking' and therefore symptomatic of the supposed reluctance of Victorian Scottish novelists to concern themselves with contemporary affairs. An awareness of 'Ravenshowe' allows us to see *Johnny Gibb* as the central section of an epic sequence nearly quarter of a million words long, encompassing almost a century of change and development in the rural North-East, which Alexander began to write in the spring of 1867 and completed probably in the winter of 1874 when the last of the stories in *Life Among my Ain Folk* appeared in the *Weekly Free Press*.[71] On the strength of his success in *Johnny Gibb*, Alexander has been seen as the doyen of rural novelists, a symbol of the apparent failure of contemporary Scots writers to engage with urban themes. But almost half his fiction is city-based. As we have hitherto been unable to place *Johnny Gibb* within the context of Alexander's other imaginative writing, we have seriously misunderstood its sophisticated Realist aesthetic and attempted to link it with the so-called Kailyard School from which it differs radically in outlook and technique.

Finally, newspaper sources show Alexander's approach to language in a wider and largely new context. He is not simply a transcriber, however gifted, of a single narrow strain of local vernacular Scots as readers familiar only with *Johnny Gibb* may have supposed. His work reflects the whole gamut of spoken register as differentiated by age, class, and education. He shows how language changes over time in a way few, if any, other writers have attempted.[72] His work is also an important—perhaps the critical—example of the implications of bi-lingualism for the evolution of fiction in Scotland during the period. In 'Sketches of Rural Life' we see in a tentative early form the strategy which attracted such favourable attention in *Johnny Gibb*, the transposition of much of the discourse into direct speech so as to allow vernacular Scots to challenge standard English as the basic narrative medium. 'Peter Grundie' uses different Scots registers within a standard English narrative matrix, but his subsequent works up to 1875 show a progressive urge to disrupt the monopolistic position of English as the language of authority and even in one short story never subsequently republished, a piece called 'Back to Macduff', he abandons the language altogether.[73]

William Alexander is a gifted and original writer whose achievement is central to the development of literary culture in Victorian Scotland. His work provides a clear example of the class-relatedness of popular fiction at this time. When the *Free Press* was able to support a cheap city edition aimed at the working-class, Alexander wrote fiction for it; and when the *Free Press* reverted to being a middle-class 'county' paper (as it did between 1856 and 1865) he ceased to do so, a further reminder, if one were needed, of the extent to which the new popular press helped created the culture it represented. Alexander committed most of his imaginative writing to the newspaper press. The fact that he could be persuaded to publish only one of his longer works—*Johnny Gibb of Gushetneuk*—in cased form is a testimony not merely to his modesty and the hectic fullness of his public life, but also to the gulf which had opened up between the London-dominated book-trade and the real world of Scottish letters.[74]

FIVE

Swallowed up in London . . .

A View of the Kailyard with some conclusions and a postscript

This is a study of writing produced in Scotland for Scottish readers through the medium of the Scottish press. It would not normally deal, therefore, with the writings of J M Barrie, 'Ian Maclaren' (Dr John Watson), and Samuel Rutherford Crockett, the main representatives of the so-called Kailyard School which dominated the Anglo-American book-market in the closing decade of the century. As they have in the past engrossed much of the discussion about Scottish fiction during this period, however, it may be useful to say a little about them here.[1]

The movement is usually considered to have been founded by J M Barrie in two books, *Auld Licht Idylls*, a collection of short stories published in London in 1888, and the novel *A Window in Thrums* which was published, also in London, the following year. They were set in a fictionalised version of his native Kirriemuir, and dealt with social and religious life in an Original Secession congregation made up largely of handloom weavers and their families at a period about half a century before his own time. Barrie got most of the stories from his mother, with whom he had an unusually close relationship, and he gave a detailed account of their genesis in his later biographical study *Margaret Ogilvie* (London 1896). In the autumn of 1884, he had been kicking his heels at home after being sacked as assistant editor of the *Nottingham Journal*, when suddenly there came to him 'as unlooked for as a telegram, the thought that there was something quaint about my native place.'[2] He worked this perception up into the first of his 'Thrums' stories, 'An Auld Licht Community'. This was at once accepted by Frederick Greenwood of the London *St James's Gazette*. As far as Barrie was concerned that was the end of the matter; but Greenwood wrote asking for more, 'so I sent him a marriage, and he took it, and then I tried him with a funeral, and he took it, and really it began to look as if we had him.'[3]

When the series was complete, Barrie tried to publish it as a book, but there were no takers. Indeed it might never have appeared in collected form but for the intervention of William Robertson Nicoll, editor of the *British Weekly* and literary adviser to the evangelical English publishing house Hodder & Stoughton.

Nicoll was the Godfather of the Kailyard. He pushed the careers of all its chief writers: he bullied one of them, 'Ian Maclaren', who as Dr John Watson of Liverpool was a leading Presbyterian divine and homiletic writer, into producing *Beside the Bonnie Brier Bush* a major bestseller in

England and America, and in the columns of his paper tirelessly championed the new wave of evangelical Scotch novelists.[4] Nicoll had himself been a Free Kirk minister before ill-health forced him to give it up. He moved into religious journalism and persuaded Hodder & Stoughton to back a new-style paper combining the moral tone of the traditional denominational press with the razzamataz of the 'new journalism'.[5] Nicoll's steely commercial instincts were seldom far beneath the surface: 'I never expected to reach the masses—' he wrote, 'But I hoped to reach the vast number of educated Nonconformists in Scotland and England who take no Christian paper, and despise the Nonconformists for their want of culture. I hope especially to get the ministers.' He added, however, 'We must have 20,000 subscribers, and there is not that number of intelligent people in the country—so we must condescend to weak minds.'[6] Apart from Barrie & Co and a number of northern theologians (more than a third of the contributors were DDs), the paper had little specifically Scottish content except for a column of 'Scotch Correspondence' bobbing about at the back among the advertisements for harmoniums and clerical hats. But the *British Weekly* carried all before it in the prosperous middle-class middlebrow Nonconformist market in England. For more than a generation, Nicoll dictated what it read. He was the great manufacturer of reputations in the world of the circulating library and the six-shilling novel. Without him the Kailyard could not have existed.

And the fact that it could, and did, springs from far-reaching changes within the literary market which Nicoll was quick to identify and exploit. During the century Scotland's population grew much more slowly than England's. The English reading public increased dramatically as a result of mass compulsory education, and Scotland became relatively insignificant as an independent market for books. The historic Anglo-American copyright agreement of 1891 set the seal upon this development. Hitherto there had been little protection for British authors in the booming American market, where something between fifty and seventy-five per cent of all published titles were pirated from British sources. The agreement extended copyright protection to British writers in the States, and, by opening up huge new sources of potential income, altered for ever the orientation of the typical British literary career. It also confirmed the London/New York axis as the dominant feature of the bookmarket in the English-speaking world. It was in New York that Barrie and Maclaren met for the first time, in October 1896.[7]

The book trade in Scotland was normally weighted against fiction in any case. In England the top places in best-seller lists were often occupied by works of popular fiction, but in Scotland, non-fiction tended to top the charts.[8] Barrie & Co were amongst the first generation of professional novelists to grow up in Scotland. But the audience lived elsewhere. *Auld Licht Idylls* shows this on nearly every page, with its simplistic explanation of Scottish religious life, its minimalist approach to the vernacular, its notes on pronunciation, like 'wright=wir-icht' (p 13) and glosses of elementary Scots words like 'toad=fox' (p 238) within the body of the text. It was initially published in England and was intended first and foremost for the English reader. One thinks, too, of S R Crockett's remarks at a public dinner in his honour in Galloway—'We authors' he said.

> cannot always do just exactly what we would like. The publisher tells you to cut down the dialect because the English public does not understand it . . . The editor must have a book on a certain subject, because public interest calls for it. The land that holds the heather and the sheep does not hold the money for the man who has to live by his pen. So that to a certain extent the author is dependent upon a more distant public.[9]

This has implications going beyond mere vocabulary and style. The aesthetics of the Kailyard were substantially different from the basically realist thrust of contemporary Scottish fiction. One can see this clearly in William Robertson Nicoll's defence of 'Ian Maclaren's' vision against charges that it was selective and sentimental, that it glossed over 'the sair bits' and that it was, therefore, false:

> It is a fair question, 'Have we true pictures in these idylls? Is it thus and thus that people act or ever acted in a Scotch parish?' It must be remembered that idylls do not pretend to give a full chronicle of life. They try to seize the moments at which the hidden beauty of the soul leaps into vision. They do not take in the whole circumference of truth, and they do not profess to take it in. But they include a far wider area than is ever compassed by cynicism. And surely it is a great and precious gift to be able to detect the divine in the carnal, and to see angels in the disguise in which we always entertain them . . . it was his avowed aim and end to bring out the idyllic elements in life, and he thus helped to slake the eternal thirst of our nature for those waters of the ideal that glimmer before us and still before us.[10]

Within a few years of the popular novel in Scotland shaking itself free from external religious constraints, there was a determined attempt by a group of expatriates in England to recover the form for the purposes of evangelical propaganda. The pietistic fiction of Barrie and Maclaren was intended as a contribution to the dilemma which called the *British Weekly* itself into existence, the acute crisis in English liberal Nonconformism during the last two decades of the nineteenth century. As such it will in time, no doubt, take its place where it belongs: in the intellectual annals of England and the United States.[11]

The milieu of the Kailyarders was in any case noticeably bourgeois. Much has been made of Barrie's lowly origins, but his family were in fact relatively well-to-do. His mother's brother, for example, was a minister and a Doctor of Divinity; his father was a small employer; both he and his brother attended university, and his sisters became teachers.[12] Crockett was a graduate and a minister.[13] Watson's father was a major public official and his mother came from wealthy farming circles in Perthshire.[14] Barrie and Crockett both published in the Scottish press, but neither identified it as the natural focus of his activities. They related to their audience through the bourgeois book-market, and looked instinctively towards its controlling centre: as Barrie wrote 'The greatest glory that has ever come to me was to be swallowed up in London . . .'[15]

The significant part of the literary market in Scotland during most of the nineteenth century was not the middle class with its subscription libraries and imported English novels, but the Scots-speaking working class and the native writers who catered for it through the medium of the popular press. Scots was the dominant medium of spoken communication throughout the Lowlands and this was reflected in the creation of a radical new speech-based vernacular prose as soon as the means of doing it became available. The language was immediately revealed as an expressive and wide-ranging discursive medium, and writers like W D Latto used it to deal with every aspect of contemporary life. Likewise in fiction. In an average year some half dozen or so novels might be published in book form which in some way dealt with Scotland and the Scottish experience; but this was dwarfed by the activities of the Scottish press.[16] Assuming that forty per cent of the papers published between 1860 and 1900 were carrying fiction and printed on average four novels a year, then during the period more than ten thousand novels addressed to a specifically Scottish readership appear in this source alone. Reducing that figure by twenty-five per cent to allow for syndication, and by another twenty-five per cent to exclude material dealing with life furth of Scotland, one is still left (even at a conservative estimate) with more than five thousand full-length Scottish novels, not counting original short stories which were published in still greater numbers, and an enormous body of folkloristic, autobiographical and social history writing springing from the same imaginative source. Taken together it amounts to a cultural achievement of massive proportions; and it is still largely unexplored.[17]

In the second half of the nineteenth century Scotland experienced a communications revolution which led to the creation of a new popular press owned, written, and distributed within the country. The new press became the main vehicle of popular culture during the period and the major locus of the imaginative life of the nation. The reading and writing of fiction as a permissible activity was extended to every social class and a secular popular fiction free from external religious constraints came into being aimed at a largely working-class audience. The demand for writing increased a thousandfold, transforming the literary market. There was a dramatic extension of the literary class thanks to widespread reader-participation in the press, a new type of professional writer represented by journalists like W D Latto and William Alexander, moving freely between the newspaper and popular publishing worlds, and a new generation of local publishing houses based on the newspaper network and reflecting the identity of the areas they served. All over Scotland people wrote fiction for the press. In places where there were many newspapers, it accumulated around practically every hedgerow and dyke in all the major genres: domestic stories, historical romances, crime fiction, tales of the supernatural, sensational stories and adventure fiction of every sort.

In his novel *Lanark*, Alasdair Gray pointed to what he saw as an enduring part of the Scottish malaise: the dismal failure of its artists and writers to invest the place with aesthetic presence: '. . . if a city hasn't been used by an artist not even the inhabitants live there imaginatively. What is Glasgow to most of us? A house, the place we work, a football park or a golf course, some pubs and connecting streets . . . And when our imagination needs exercise we use these to visit London, Paris, Rome under the Caesars, the American West at the turn of the century, anywhere but here and now.'[18] With regard to much of the twentieth century the criticism is, perhaps, a just one. Victorian Scotland, however, was a completely and lovingly imagined place, and a very different one from that visible through the narrow and distorting perspective of the printed book. The market for imaginative writing was much more complex and extensive than has sometimes been supposed, and we have come to misleading conclusions by looking at only one part of it. Many of our conventional ideas about the period are at best only partly true, and some are quite false. On the whole popular fiction in Victorian Scotland is not overwhelmingly backward-looking; it is not obsessed by rural themes; it does not shrink from urbanisation or its problems; it is not idyllic in its approach; it does not treat the common people as comic or quaint. The second half of the nineteenth century is not a period of creative trauma or linguistic decline; it is one of the richest and most vital episodes in the history of Scottish popular culture.

As the century neared its end the newspaper world began to change. Papers sold at or below cost and they had to outdistance their rivals in the struggle for advertising revenue if they wanted to stay in business. To do this they had to outstrip them in circulation. They had to get big and then get bigger, with all that implied in terms of amalgamation, elimination of rival titles, and the progressive loss of local control. They strained to attract more readers, readers who were less discriminating, drawn from those 'involuntary literates' with whom compulsory education was flooding the market. This exerted a sustained downward pressure upon the press from about the mid eighteen-eighties onwards. By 1900 the 'new journalism' was firmly entrenched and the long trivialisation of the Scottish press had begun.

The cultural autonomy of the press began to weaken from about the same period. As mass-produced stereotyped copy became available in quantity, the flow of distinctive original writing faltered and imported agency fiction bought on the cheap from English syndicates became increasingly common, even in wealthy and powerful papers like the *People's Journal*.[19] Public libraries, cheaper books, and growing affluence changed popular reading habits, and by the second decade of the new century newspapers had generally ceased to function as a source of popular fiction for the upper working or the lower middle class. Acute paper shortages during the 1914–18 war delivered the final blow. When the Scottish press emerged on the other side of that great divide, it found itself in a new and bleaker age.

Notes

Locations of newspapers cited below may be found in Joan P S Ferguson (ed), *Directory of Scottish Newspapers* (Edinburgh 1984).

Lionel Madden and Diana Dixon, *The Nineteenth-Century Periodical Press in Britain—a Bibliography of Modern Studies 1901-1971* (New York & London 1976), gives a full listing of Scottish papers together with holding libraries, secondary sources, and the dates of centenary and other commemorative numbers.

Papers cited frequently in the notes appear in abbreviated form as follows:

PJ: *The People's Journal*

AFP: *Aberdeen Free Press* (published weekly until 1865 then bi-weekly until 1872; daily thereafter).

WFP: *Weekly Free Press*. (For the sake of convenience, I refer to the *Aberdeen Free Press* group's weekly paper by this title throughout after 1872; the actual title changed from time to time as follows: from 1876, *Herald and Weekly Free Press* (following acquisition by *Free Press* of *Aberdeen Herald*); from 1889 onwards, *Weekly Free Press and Aberdeen Herald*.)

INTRODUCTION

1 R M W Cowan, *The Newspaper in Scotland a Study of its First Expansion 1815-1860* (Glasgow 1946), pp 409-10. For the English press *see*: George Boyce, James Curran and Pauline Wingate (eds), *Newspaper History from the Seventeenth Century to the Present Day* (London 1978); Alan J Lee, *The Origins of the Popular Press in England 1855-1914* (London 1976); Stephen Koss, *The Rise and Fall of the Political Press in Britain*, Volume One: The Nineteenth Century (London 1981); Maurice Milne, *The Newspapers of Northumberland and Durham A Study of their Progress during the 'Golden Age' of the Provincial Press* (Newcastle, n.d.).

2 For Watson *see* James Grant, *The Metropolitan Weekly and Provincial Press* (London 1872), pp 410-14; for Ruddiman, *see* Douglas Duncan, *Thomas Ruddiman a Study in Scottish Scholarship of the 18th Century* (Edinburgh 1965), pp 4, 76-7; for Scott *see* Grant op.cit. pp 424-8, 474, William Norrie, *Edinburgh Newspapers Past and Present* (Earlston, 1891), p 20, and *The Progress of British Newspapers in the 19th Century. Supplement to Sell's World Press Guide* (London 1907), p 132; for Wilson, Lockhart and Hogg, *see* James Bertram, *Some Memories of Books Authors and Events* (London 1893) p 93; for Hugh Miller *see* Cowan op.cit. p 279, Norrie op.cit. pp 42-4; for Alexander *see* within pp 101-44; for C M Grieve, *see* Duncan Glen, *Hugh MacDiarmid and the Scottish Renaissance* (Edinburgh 1964), p 71; and for James Leslie Mitchell, *see* Ian S Munro, *Leslie Mitchell: Lewis Grassic Gibbon* (Edinburgh 1966), pp 24-5.

CHAPTER ONE

1 This figure is derived from Joan P S Ferguson op.cit.

2   Alexander Sinclair, *Fifty Years of Newspaper Life, 1845-1895: Being Chiefly Reminiscences of that Time* (Glasgow, privately printed, n.d. [1895]), a superb source, covering every aspect of the Victorian newspaper press in Scotland in great detail: *see especially* pp 34-6, 87, 143-4. See also *The Aberdeen Journal and its History* (Aberdeen 1894), pp 9-10; Cowan, *The Newspaper in Scotland . . .*, op.cit. pp 143-5, 148-9, 169-70.

3   *Dundee Advertiser Festival* (Dundee 1876), p 12. For the history of the *Advertiser* group during the nineteenth century, *see* A H Millar, *The Dundee Advertiser, 1801-1901. A Centenary Memoir* (Dundee 1901), *passim*; also *How a Newspaper is Printed* (Dundee n.d. but 1890), pp 41-51; a concise but detailed account of the rise of the *Advertiser* group during the nineteenth century is also given in [H A Boswell], *About Newspapers: Chiefly English and Scottish* (Edinburgh 1888), pp 72-80.

4   Sinclair op.cit. pp 2-3, 11-12, 15-17; *see also* William Lindsay, *Some Notes: Personal and Public* (Aberdeen 1898, privately printed), pp 122-9; Cowan op.cit. pp 23, 165-6; *Jubilee of the People's Journal 1858-1908* (Dundee 1908), p 34.

5   Boyce, Curran and Wingate (eds), *Newspaper History from the Seventeenth Century to the Present Day*, op. cit. pp 46-9, 55-61.

6   *Report from the Select Committee on Newspaper Stamps*, pp 241-57; 'The Newspaper Stamp', *AFP*, 8 Dec 1854, p 5, 26 Jan 1855 p 5, 16 Feb 1855, p 8. Magnus Magnusson *et al. The Glorious Privilege: the History of 'The Scotsman'* (London 1967), pp 32-3; there is an affectionate and amusing sketch of Russel in Henry Grey Graham, *Literary and Historical Essays* (London 1908), pp 219-72.

7   Sinclair op.cit. p 3; for a personal memoir of the explosive growth of the Scottish press, *see* Andrew Aird, *Reminiscences of Editors, Reporters, and Printers, during the last Sixty Years* (Glasgow 1890), pp 26-7; 36-7; 80-8.

8   Michael L Turner, 'The Syndication of Fiction in Provincial Newspapers 1870-1939. The Example of the Tillotson "Fiction Bureau"'. Unpublished B.Litt thesis, Oxford University 1968, p 6.

9   [William Alexander], *Twenty-Five Years: A Personal Retrospect* (Aberdeen 1878), pp 1-3; for the foundation of the paper, *see* Lindsay op.cit. pp 303-5; [Boswell] op.cit. pp 71-2.

10   For the profitability of one successful title *see* A D Campbell 'The *Herald* Partners a Financial Survey' in *The Glasgow Herald 1783-1958* (Glasgow 1958), p 43: during the 1870s the *Herald* was clearing £20,000 per annum—by the end of the century the annual profits were in excess of £40,000. One freesheet, the *Northern Advertiser*, was supplied *gratis* to all householders in its area but only if they paid police and parochial taxes on a rent of £5 and upwards. See also *Jubilee* op.cit. p 39.

11   William Harvey, *Printing in Stirling, Charles Randall and his Successors, The Story of the 'Stirling Observer' Press* (Stirling 1923), pp 12-78; *The 'Stirling Observer' Press Ninety Years' Progress 1836-1926* (Stirling 1926), pp 14-32; *Eighty Years of the Falkirk Herald 1845-1925* (Falkirk 1925), pp 17-18.

12   *The Buteman* 'Centenary Number', 10 Dec 1954.

13   For a brief history of the paper see *Hamilton Advertiser*, 'Centenary Supplement', 5-7 July 1956.

14   John Mowat, 'Romance of the Orkney and Shetland Press' in *Proceedings of the Orkney Antiquarian Society*, 1937, pp 31-7; see also *Eighty Years of the Falkirk Herald*, p 23; *Paisley & Renfrewshire Gazette*, 'Prospectus', 29 Oct 1864, p 4.

15   Mowat op.cit. pp 34-5; also 'Local Publications at the *Brechin Advertiser* Office' bound in with D H Edwards, *Glimpses of Men and Manners About the Muirside*

(Brechin 1920); *The 'Stirling Observer' Press Ninety Years' Progress* op.cit. p 72; and 'Local Publications . . . David Scott, Printer &. Publisher, Sentinel Office, Peterhead', in J Longmuir, *Address to the Statue of Marshal James Keith* (Peterhead 1874).

16 *Peterhead Sentinel* 'Prospectus', 6 June 1856.

17 James Annand, born Longside, Aberdeenshire, 1843, son of blacksmith/crofter, largely self-taught, became teacher at Coldwells near Cruden Bay, then followed Hugh Gilzean Reid as editor of the *Buchan Observer*, 1865-71. *See* George B Hodgson, *From Smithy to Senate: the Life Story of James Annand, Journalist and Politician* (London 1908), pp 4-51; J L McCallum, *James Annand, MP, a Tribute* (Edinburgh 1908), pp 26-46.

  Hugh Gilzean Reid, born 1836, at Cruden, entered journalism from teaching following encouragement by William McCombie; reporter on *Banffshire Journal*, editor *Peterhead Sentinel* 1856/7-59, editor and part-proprietor *Buchan Observer* 1862-5, wrote serial fiction for latter paper, *see* 'Sir Hugh Gilzean Reid' in Adam Mackay, *Distinguished Sons of Cruden* (Peterhead 1922), pp 135-90; also Hodgson op.cit. pp 21, 28-9, 38-9.

18 Cowan op.cit. pp 30, 307.

19 Aird op.cit. pp 17-20; Norrie op.cit. p 23—but *see also* W J Couper in *Scottish Notes and Queries*, Vol IV, 2nd series, June 1903, pp 182-3.

20 At least one paper had a female editor: when it first started in 1817, the *Inverness Courier* was nominally under the direction of Mr John Johnstone, but the paper was actually edited by his wife, who later went on to edit *Tait's Magazine* in Edinburgh—*see* Grant, *Metropolitan Weekly and Provincial Press*, p 549. For the backgrounds of various of her male colleagues during the century see *Henry Alexander, a Memoir* (Aberdeen 1915), and the *Perthshire Advertiser* 'Centenary Number', 12 Aug 1929, pp 9-11.

21 [Alexander] *Retrospect*, pp 6-8.

22 For an assessment of Forsyth as editor of the *Journal*, *see* Cowan op.cit. p 292; a fuller account of his life and works is prefixed to *Selections From the Writings of the Late William Forsyth, Editor of the 'Aberdeen Journal'* (Aberdeen 1882) pp iii-xv.

23 Ian Carter, *Farmlife in Northeast Scotland 1840-1914 the Poor Man's Country* (Edinburgh 1979), pp 165-75, gives an outline account of the involvement of the *Free Press* and of William Alexander in Liberal politics in the region notably with regard to the land question.

24 Sinclair op.cit. pp 40-4; [Boswell] op.cit. pp 100-2; *see also* James Grant, *The Newspaper Press: its Origin—Progress—and Present Position*, Vol II (London 1871), pp 141-4.

25 William Forsyth, *Idylls and Lyrics* (Edinburgh 1872).

26 Quoted in National Register of Archives (Scotland) Survey No. 1500 'Irvine of Drum', Bundle 422, 'Miscellaneous personal and official correspondence addressed to Alexander Forbes Irvine, 20th of Drum, 1866-69.'

27 Although few business records of Victorian newspapers have survived, directors' minute books, miscellaneous ledgers, wage-books and stock-inventories are available for the Aberdeen and North of Scotland Newspaper and Printing Co Ltd from March 1876 onwards (Aberdeen University Library, MS 2770) and the account of the *Aberdeen Journal* which follows is largely based on this source, in particular the Minute Books of Directors, March 1876-Jan 1882, May 1884-Dec 1894, and the Minute Book of the Business Committee, Nov 1877-June 1883.

28 Although there is no formal biography of John Leng, details of his career are preserved in a number of sources, several of them collected as *In Memoriam: Sir John Leng* (Dundee 1906); *see especially* pp 5-12, 34-6, 38, 44, 49. *See also* 'Journalistic Autobiographies, 1.—Sir John Leng', in *The Bookman*, Feb 1901, pp 156-8; A H Millar, op.cit. pp 20-26; *Dundee Advertiser Festival*, op.cit. pp 14-15; the reader will also find references to Leng in William Walker, *Juteopolis: Dundee and its Textile Workers 1885-1923* (Edinburgh 1979).

29 Cowan op.cit. pp 279, 286, 290-91. *Eighty Years of the Falkirk Herald*, pp 7-8, 33-5.

30 For a lively account of *Chambers' Journal* and the popular literature trade in Edinburgh during the 1830s and 1840s, *see* Bertram, *Some Memories of Books, Authors and Events* (London 1883) pp 137-45. The flavour of the magazine is well conveyed by 'The Editor's Address to his Readers', *Chambers' Edinburgh Journal*, No. 1, 4 Feb 1832, pp 1-2. On the rise of cheap literature generally during the period, *see* 'The Market of Literature' in Lindsay op.cit. pp 287-300. For the drift of Scottish periodicals to the south *see* Louis James, *Fiction for the Working Man 1830-1850* (London 1963), pp 14-15, and Duncan Ferguson, *The Scottish Newspaper Press* (Edinburgh 1946), p 34.

31 Sinclair op.cit. p 63. For an indication of the extent to which Scottish book-fiction was produced for a predominantly English market from the earliest years of the nineteenth century onwards, *see* David Craig, *Scottish Literature and the Scottish People 1680-1830* (London 1961), pp. 213-31, 297-300; for evidence of increasing absorption of Scottish publishing houses in a London-dominated all-U.K. literary market see F D Tredrey, *The House of Blackwood 1804-1954* (Edinburgh 1954), pp 85-188. It may be questioned how far there was a separate Scottish trade in book-fiction: for example, Collins of Glasgow, one of the greatest Scottish publishing houses carried little or no fiction during the period, they specialised in bibles and devotional works, reference books, dictionaries, educational and scientific textbooks, and when they did begin to turn their attention to fiction at about the start of the century, it was, significantly perhaps, children's fiction that became their speciality—*see* David Keir, *The House of Collins The Story of a Scottish Family of Publishers from 1789 to the Present Day* (London 1952), pp. 156-216. Throughout this study, I adopt as a working definition of 'popular literature' material which has been written specifically for publication in newspapers.

32 For testimony to similar effect from inside the working class *see* 'To the Editor, etc . . . A Ploughman' in *AFP*, 16 March 1855, p 8.

33 *See* 'Reading for the Million' on Brougham's conversion to the psychological necessity of popular fiction, *AFP*, 22 Oct 1858, p 3, 5 Nov 1858, p 5.

34 *The Buchan Clown, A New Periodical, of an Amusing and General Literary and Moral Character* (Peterhead 1838), No. 1, p 2.

35 *AFP*, 14 Jan 1853, p 8.

36 Alastair R Thompson, 'An Enquiry into the Reading Habits of the Working Classes in Scotland from 1830-1840'. Unpublished B. Litt thesis, Glasgow 1962, p 29; *see also* Laurence J Saunders, *Scottish Democracy 1815-1840* (Edinburgh 1950), pp 241-303.

37 *AFP*, 23 Nov 1860, p 6.

38 'Clodpole on the results of "Popular Ignorance"', *PJ*, 26 June 1858.

39 *AFP*, 30 April 1867, p 4.

40 D H Edwards, *Glimpses of Men and Manners . . .* , op.cit. p 9.

41 Thompson op.cit. pp 55, 58; for the situation in England *see* Richard D Altick, *The English Common Reader: a Social History of the Mass Reading Public 1800–1900* (Chicago 1957), pp 9–10.

42 For the difficulties of matching newspaper growth to literacy gains in England, *see* Alan J Lee, *The Origins of the Popular Press in England 1855–1914* (London 1976), pp 34–5.

43 Lindsay op.cit. pp 85–90, 125–98, 202–3, 241–2, 280–7.

44 For the pre-repeal Scottish press as an advertising medium, *see* Sinclair op.cit. pp 4–6.

45 *Chambers' Edinburgh Journal*, No. 42, New Series, 19 Oct 1844, p 249; No. 47, New Series, 23 Nov 1844, pp 335–6 contains a letter from a flax-heckler at Dundee giving a detailed account of the reader-system there. William Chambers himself when young was a reader in a bakery, Bertram op.cit. p 102.

46 Lindsay op.cit. pp 25–30; *see also*, pp 32–3.

47 Walter Gregor, *An Echo of the Olden Time from the North of Scotland* (Edinburgh 1874), pp 32–4; *see also AFP*, 21 Jan 1868, p 4.

48 *AFP*, 12 May 1854, p 6.

49 Lindsay op.cit. p 256.

50 *PJ*, 14 March 1868, p 2.

51 *PJ*, 27 Nov 1869.

52 Millar op.cit. pp vii, 53.

53 *Jubilee* op.cit. pp 32, 42–8.

54 Millar op.cit. p 33; *Jubilee* op.cit. p 47.

55 Millar op.cit. p 53.

56 Ernest Frank Carter, *An Historical Geography of the Railways of the British Isles* (London 1959), p 350; Sinclair op.cit., pp 104–6.

57 Lindsay op.cit. pp 252–7.

58 *PJ*, 8 Feb 1868, p 2.

59 Ibid. 19 June 1875.

60 *How a Newspaper is Printed*, p 10.

61 Millar op.cit. pp 36–45; see also *How a Newspaper is Printed*, pp 29–31, 33–7; *Jubilee* op.cit. p 4.

62 Walker op.cit. p 255.

63 The main sources for Latto's life are the long obituary 'Mr W D Latto' published in *The Dundee Year Book*, 1899, pp 68–71, and 'Mr W D Latto, Editor of *The People's Journal*, Dundee', in *The Biographical Magazine*, April 1887, pp 333–49, probably compiled by Latto himself; the present study relies heavily upon these for biographical detail concerning this writer; see also *Jubilee* op.cit. p 5.

64 For an account of the Scottish National Reform League, *see* James D Young, *The Rousing of the Scottish Working Class* (London 1979), pp 112–17.

65 One would obviously have to add to this a strong existing interest in these subjects on the part of his readers: *see* Young op.cit. pp 52–3, 56–9, 81–2.

66 *PJ*, 20 May–16 Dec 1876.

67 Some theorists have represented popular culture as essentially negative in character, something manufactured for profit and consumed by a passive paying audience, *see*, for example, Herbert J Gans, *Popular Culture and High Culture An Analysis and Evaluation of Taste* (New York 1974), p 19, and James op.cit. pp 28–9. Dwight MacDonald presents this view in its most trenchant form: 'Mass Culture is imposed from above. It is fabricated by technicians hired by businessmen; its audiences are passive consumers, their participation limited to the choice between buying and not buying. The Lords of *kitsch*, in

short, exploit the cultural needs of the masses in order to make a profit and/or to maintain their class rule . . . (It is very different to *satisfy* popular tastes, as Robert Burns' poetry did, and to *exploit* them, as Hollywood does.) Folk Art was the people's own institution, their private little garden walled off from the great formal park of their masters' High Culture. But Mass Culture breaks down the wall, integrating the masses into a debased form of High Culture and thus becoming an instrument of political domination.' Bernard Rosenberg and David Manning White (eds), *Mass Culture The Popular Arts in America* (London 1964), p 60. In traditional culture it is held that the individual can act both as producer and consumer—having a set of internalised rules which enable him to generate his own cultural products; in the prevailing view of popular culture, however, the individual cannot modify the structure in this way.

A number of commentators regard the popular press in a similar light, *see*, for example, James Curran, 'The Press as an agency of social control: an historical perspective' in Boyce, Curran and Wingate op.cit. pp 51–75. On the evidence of the present study, there are serious difficulties in both these positions at least in their simple form. For a useful overview of the concept of popular culture in a historical setting *see* Zev Barbu, 'Popular Culture a Sociological Approach' in C W E Bigsby (ed), *Approaches to Popular Culture* (London 1976), pp 39–68, especially p 67.

68 *PJ*, 16 Jan 1858.
69 Ibid. 27 Feb 1858.
70 Ibid. 6 Feb 1858, 6 March 1858.
71 Ibid. 13 March 1858.
72 Ibid. 4 June 1859.
73 'Literary Culture', *PJ*, 22 July 1865, p 2.
74 Ibid. 29 Dec 1866, p 2.
75 *PJ*, 6 Nov 1869.
76 *How a Newspaper is Printed*, pp 53–5.
77 *People's Friend*, 5 Jan 1870.
78 A number of Scottish papers took up the competition idea including *AFP*, the *Buchan Observer*, and the *Glasgow Herald*; *see* Sinclair op.cit. p 184.
79 *Perthshire Advertiser* 'Centenary Number', op.cit. pp 9–11.
80 See Roger Lewis, 'Captain America Meets the Bash Street Kids: the Comic Form in Britain and the United States', in C W E Bigsby (ed), *Superculture American Popular Culture and Europe* (London 1975), pp 175–89. Strip cartoons also feature in the Aberdeen comic paper *Bon-Accord*, during the 1880s: *see*, for example, Vol 1, No. 14, 3 April 1880, p 3.
81 For a strongly-worded comment on the 'new journalism' in Scotland, from the pen of James Leatham *see* 'Twa Newspaper Billies', *Peterhead Sentinel*, 8 April 1905, p 4. For the rise of the phenomenon in England *see* Lee op.cit. pp 117–30; Milne op.cit. pp 191–2.
82 *Jubilee* op.cit. p 35.
83 *PJ*, 21 Jan 1860, p 4.

CHAPTER TWO

1 Thompson, 'An Enquiry into the Reading Habits of the Working Classes . . .' op.cit. pp 150–75, 226; *see also* William Harvey, *Scottish Chapbook Literature*, Paisley 1903, p 138.

2   Mairi Robinson *et al.* (eds), *The Concise Scots Dictionary* (Aberdeen 1985), p xi; *see also* Craig, *Scottish Literature and the Scottish People* . . ., op.cit. pp 57, 158 *n.1*, 303-4, 313.

3   Henry Grey Graham, *The Social Life of Scotland in the 18th Century* (5th edn London 1969), p 119; it may be fair to point out that Sheridan also lectured all over England, including in Oxford.

4   Aberdeen University Library, Local Collection, Box PΛ Periodical Sco (Q-Z).

5   Quoted in *Brown's Bookstall*, No. 9, Sept 1892, p 127.

6   Gregor, *An Echo of the Olden Time* . . ., op.cit. pp 38-9; *see also* Edwards, *Glimpses of Men and Manners* . . ., op.cit. for the complete Scots alphabet with equivalent phonetic values, pp 212, 215-16.

7   [Alan Reid], *Howetoon—Records of a Scottish Village by a Residenter* (Paisley, 1892), pp 54-8; see also *Rob Lindsay and his School, By one of his old Pupils*, (London n.d.), pp 17-19; [W S MacGillivray], *Cotbank and its Folks* [London 1911], pp 20-1; Alexander Whamond, *James Tacket A Humorous Tale of Scottish Life* (London n.d.), pp 11-14, 35-6, 96 ; 'The Story of a Tatie-Boodie', *WFP*, 1 June 1895, p 3. Bright children received little formal English instruction in school in any case, most of what went on was in Latin, although they would have experience of *writing* English as the language into which the original text was translated, *see* Robert Wilson, *George Mathieson, MA Schoolmaster of Inverallochy* (Aberdeen 1911), pp 12-14.

8   'The Rivals', *WFP*, 3 Jan 1880, p 2, shows Dr Melvin of Aberdeen Grammar School using Scots in class (although clearly not habitually).

9   *See* 'Notes and Notions by an Ex-Cow-Baillie', *AFP*, 7 Nov 1856, p 7.

10 James Will, 'On Buchan Humour', *Buchan Club Transactions*, Vol XIII, 1924-8, pp 13-16.

11 *WFP*, 26 May 1894, p 2; *see also* Gregor op.cit. pp 39-40.

12 *Jubilee* op.cit. p 8.

13 For the tradition of the epistolary leading article which lies behind the 'Sandy' letters and those of W D Latto, *see* Cowan, *The Newspaper in Scotland* . . . op.cit. p 27.

14 For correspondence attacking this vulgar Dundonian habit, see *PJ*, 8 May, 15 May 1858.

15 Ibid. 13 March 1858.

16 In a section 'To the reader' prefixed to *The Bodkin Papers*, Second Series, (Dundee 1883), Latto estimated that even by that stage he had written between three and four hundred Tammas Bodkin essays for the *People's Journal*. The column became a national institution, and William Lindsay often found that subscribers would take the *People's Journal* for the sake of Bodkin although otherwise hostile to the paper's radicalism. 'It was not until the *People's Journal* was introduced into Aberdeen that a really determined and successful effort was made by its proprietors to establish newsagencies over the North of Scotland. Acting as local publisher of that paper I found, in my wanderings to appoint agents, the greatest disinclination on the part of many booksellers of that day to accept an agency for a paper promulgating Radical politics. I endeavoured, invariably, to secure the services of the established booksellers in the first place, which they almost invariably declined, the result of this being that, by the year 1863-4, merchants in different branches of trade sold the *People's Journal* over many parts of the North of Scotland.

    In the appointment of news-agents I found the *nom de plume* "Tammas Bodkin" a name to conjure with. Once, when trying to induce a merchant to accept an agency, I heard a clear treble voice coming from a part of the premises I had not noticed before, saying, "Is that the paperie that Tammas Bodkin's funny stories are in, because, if it is, we'll tak it." At this point the good man, with a smile on his countenance, looked across at me and settled the matter by saying—"Weel, weel, if the wife's wintin't, we'll jist try it." I had many experiences similar to this.' Lindsay op.cit. pp 297-8. For William Robertson Nicoll's account of the impact of *PJ* and Tammas Bodkin on the village of Lumsden, Aberdeenshire, where he spent his boyhood, see *Jubilee* op.cit. pp 32-3.

17 pp v-vii.

18 'To the reader', *Bodkin Papers* op.cit.

19 *PJ*, 11 May 1867.

20 Ibid.

21 Ibid. 25 May 1867.

22 Ibid. 15 June, 29 June 1867, p 2.

23 *Hamilton Advertiser*, 19 Jan 1867-13 June 1868; a selection of the 'Geordie Short' papers were included in *Clydesdale Readings: being Humorous Sketches of Scottish Life, and Choice Selections from the 'Life of James Tacket,' and the writings of 'Geordie Short', 'Tam Jenkins', etc.*, 2nd edn (Hamilton, 1880), pp 65-163; The 'Jeems Sim' essays were subsequently reprinted in book-form, see J Cowe, *Jeems Sim: A Reprint of his Epis'les to the Northern Figaro* (Aberdeen 1887); *Sir Jeems Sim Letters* (Aberdeen n.d.). Leatham acknowledged authorship of 'Airchie Tait' in *Gateway*, Vol 1, No. 6, p 30.

24 Alexander John Ellis, *A Plea for Phonetic Spelling; or, the Necessity of Orthographic Reform* (London 1848), p 82. [Boswell] op.cit. pp 108-112; Sinclair op.cit. pp 45-6.

25 Ellis op.cit. pp 14-15, 16-17n, 54-5, 80-1.

26 *Phonetic Journal*, May 1848, pp 145-8.

27 For early articles referring explicity to Pitman and Ellis's work, and emanating from the circle of the youthful William Alexander, see *The Rural Echo*, No. III, pp 11-13, No. V, pp 8-10, 'The Spelling Reform and Education': these reveal, *inter alia*, that the Phonetic Society, founded in 1843, already had 3,000 members, and offered instruction through the post, free; see also *AFP*, 10 Feb 1854, p 7, 3 March 1854, p 6.

28 There is an entry for Anderson in *Boase*. I am indebted for this example to Mr John J Graham, compiler of *The Shetland Dictionary* (Stornoway 1979).

29 Graham op.cit., pp xx-xxvii.

30 *AFP*, 5 Nov 1858, p 6.

31 *East Fife Record* 17 March 1876, p 3; *see also* 'Heritors' Meeting at Crail', 7 March 1873, p 2, 'Oor Skule Baird', 26 March 1875, p 3, 'Crail School Board', 4 June 1875, p 3, and 'Crail Skule Boord', 24 March 1876. I am indebted for these references to the North East Fife District Library Service.

32 For further examples see the *Bailie*, Glasgow, and *Bon Accord* of Aberdeen.

33 *Seestu*, 1 March, p 3, 15 March, p 3, 29 March p 3, 19 April 1881, p 8.

34 *Seestu*, 30 Nov 1880, p 4.

35 *PJ*, 20 April 1861, p 2.

36 *See*, for example, 'The Phonetic Representation of Cockney' in P J Keating, *The Working Class in Victorian Fiction* (London 1971), pp 246-68. N F Blake, *Non-Standard Language in English Literature* (London 1981), pp 147-62; Martha Vicinus, *The Industrial Muse a Study of 19th century British Working Class Literature* (London 1974), pp 185-237. For dialect writing in West Indian

newspapers, see the entries for Michael McTurk and Edward A Cordle in Paula Burnett (ed), *The Penguin Book of Carribbean Verse* (Harmondsworth 1986), pp 374–5.

37 *See* Leo Marx, 'The Vernacular Tradition in American Literature' in Joseph J Kwiat and Mary C Turpie (eds), *Studies in American Culture Dominant Ideas and Images* (Minneapolis 1960), pp 109–22.

38 *Dictionary of American Biography*, XVII, pp. 39–40; III, pp 162–4; VIII, pp 312–14.

39 *The Paisley and Renfrewshire Gazette*.

40 *Yankee Drolleries. The Most Celebrated Works by the Best American Humorists* (London 1868); *More Yankee Drolleries. A Second Series of Celebrated Works by the Best American Humorists* (London n.d. [but 1869]).

41 Andrew Hook, *Scotland and America: A Study of Cultural Relations 1750–1835* (Glasgow 1975), *passim*; Bernard Aspinwall, *Portable Utopia, Glasgow and the United States 1820–1920* (Aberdeen 1984), *passim*; see also Young, *The Rousing of the Scottish Working Class*, op.cit. pp 34–5, 42–3, 108, 119, 148–9, 153–5, 160, 169.

42 Pirated American fiction using American English dialogue circulated fairly extensively in Victorian Scotland; *see*, for example, *Clara's Rescue; or Ned Wentworth's Vow* (Glasgow 1871), an early Western of some 30,000 words published in enlarged chapbook form. For a typical example of the stereotyped American in book-length fiction see Col Washington Dodge, Sheriff of Coontail County, State of California, villain of the serial novel 'Polly, The Tearoom Girl; or, A Heroine of Glasgow', *PJ*, 13 Nov 1897–30 April 1898, p 4; or Robert Buchanan's coolly slaughterous sheriff in 'A Hero in Spite of Himself', *WFP*, 4 Dec 1886, p 2. A number of Scottish papers carried the syndicated column 'Yankee Humour', and there are several explicit Scots imitations of 'Artemus Ward', *see* 'To the Editor of the Hoo'let' in *The Hoo'let* 'intended to be a source of amusement and political instruction to the inhabitants of Paisley . . .', No. 1, in *Paisley Comic Serials, Issued During the Parliamentary Election of 1868* (n.p. [but Paisley] 1868).

43 *Josh Billings, His Sayings* (New York 1866), pp 40–1; speech-influenced departures from standard orthography have been made the subject of phonological field research in the United States—*see*, for example, Sumner Ives, *The Phonology of the Uncle Remus Stories*, Publications of the American Dialect Society, No. 22 (Gainesville 1954), *passim*, but especially pp 3–7.

44 Burgess op.cit. p 9; the poem was originally published in *PJ*, 18 March 1865; *see also* an enlarged edition of Burgess' poems, *'Poute!' Being Poutry, Poetry, and Prose By the late Alexander Burgess, Coupmyhorn, Kennoway* (Cupar n.d.) which includes a brief life, pp iii–iv.

45 'A Visit to an Aberdeenshire Warlock', *WFP*, 28 June–19 July 1879, p 2. 'A Criminal Officer of the Old School. Being Passages in the Life and Professional Experiences of George Webster, Sheriff and Criminal Officer, Oldmeldrum' *WFP*, 18 Jan–24; May 1879, p 2. The latter is attributed to William Alexander in *AFP*, 21 Feb 1894.

46 12 Oct 1895, p 1.

47 3 Aug 1895, p 1.

48 Ibid.

49 For David Scott and the *Sentinel* see W L Taylor, *Bibliography of Peterhead Periodical Literature* (privately printed 1889), pp 7–11; the fullest account of Scott, an intriguing figure in his own right, is contained in James Leatham's biographical study *Daavit: the True Story of a Personage* (Turriff n.d. [but? 1929]).

50 My account of James Leatham is drawn from the following sources: Bob
    Duncan, *James Leatham* (*1865-1945*), (Aberdeen 1978), *passim*; Leatham's own
    autobiographical articles entitled 'Sixty Years of World Mending', beginning in
    Gateway, Vol XXVIII-XXIX, April-May 1940 and continuing irregularly
    thereafter, and his semi-autobiographical novel, *D'ye Mind Lang Syne? A Matter
    of Fact Romance* (Huddersfield, n.d.); the social and linguistic attitudes of the
    'Airchie Tait' column may be compared with his earlier statements in *The
    Ancient Hind: A Monologue in the Aberdeenshire Dialect* (Aberdeen 1891),
    especially pp 26-8; for his continuing interest in spoken Scots *see* his *Fisherfolk
    of the North-East* (Turriff n.d. [but post 1930]), especially pp 26-8, 49-50; for the
    S.D.F. in Scotland, *see* Young op.cit. pp 145-9, and in England, Chushichi
    Tsuzuki, *H M Hyndman and British Socialism* (Oxford 1961), pp 64-109.
51 For a brief history of the *Buchan Observer see* W. L. Taylor op.cit. pp 12-14.
52 'Printing in Peterhead', *Peterhead Sentinel*, 15 Oct 1884, p 5; this also gives an
    account of the printing activities of the ballad collector Peter Buchan.
53 James Leatham, 'Paper on "An Aberdeenshire Classic—Centenary of Dr William
    Alexander"' in *Buchan Club Transaction*, Vol XIII, 1926, p 123.
54 *Peterhead Sentinel*, 10 Sept. 1904, p 5. (The Buchan district poorhouse was
    situated at Maud.)
55 Ibid. 5 Nov 1904, p 5.
56 *see* n. 49 above.
57 *Peterhead Sentinel*, 6 June 1903, p 4; 19 Dec 1903, p 5.

CHAPTER THREE

1 On 'Tam o'Shanter' *see* Cowan, *The Newspaper in Scotland* . . ., op.cit. pp 9-10;
    ibid. pp 43, 47-8 for the *Elgin Courier* and *Berwick Advertiser* (a fuller account of
    the literary content of the *Courier* is given by James Grant, its former editor in
    Metropolitan Weekly and Provincial Press, pp 426-7); Norrie, *Edinburgh
    Newspapers Past and Present* op. cit. p 20 is the authority for the newspaper
    serialisation of Scott; *see also* Graham Pollard, 'Serial Fiction' in John Carter (ed),
    New Paths in Book Collecting (London 1934), pp 245-77, but especially pp 257-8.
 2 Altick, *The English Common Reader* . . . op. cit. pp 262-4.
 3 James, *Fiction for the Working Man* . . . op. cit. p 8.
 4 Bertram, *Some Memories of Books, Authors and Events*, op. cit. pp 103-4; *see
    also* pp 86-7. For number publication in England, *see* Altick op.cit. pp 279-80.
    For the last stage in the evolution of the chapbook when it began to merge with
    the sensational novella see John Fraser, *The Humorous Chapbooks of Scotland*,
    Part One (New York 1873) pp 141-2: at least one example cited by Fraser
    survives, see *Clara's Rescue* (Ch 2 *n*. 42 above); for an interesting neo-gothic
    example see *The Iron Shroud; or, Italian Revenge* (Paisley: Printed by Caldwell
    and Son, 2 New Street, 1839). For more information concerning the Caldwell
    Press *see* 'John Strathesk' (ed), *Hawkie The Autobiography of a Gangrel* (Glasgow
    1888), pp 34-5, 96.
 5 1 Aug 1838, p 47.
 6 1 March 1838, p 5.
 7 Ibid. pp 5-6.
 8 2 April 1838, pp 14-15.
 9 For the traditional basis of several of these stories see H[ugh] G[ilzean] Reid
    (ed), *Lowland Legends: chiefly relating to the Buchan District* (Edinburgh 1865),
    passim.
10 1 May 1838, pp 21-3; *see also* Margaret Dalziel, *Popular Fiction 100 Years Ago An*

Unexplored Tract of Literary History (London 1957), pp 129–34; *see also* John R Reed, *Victorian Conventions* (Ohio UP, 1975) pp 105–15.

11   1 Aug 1838, pp 43–7; 1 Sept 1838, pp 51–2; *see also* Reed op. cit. pp 268–88.

12   1 June 1838, pp 29–31.

13   *PJ*, 12 June 1858.

14   For a useful account of serialisation although wholly from an English point of view, *see* Pollard op.cit. pp 245–77.

15   I am indebted for biographical details concerning David Pae to his grandson Mr David G Pae, and the following published sources: 'Sudden Death of Mr David Pae, of the *People's Friend*', *Dundee Advertiser*, 10 May 1884; 'Funeral of the Late Mr David Pae', *Dundee Advertiser*, 14 May 1884; 'Memorial Papers on the Late David Pae, Esq of Craigmount, Newport, Fifeshire', reprinted in *Eustace the Outcast: or, The Smugglers of St Abb's* (Dundee 1884), pp 385–96; *see also* Norrie op.cit. p 24.

16   Later published as a novella with the title 'The Next of Kin; or, A Christmas Day in a Lawyer's Office', in the *People's Friend*, 3rd Series Vol II, No. 94, 22 Dec 1875, pp 801–12.

17   *See* A C Cheyne, *The Transforming of the Kirk—Victorian Scotland's Religious Revolution* (Edinburgh 1983), pp 60–87; for the work of the Evangelical Union in spreading the gospel of unlimited atonement, and how the doctrines of self-help and self-improvement undermined old style Calvinism, *see* Lindsay, *Some Notes: Personal and Public* op. cit. pp 272–9, 326–8; *see also* Stewart J Brown, *Thomas Chalmers and the Godly Commonwealth in Scotland* (Oxford 1982), pp 138, 150, 213–16. On the obligation to provide mental as well as physical nourishment to lower social classes see 'The "Working Classes" and their Literature: what it is and what it ought to be', No. 1–4, *Edinburgh Christian Magazine*, April–Sept 1856, pp 10–13, 37–41, 123–7, 179–82.

18   [David Pae], *Two Years After and Onwards; or, The Approaching War amongst the Powers of Europe* (London 1864), p 4.

19   The first of these in particular created a great stir, running through several editions; it was even translated into Welsh.

20   *Two Years After . . .*, p 150.

21   *See* J F C Harrison, *The Second Coming Popular Millenarianism 1780–1850* (London 1979), pp 3–10; 222–7; *see also* Andrew Landale Drummond, *Edward Irving and his Circle* (London n.d. [but 1934]), pp 56–7, 110–64.

22   For reviews of Pae novels in the denominational press *see The Scottish Christian Journal*, 3rd Series (Edinburgh 1858), pp 149–50, 198, 316–17.

23   p 33.

24   Bound in with the National Library of Scotland copy of Pae's *The Merchant's Daughter* (Edinburgh [1857]), is a publisher's advertisement which sandwiches *George Sandford* between Ralph Erskine's *Gospel Sonnets* and a treatise on *The Life, Prophecies and Times of Alexander Peden*.

25   For the corrupting tendencies of chapbooks, *see* William Alexander, 'Literature of the People—Past and Present', *Good Words*, Vol xvii, 1876, pp 92–6; *The Third Annual Report of the Aberdeen Book Agent and Colporteur Society*, 1859, gives an interesting account of the distribution of religious books and tracts in the North-East with lively bothy scenes including dialogue: 'The farmer swore terribly and said "Fit am I needin wi' reeligion, man . . .'", Aberdeen City Library, Pamphlets 000/016.299; *see also* 'Diffusion of a Healthy Literature', *AFP*, 6 March 1857, p 2; 'The Colporteur's Work', *WFP*, 1 March 1873, p 5, stresses that chapbooks and song-slips were particularly prized by the common people if they had the 'threadie o' blue'.

26   Harvey, *Printing in Stirling*, pp 78–9; *The "Stirling Observer" Press* op.cit. pp 35–9.

27   Harrison, op.cit. pp 50–54. For a brief account of the tractarian movement in England, see Altick, op.cit. pp 72–96.

28   *Christian Advocate*, Vol III, No. 9, Sept 1859, p 4; *see also* Craig, *Scottish Literature and the Scottish People . . .* op. cit. pp 199–206.

29   'The "Working Classes" and their Literature . . .', op.cit. pp 37, 39, 124, 181.

30   Richard Stang, *The Theory of the Novel in England 1850–1870* (London 1959), pp 48, 67–72.

31   For the development of the orphan theme in England, especially as related to love and class-difference, *see* James op.cit. pp 102–9; *see also* Raymond Williams, *The Long Revolution* (Harmondsworth 1975 [first pub London 1961]), pp 84–8; and Reed op. cit. pp 250–67.

32   *Jessie the Bookfolder; or, The Heroism of Love* (Leeds 1865), pp 320–1.

33   It is one of the paradoxes of the period that liberal evangelicals were in the forefront of the movement towards secularisation; so, Norman Macleod as editor of *Good Words* was amongst the first to solicit fiction contributions from established secular novelists for an explicitly religious periodical; *see* Altick op.cit. p 125, W J Couper, 'Bibliography of Edinburgh Periodical Literature' in *Scottish Notes and Queries*, Vol V, 2nd Series, Oct 1903, pp 56–7. Dalziel op.cit. quotes the 'essential rules of healthful fiction' laid down by the Religious Tract Society in its *64th Annual Report*, 1863, p 10: stories should be
     (1)   *Moral*—no vice being invested with interest;
     (2)   *Natural*—true both to nature and to fact, free from false representations of life and exaggerations of character;
     (3)   *Unexciting*—leaving the spirit calm and the passions not unduly moved.'
                                                                                                     (p 67)

34   Norrie op.cit. pp 23–4.

35   'Funeral of the late Mr David Pae', *Dundee Advertiser*, 14 May 1884.

36   Quotations from the *Middlesborough News* and the *North Briton* cited from publisher's advertisement bound in with Pae's novel *The Merchant's Daughter* (Edinburgh [1857]).

37   *Jubilee* op.cit. pp 18, 34.

38   William Power, *Literature and Oatmeal* (London 1935), pp 163–4.

39   George Blake, *Barrie and the Kailyard School* (London 1951), pp 9–13; *see also* pp 14–16.

40   Francis Russell Hart, *The Scottish Novel* (London 1978), p 87; *see also* p 89.

41   Cowan op.cit. p 301.

42   'The Factory Girl, or the Dark Places of Glasgow, Showing Evil overruled for Good, Iniquity Punished and Virtue Rewarded', *PJ*, 5 Sept 1863–23 April 1864; the title varies between newspaper and book editions, *see* note 57 below. For a near contemporary response to the story *see* 'Lucy the Factory Girl Was Willie Erskine's Favourite' in *Airdrie & Coatbridge Advertiser*, 'Centenary Supplement', 5 March 1955: '. . . the serial story featured from week to week and eagerly followed as a Saturday night's entertainment as we anxiously awaited the sequel to the previous week's instalment, which had left the heroine in deadly peril. The one to which I would like to devote special attention was called 'Lucy, the Factory Girl.' . . . I think I might be about ten years of age when this story was appearing and I used to go and read the current chapter or two to an elderly widow who had a small confection and fruiterer's shop in High Street at that time. This was always on Saturday forenoon in her back-room after the shop was opened and before a nice fire with the kettle singing on the hob, I read

the latest instalment to her often in a broken voice and between sobs while the old lady kept wiping her eyes on her clean white apron, as the story described the hardships and misfortunes that befel poor Lucy. Ultimately it transpired that Lucy was the real owner of the factory where she had worked and endured so much, having been wrongfully deprived of her estate by a wicked uncle.' For a sophisticated contemporary appreciation, see William Westall, 'Newspaper Fiction', *Lippincott's Monthly Magazine*, Vol XL, 1890, pp 77–88, especially pp 81–5, 87. The *PJ* serialisation was not the first appearance of the novel in print; correspondence in the possession of the family shows Pae at work on the story during the winter of 1858/9, and the earliest of the book editions, *Lucy, the Factory Girl; or, the Secrets of the Tontine Close* (Edinburgh 1860), had actually been published some three years before.

43 *PJ*, 20 Feb 1864, p 2.

44 Strathesk, op.cit. *passim*, but especially p 33.

45 *See*, for example, Thackeray's splendid satire on the affectation of thieves slang by the Bulwer/Ainsworth school which gives a vivid idea of their style:

> One, two, three! It is the signal that Black Vizard had agreed on. 'Mofy! Is that your snum?' said a voice from the area. 'I'll gully the dag and bimbole the clicky in a snuffkin.'
> 'Nuffle your clod, and beadle your glumbanions,' said the Vizard, with a dreadful oath. 'This way, men: if they screak, out with your snickers and slick! Look to the pewter room, Blowser. You, Mark, to the old gaff's mopus box! and I', added he, in a lower but more horrible voice, 'I will look to Amelia!'

Quoted in Keith Hollingsworth, *The Newgate Novel 1830–1847* (Detroit 1963) p 206.

46 *PJ*, 19 Sept 1863, p 2.

47 *See*, for example, 'Haggart, the Housebreaker; or, Stranger than Fiction. By the Author of "Experiences of an Edinburgh Detective"', which began its run in *PJ*, 11 Nov 1876, a story with strong elements of social realism which takes the reader into the Edinburgh Bridewell and the world of the city's teenage gangs; the professional criminal element all use Pae-type jargon, as do the underworld characters in a story published near the end of the century, 'Polly The Tearoom Girl; or, a Heroine of Glasgow', *PJ*, 13 Nov 1897–30 April 1898, p 4, as for example in the instalment for 29 Jan 1898.

48 'Ali Baba' circulated in Scotland as a chapbook during the first half of the nineteenth century, *see* William Harvey, *John Fraser An Old Stirling Printer and Teacher* (Stirling 1926), p 7.

49 *See* J F C Harrison, *Robert Owen, and the Owenites in Britain and America* (London 1969), p 15.

50 *PJ*, 20 Feb 1862, p 2.

51 *See* J Butt, 'Robert Owen of New Lanark: his critique of British Society', in J Butt and I F Clarke, *The Victorians and Social Protest* (Newton Abbot 1973), pp 13–32, especially p 19.

52 For a brief discussion of George MacDonald's use of this motif at a slightly later period, *see* Hart op.cit. pp 101–2, 116–17.

53 Harrison, *Robert Owen* . . . p 60.

54 Dalziel, op.cit. p 96; *see also* Williams op.cit. pp 78–81 and Reed op.cit. pp 59–76.

55 *PJ*, 3 Oct 1863, p 2.

56 'Our Closing Remarks', *PJ*, 23 April 1864, p 2.

57 Pae novels published in book form in order of publication are as follows:

George Sandford; or, the Drapers Assistant (Edinburgh 1853); *Jessie Melville; or, The Double Sacrifice* (Edinburgh 1856) [reprinted as *Jessie the Bookfolder; or, The Heroism of Love* (Leeds 1865)]; *Fraud and Friendship; or, The Orphan and the Foundling of the King's Printing-House* (Edinburgh 1857); *The Merchant's Daughter; or, Love and Mammon* (Edinburgh 1857); *The Cloud on the Home; or, a Wife's Devotion: a Temperance Tale* (London 1858); *Lucy the Factory Girl; or, the Secrets of the Tontine Close* (Edinburgh 1860); *Mary Paterson; or, the Fatal Error. A Story of the Burke and Hare Murders* (London 1866); *Eustace the Outcast; or, the Smugglers of St Abb's* (Dundee, 1884); *'Hard Times'; or, the Trials and Sorrows of the Linwood Family. A Tale of the Lancashire Cotton Famine* (2nd edn Manchester 1886); *Grace Darling, the Heroine of the Longstone Lighthouse; or, The Two Wills. A Tale of the Loss of the 'Forfarshire '* (Dundee 1888).

In an essay attached to the memorial edition of *Eustace the Outcast* (1884, as above) Andrew Stewart, deputy editor of the *People's Friend* and a long-term associate, gave a list of more than forty serial novels by Pae in their order of publication; it is reproduced below, with full titles supplied from other sources wherever possible, additions appearing within square brackets: 'Jessie Melville, or the Double Sacrifice'; 'The Merchant's Daughter, or Love and Mammon'; 'Frederick the Foundling [and Ellen Campbell; or, Lights and Shades of City Life. A Tale of Lanarkshire and Midlothian]'; 'Fraud and Friendship'; 'Clara Howard, or the Captain's Bride'; 'Lucy the Factory Girl, or the Secrets of the Tontine Close'; 'The Heiress of Wellwood'; 'Nelly Preston, or the Lawyer's Plot'; 'George Dalton, or the Convict's Revenge'; 'Norah Cushaleen, or the Murdered Wife'; 'Biddy Macarthy, or the Hunted Felon': 'Flora the Orphan, or Love and Crime'; 'Basil Hamilton, or the Ticket of Leave'; 'Very Hard Times, a Tale of the Cotton Famine'; 'Helen Armstrong, or the Rose of Tweedside'; 'Effie Seaton, or the Dark House in Murdoch's Close'; 'Captain Wyld's Gang, a Glasgow Tale'; 'The Smuggler Chief'; 'Mary Paterson, or the Fatal Error'; 'The Cloud on the Home'; 'The Gipsy's Prophecy [or the Hermit of the Glen]'; 'The Haunted Castle, or a Brother's Treachery'; 'Eustace the Outcast'; 'Jeannie Sinclair, or the Lily of the Strath'; 'The Heir of Douglas'; 'Cast on the World, [or, the Border Marriage: a Story of the Great Glasgow Bank Robbery']; 'Annie Grey'; 'The Laird of Birkencleuch [or, The Maiden's Choice. A Tale of the Convenanters]': 'Clanranald [or, The Fugitives. A Tale of the 'Forty-Five']'; 'Isaac Barton's Crime [or, Guilty but Not Proven]'; 'Helen Moir, or Love and Honour. [A Tale of the Clyde]'; 'The Foster Brother [or, the Orphan of the Wreck]'; 'Annabel, or the Temptation'; 'Mayhew the Millspinner [or, The Stolen Will]'; 'Victor Mordaunt [or, The Lost Ships. A Glasgow Story of 50 Years Ago]'; 'Harold the Outlaw [or, The Gauger of Skene]'; 'A Shadowed Life [or, the Mystery of Greystone Quarry]'; 'Mabel's Love [or The Beauty of Raystock]'; '[Am Fogarrach Gealach; or] The Exploits of Rob Roy'; 'Paul Jones [the Robber of the Seas; or Twenty Years in Exile. A Tale of the Solway]'; 'Deacon Brodie [or, Death in the Dice Box]'; 'Grace Darling'; 'The Lost Heir of Glencorran' [or, The Emigrants. A Tale of Highland Eviction]'. Stewart acknowledged that the list was probably incomplete (*Eustace the Outcast*, p 388) and at least a further two titles, 'Wild Oats; or, Sowing and Reaping', and 'The Forged Will or, The Orphan and the Foundling' might perhaps be added to it, on the grounds of their inclusion as Pae's by syndicating newspapers amongst various other titles known to be by him.

58 [Boswell] *About Newspapers . . .*, op.cit. pp 113-7.

59 Turner, 'The Syndication of Fiction in Provincial Newspapers . . .', op.cit. pp 12-30.

60 *See* 'The Stereotyping Process' in *How a Newspaper is Printed*, pp 23-5.

61 Turner op.cit. pp 39-48.

62 *See* Conrad Eugene Tanzy, 'Publishing the Victorian Novel: A Study of the Economic Relationships of Novelists and Publishers in Victorian England' (Ann Arbor University Microfilms 1961), pp 55-7, 114-58.

63 Aberdeen and North of Scotland Newspaper and Printing Co Ltd, Business Committee Minute Book, Nov 1877-May 1883, Aberdeen University Library, MS 2770, 15 March, 29 March 1878.

64 Ibid. 4 Oct 1878.

65 Ibid. 29 Oct 1880.

66 Sinclair, *Fifty Years of Newspaper Life*, . . ., op.cit. p 184.

67 Westall op.cit. pp 77-88.

68 For what a writer could earn by doing this, *see* 'The Newspaper Press', *Quarterly Review*, Vol CL, Oct 1880, pp 498-537, especially pp 533-4.

69 Aberdeen University Library, MS 2770, Directors' Minute Book, May 1884-Dec 1894, 14 Nov 1884, 13 Feb 1885.

70 The *Fife Free Press & Kirkcaldy Guardian*, 15 April 1871; 22 April 1871; 29 April 1871; *see also* 20 May 1871: 'To our Readers. Since the introduction of the excellent and interesting Story now appearing in its columns, the circulation of the "Fife Free Press" has been steadily on the increase; and, at the request of numerous readers, we have resolved to cultivate this feature of the paper, and with that in view, we have pleasure in announcing A NEW STORY from the pen of a popular writer, entitled "The Forest Girl".

The new story is, like the one now appearing in the columns of the "Fife Free Press", founded on fact, abounding in incident and anecdote, and is written in a style which we unhesitatingly guarantee to interest, delight, and captivate the reader.' For a further comment on the effect of serial fiction on newspaper circulations, see Turner op.cit. p 89, and Westall, op.cit. p 80.

71 *Jubilee*, pp 7-8; 'Sudden Death of Mr David Pae, of the *People's Friend*', *Dundee Advertiser*, 10 May 1884.

72 *PJ*, 22 Oct 1881, p 2—17 June 1882, p 2.

73 The novel has obvious topical reference: the Crofters' War started in 1879 and 1882 saw the setting up of the Napier Commission into the condition of the crofters and cottars in the Highlands, *see* Eric Richards, *History of the Highland Clearances* (London 1982), pp 472-501.

74 For the changing climate of belief and social practice in Scotland at this period *see* Cheyne op.cit. 157-74.

75 Westall op.cit. pp 80-1.

CHAPTER FOUR

1 Hart, *The Scottish Novel* op.cit. p 88; *see also* 87-92.

2 This first appeared in serial form in the *Daily Free Press*, 22 March 1875-27 Sept 1875, p 4. All subsequent references are to the Carter edition (Finzean 1981).

3 Alexander Mackilligan, 'Paper on "Johnny Gibb of Gushetneuk"', *Buchan Club Transactions*, Vol XIII, 1926, pp 96-120; 'The Late Mr William Alexander, LL D', *Daily Free Press*, 21 Feb 1894, p 4; *'see also* 'Death of Mr Wm Alexander, LL D', *Aberdeen Journal*, 20 Feb 1894, p 4.

The fact of the estrangement is noted by Ian Carter in '"To roose the countra fae the caul' morality o' a deid moderatism"; William Alexander and *Johnny Gibb of Gushetneuk', Northern Scotland*, Vol II, No. 2 1976-7, p 155 *n* 4, quoting a letter from Alexander Mackilligan, the best of Alexander's earlier biographers, to Dr Malcolm Bulloch: 'I have known nothing more painful in journalism than the long and bitter estrangement between Dr Alexander and the other proprietors of the "Free Press"—especially Mr Henry Alexander and Mr William Watt—on the Home Rule issue . . . The quarrel clouded Dr Alexander's later years.'

4   [Alexander], op.cit. p 8.

5   The standard bibliography of William Alexander's works published in book or pamphlet form is contained in *Buchan Club Transactions*, Vol XIII, 1926, pp 120-1, compiled by R Murdoch Lawrence.

6   *WFP*, 25 Nov 1876, p 4; *Daily Free Press*, 21 Feb 1894, p 4; see also *WFP, 24 Feb 1894*, p 5.

7   Quoted in 'The Alexander Family', *Bon Accord*, New Series No. 8, 5 June 1926, pp 4-6.

8   Alexander's standard account of the rage for improvement is contained in *Notes and Sketches* op.cit.; his series of articles entitled 'The Peasantry of North-Eastern Scotland', *United Presbyterian Magazine*, Sept, Oct, Dec, 1884, pp 377-9, 426-9, 519-23, is a useful summary and extension of this. For a modern account *see* Carter *Farmlife . . .*, op.cit. pp 10-75; a convenient summary of Carter's views will be found in 'Class and Culture among Farm Servants in the North-East, 1840-1914' in A Allan MacLaren (ed), *Social Class in Scotland: Past and Present* (Edinburgh n.d.), pp 105-27.

9   For the ambience of folklore in the Aberdeenshire of Alexander's boyhood and youth, see *Northern Rural Life* op.cit. pp 16, 137-8, 154-8.

10 'The Late Mr William Alexander, LL D', *Daily Free Press*, 21 Feb 1894, p 4.

11 For a brief account of Alexander's early life *see* Mackilligan op.cit. pp 98-9; for a typically slighting assessment of parochial schoolmasters *see* 'The Late William McCombie, Esq', *AFP*, 13 May 1870, p 5.

12 *See* Alexander's short story 'Isaac Ronald the Dominie' in *Life & Work*, Vol IV, Jan pp 3-7, Feb pp 19-21, March pp 35-8, April pp 59-61, May pp 67-70, June pp 83-5, July pp 99-102, Aug pp 115-17, 1882; especially Ch IX—'A School Day'.

13 For a useful account of McCombie's life and character *see* Robert Harvey Smith, *An Aberdeenshire Village Propaganda Forty Years Ago With an Introduction by William Alexander*, LL D (Edinburgh 1889), pp 50-119.

14 Edinburgh 1835 and London 1842 respectively; *see also* Smith op.cit. p xi.

15 Obituary, 'William McCombie' by James Macdonnell in the *Spectator*, reprinted in *AFP*, 20 May 1870; his paper's own obituary 'The Late William McCombie, Esq,' is almost certainly by William Alexander see *n*. II above.

16 Ibid.

17 Smith, op.cit. *passim*, gives the history of the Mutual Instruction Union; *see also* Ian Carter, 'The Mutual Improvement Movement in North-East Scotland in the 19th Century', *Aberdeen University Review*, 1976, Vol XLVI, pp 383-92.

18 Mackilligan op.cit. p 99; Smith op.cit. pp 37, 40*ff*.

19 *The Rural Echo, and Magazine of the North of Scotland Mutual Instruction Associations*. January to June 1850. Conducted by the Lentush Club (Aberdeen 1850).

20 Ibid. II, pp 11-13; *see also* No. III, pp 4-6, 'The Observing Faculties.'

21 The compilers of the *Rural Echo* gave amongst their reasons for stopping publication that 'certain of us wish to make ourselves acquainted with the

French and German languages, in order the more effectually to study the philosophical tendencies of the present age.' No. VI, p 16.

22   Smith op.cit. pp 110–26.

23   Smith op.cit. p 85; 'Aberdeen Newspaper Life', *WFP*, 10 March 1888, gives the history of the *North of Scotland Gazette* and those connected with it.

24   The *Rural Echo* declared 'the management of a debate, or rational conversation, is . . . the principal object of consideration.' No. I, p 4.

25   *North of Scotland Gazette*, 25 March 1853, p 2.

26   Mackilligan op.cit. p 100.

27   *AFP* 24 June 1853, p 6; 8 July 1853, p 6.

28   *Penny Free Press*, 24 July 1855, p 2.

29   Ibid. 31 July 1855, p 2.

30   Ibid. 21 Aug 1855, p 2.

31   Cheyne, *The Transforming of the Kirk . . .* , op.cit. pp 114, 118; for possible influence on Alexander by the later social theories of Thomas Chalmers, *see* Brown, *Thomas Chalmers and the Godly Commonwealth . . .* pp 68, 285–96, 350, 367–8; *see also* J F C Harrison, *Robert Owen . . .*, op.cit. pp 15–31, 47–51.

32   *Penny Free Press*, 23 Oct 1855, p 2.

33   Ibid.

34   James Leatham, 'An Aberdeenshire Classic—Centenary of Dr William Alexander', *Transactions of the Buchan Club*, Vol XIII, 1926, pp 123–34, especially p 124; Mackilligan, op.cit. pp 106, 107.

35   [Alexander], pp 4–5.

36   *AFP*, 17 Oct 1865, p 4.

37   Ibid. 29 Jan 1866 p 4.

38   Ibid. 13 Feb 1866, p 4.

39   *AFP*, 20 Aug 1862–16 Jan 1863, p 7; 11 Dec 1863–1 Jan 1864; only one number traced, 6 May 1864, p 9.

40   For Alexander's account of improvements in transport and communication in the North-East at about this time see *Northern Rural Life* op.cit. Chs XII–XIII.

41   *AFP*, 28 April 1868, p 4.

42   Ibid. 26 March 1867, p 4.

43   *See* 'The Peasantry of North-Eastern Scotland', *United Presbyterian Magazine*, Sept 1884, pp 378–9; Oct, p 428.

44   *Onward and Upward*, Vol IX, August 1891, pp 220–1; for Alexander's comments on hereditary characteristics amongst the fisher population of North-East Scotland, see *Gordonhaven: Scenes and Sketches of Fisher Life in the North. By an Old Fisherman. With an introduction by W Alexander, LL D* (Edinburgh 1887), pp v–ix.

45   See *Northern Rural Life* op.cit. p 26.

46   For an account of the genesis of this work, *see* Mackilligan op.cit. pp 107–8.

47   *WFP*, 23 Jan–27 Feb 1872; for a personal account of deteriorating conditions for the agricultural workforce *see* 'Eleven Years at Farm-Work: being A True Tale of Farm-Servant Life', *WFP*, 26 July–11 Oct. 1879 p 2.

48   For another comment on this *see* 'The Peasantry of North-Eastern Scotland', *U.P.Mag.*, Sept 1884, p 379, Oct, 1884, p 427.

49   This story has been reprinted in Douglas Gifford (ed), *Scottish Short Stories 1800–1900* (London 1971), pp 179–201.

50   *WFP*, 21 Dec 1872, p 2.

51   *Life Among my Ain Folk*, pp 134–7.

52   *See also* the author's Preface to *Johnny Gibb of Gushetneuk* (Aberdeen 1871):

'The intention of the writer was to portray, as faithfully as he could, some forms of character not uncommon in the rural life of Aberdeenshire a quarter of a century ago, at least; the effort being to make the purely ideal persons introduced literally "true to nature", as it had manifested itself under his own eyes, or within his own experience, in their habits of thought and modes of speech.'

53 It has even been *condemned* because of its realism, Leatham op.cit. pp 127-30, 133.

54 Alexander Mackie 'Introduction and Appreciation' prefixed to the 15th edn of *Johnny Gibb* (Edinburgh 1908), pp xiv-xviii: [a subtle and perceptive essay, easily the best of the older studies]; Leatham op.cit. p 132.

55 Robert Anderson, 'An Aberdeenshire Author', *Caledonia*, I/II, 1895, pp 47-53; 137-43; Leatham op.cit. is typical of this position, he notes that 'William Alexander is in method a realist, probably without having had any theory about his art at all. His is simply the dry, caustic, unromantic, and generally unemotional style of a man of the bothy with a pen in hand' (p 130).

56 Ibid. pp 125-6.

57 A source close to Alexander discusses his linguistic intentions in *Johnny Gibb* in the following terms: 'Philologically, "Johnny Gibb" is a work of very great value. The author is as successful in the mode of speech he represents his characters as using, as he is in delineating otherwise their manners and customs. The dialect the interlocutors speak is what is distinguished as the Buchan Scotch. It differs somewhat, not very widely, from the dialects of the districts adjoining its seat; but Aberdeenshire Scotch, of which it may be reckoned a sub-dialect, differs considerably from the Scotch for which a place has been won in literature by the writings of Robert Burns and Walter Scott. Of the dialect it exemplifies, "Johnny Gibb" is, out of sight, the best specimen in existence. The peculiarities are accurately preserved, and this without straining, without even a sentence having the appearance of being manufactured to introduce some particular word or phrase . . . Many of these forms of speech are exceedingly forcible and expressive, and it is frequently difficult, sometimes it is impossible, to convert them into English equivalents. The task of compiling a glossary in a case like the present is a very formidable one, but the difficulty has been faced . . . and fairly overcome. The idioms prevalent in this locality, many of which were altogether unknown to Jamieson, and have been passed unnoticed by minor lexicographers, are accurately and clearly explained in the glossary now appended to this volume. This adds very materially to the value of the book, since it has found and will continue to find, many readers whose ignorance of the dialect prevents their proper appreciation of it, and whose enjoyment must be greatly enhanced by the explanations and hints given here of the meaning of dialectic peculiarities. A Note prefixed to the glossary contains a few sensible remarks on Aberdeenshire modes of speech. The history and genesis of local words and idioms such as are here commented on are well worthy of the attention of the student of language. The service which the author of "Johnny Gibb" has rendered to philology is all the greater that the expressions thus preserved, and presented, not as bare expressions, but in their natural connections, are falling every year into disuse. Ere another generation pass away, many of them will cease to be employed by the people. All the more honour is due on this account to him who stores up in a book like this what explorers in after times will recognise as fossil language *in situ*.' 'Literature', *WFP*, 5 July 1873, p 2; see also *Northern Rural Life*, p 16.

58 Mackilligan op.cit. p 96, 110.
59 Mackie op.cit. pp v–xxiv: *see* especially p v.
60 Ian Carter, "'To roose the countra fae the caul' morality o' a deid moderatism'";
    William Alexander and *Johnny Gibb of Gushetneuk'*, *Northern Scotland*, Vol II,
    No 2, 1976–7, pp 145–62.
61 *See*, for example, 'The Social Conditions of Farm Servants', *WFP*, 11 May 1872,
    pp 4–5, 'The Domestic Servants Question', *WFP*, 25 May 1872, pp 4–5; 'Farm
    Servants and Emigration', *WFP*, 1 June 1872, pp 4–5; 'How we Manage at our
    Board', *WFP*, 8 June–22 June 1872, p 5; 'Land Tenure at Home and Abroad',
    WFP, 13 July 1872, pp 4–5; 'The Footdee Fishers and their Dwellings' *WFP*, 7
    Dec 1872, p 2; *see also* Carter, *Farmlife*, pp 165–75.
62 'Literature', *WFP*, 5 July 1873, p 2.
63 For an excellent introduction to Realist aesthetics at this period *see* George J
    Becker (ed), *Documents of Modern Literary Realism* (Princeton 1963), pp 3–38.
64 'Isaac Ronald the Dominie', *Good Words*, Ch III, p 5; 'Aberdeenshire Character
    and Characteristics: Old and New', *Onward and Upward*, Vol 1, No. IX, 1891,
    pp 218–21; Vol I, No. XI, 1891, pp 274–6; *see also Life Among my Ain Folk*, pp 74,
    100, 204–7, 213, 230. For the application of the assumptions of physical science
    to human behaviour at this time and the important role played by Scottish
    philosophy in this movement, *see* J F C Harrison, *Robert Owen . . .*, op.cit.
    pp 78–87.
65 *WFP*, 2 Dec 1876, p 2.
66 Ibid. 9 Dec 1876, p 2.
67 Ibid. 16 Dec 1876, p 2.
68 Ibid. 6 Jan 1877, p 2.
69 Ibid. 3 March 1877, p 2.
70 Stang op.cit. pp 153–90. I take a positive view of the structure and intention of
    'My Uncle the Baillie'; Becker would regard it as a classic failure of the realist
    method; for a discussion of this point in relation to Zola's *Germinal see* op.cit.
    pp 32–3.
71 Viewed thus, these works of Alexander's have interesting similarities with a
    later trilogy, James Leslie Mitchell's *Scots Quair*. [The location of the final *Life*
    stories is uncertain because there are gaps in the Aberdeen holdings June
    1874–May 1876, April 1883–Sept 1884, Jan–March 1886, Jan–March 1887, July
    1887–Jan 1888, April–July 1888, Oct 1888–Jan 1891, July–Oct 1891, Jan–Dec
    1892.]
72 'As the dialect in which the various personages in the story naturally utter
    themselves is one of great force and expressiveness, some pains were taken to
    render it accurately, both as to idiom and orthographical form.' *Johnny Gibb of
    Gushetneuk* (De Luxe Edition, Edinburgh 1880), Preface.
73 *WFP*, 21 Sept–5 Oct 1872, p 2. This device, although hardly common, is not
    confined to Alexander—*see* 'Adoption: a Glesca' Story', *Glasgow Weekly Herald*,
    28 Dec 1876, p 2. In a number of short stories by George Roy, also set in
    Glasgow, both narrative and dialogue are in demotic Scots, *see*, for example,
    'The Stairhead Battle', in *PJ*, 10 April 1858, p 2. *See also* David Grant's 'The
    Sexton's Story' in *The Chronicles of Keckleton* (Elgin, 2nd edn n.d.), pp 27–52,
    published in *WFP*, 2 May–27 June 1885. *The Chronicles* are interesting from a
    language point of view, written in various different registers to reflect the
    whole social range of a typical northern community, from the Scots-speaking
    business people to the flash colloquial English of the local newspapermen and
    the pedantic and latinate style of the schoolmaster.

74   A source close to the author states that it was not his original intention to publish *Johnny Gibb* in book-form: 'Literature', *WFP*, 5 July 1873, p 2; *see also* 'The Late Mr William Alexander, LL D', *Daily Free Press*, 21 Feb 1894, p 4.

CHAPTER FIVE

1   The fullest recent study of the Kailyard, Thomas D Knowles, *Ideology, Art and Commerce: Aspects of Literary Sociology in the Late Victorian Kailyard*, Gothenburg Studies in English, 54 (Gothenburg 1983) also stresses its 'British' dimension.

2   Op.cit. pp 62-3.

3   Ibid. p 64.

4   T H Darlow, *William Robertson Nicoll Life and Letters* (London 1925), pp 329-31; for a less enthusiastic appraisal of Nicoll as a literary entrepreneur, *see* John Attenborough, *A Living Memory Hodder and Stoughton Publishers 1868-1975* (London 1975), pp 30-59.

5   'The BRITISH WEEKLY is an attempt to supply in a religious paper the freshness, vivacity, ability, and energy of the New Journalism.'—Advertisement for the *British Weekly* bound in with J M Barrie, *A Window in Thrums* (London 1889); *see also* Attenborough op.cit. p 37.

6   Darlow op.cit. pp 73, 70, 329.

7   Darlow op.cit. pp 135, 137-8, 143-4, 335; Knowles op.cit. p 71; Tanzy, Publishing the Victorian Novel . . ., op.cit. pp 173-7; Turner, 'The Syndication of Fiction . . .,' op.cit. pp 58, 71; Hodder and Stoughton had long been heavily engaged in the American and Canadian market—*see* Attenborough op.cit. pp 25-9.

8   *See* 'Sales of Books during the Month' in *The Bookman*, starting in Vol I, No. 1, Oct 1891, a regular feature listing best-selling titles in a number of British cities: *see especially* the contrast between Edinburgh and London in Vol III, No. 13, Oct 1892, p 24, and Vol III, No. 18, March 1893, p 195.

9   M M Harper, *Crockett and Grey Galloway* (London 1907), pp 164-5. He added '. . . some day, when editors cease a little from troubling and publishers from dictating, I will write for you of Galloway, and for you, brither Scots, akin to her, a real Galloway book, in the full dialect, to be understood only by those to the manner born. I did not think until the other day that such a book would find a publisher, but I met a friend who said, "I'll publish it when you write it". We poor authors may get our fame and our inspiration from our homelands, but we have to get our money elsewhere than where the heather grows' (p 162).

The English market was prepared to tolerate the vernacular to an extent, but only in a diluted and standardised form; *see*, for example, the review of *Malcolm* in *Blackwood's Magazine*, Vol CXVII, 1875, pp 634-5 where George Macdonald is castigated for adopting a regional standard for his Scots-speaking characters: 'Why will Mr Macdonald make all his characters, almost without exception, talk such painfully broad Scotch? Scotch to the fingertips, and loving dearly our vernacular, we yet feel it necessary to protest against the Aberdeen-awa' dialect . . . which bewilders even ourselves now and then, and which must be almost impossible to an Englishman. So many beautiful thoughts, tender, and delicate, and true, must be obscured to the reader by this obstinate purism, that we feel angry, disappointed, and impatient at the author's perseverance in this mistaken way . . . It is poor art, and not truth at all, to insist upon this desperate accuracy. Sir Walter's Scotch was never like this.'

10 W Robertson Nicoll, 'Ian Maclaren' Life of the Rev John Watson DD (London 1908), pp 179-80.
11 Knowles op.cit. p 90; Darlow op.cit. pp 323-4; see also Stephen Koss, Nonconformity in Modern British Politics (London 1975), pp 15-41; Hector Macpherson, The Intellectual Development of Scotland (London 1911), p 211.
12 Janet Dunbar, J M Barrie the Man behind the Image (London 1970), pp 14-17, 23, 120.
13 Harper op.cit. pp 59-110.
14 Nicoll op.cit. pp 11-12.
15 Quoted in Allen Wright, J M Barrie Glamour of Twilight (Edinburgh 1976), p 22.
    For the extent to which Scottish book-fiction was produced for a predominantly English market from the earliest years of the nineteenth century onwards, see Craig, Scottish Literature and the Scottish People . . . op.cit. pp 213-31, 297-300. For recent attempts to make sense of the Kailyard in a basically Scottish setting, see Ian Carter, 'Kailyard: the Literature of Decline in Nineteenth Century Scotland' in The Scottish Journal of Sociology, Vol 1, No. 1, (1976) pp 1-13; Ian Campbell, Kailyard. (Edinburgh 1981), passim, and 'The Liberals in the Kailyard' in Hart, The Scottish Novel . . ., op.cit. pp 114-30. Christopher Harvie, 'Behind The Bonnie Brier Bush: "The Kailyard" Revisited', in Proteus, No. 3 June 1978, pp 55-70, links the phenomenon with the wider world of British literary capitalism, a line developed in Knowles, op.cit. passim, but especially pp 27, 49-50, 71, 87, 96, 216.
16 I derive this figure from contemporary book-reviews in the Scottish press during the 1860s and 1870s; it may be on the high side.
17 For a representative sample of social history and popular culture material see 'East Neuk Chronicles or Rambling Reminiscences of an East Ender' [working-class life in mid-Victorian Aberdeen], Aberdeen Weekly Journal, 29 April 1896, p 3 ff; 'Local Days in the '45', AFP, 19 Nov-17 Dec 1867, p 4; 'Epitaphs and Inscriptions from Burial Grounds, Old Buildings, &c. in the North East of Scotland', WFP, 13 July 1872, ff; 'Random Scraps Connected with the Cordwainers and the Cordwainer Craft, Freemen of the Burgh of Aberdeen', WFP, 6 Oct 1872 ff; 'Reminiscences of Woodside. By an Auld Residenter', WFP, 13 Oct 1877, p 2 ff; 'A Midnight Gathering in the Glentons; or My Initiation into the Mysteries of the Horseman Word', WFP, 2 March 1872; 'Shiprow-Foot in Bygone Days', WFP, 9 March 1878; 'Second-Sight, Omens and Apparitions', WFP, 15 June 1878 ff; 'The Sports and Pastimes of the Scotch', WFP, 6 Sept 1879-24 July 1880, p 2; 'Eminent Ecclesiastics of Aberdeen and the North', WFP, 31 July 1880 ff; 'The Bards of Bon-Accord', WFP, ?[gap in Aberdeen holdings] Dec 1883 ff; 'Sketches of and in Aberdeen', WFP, 8 Nov 1884 ff; 'Aberdeenshire a Hundred Years Ago', WFP, 28 March 1885, p 2 ff; 'Deeside Smuggling Sixty Years Ago—Recollections of an Old Aberdonian', WFP, 25 June 1887, p 2 ff; 'The Laird and the Laird's Tenants in the Auld Time', 24 March 1888, p 2 ff; 'Random Recollections of Buchan and Buchan Worthies. By a Septuagenarian', WFP, 13 June 1891, p 2 ff; 'Sketches of Life in a Jute Mill', PJ, 14 May 1881, p 2 ff; 'Typical Aberdeenshire Farms', PJ, 8 Jan 1898, p 8 ff; 'Scotch Radicalism Fifty Years Ago', PJ, 26 Sept 1868 ff; 'Traditions and Superstitions of the Mearns', PJ, 5 June 1869-26 June 1869 [bearing witness to widespread survival of folk belief among older members of the current generation]; 'Songs for the Million' [an appreciative comment on song-slips], PJ, 10 Oct 1862, p 2; 'The Jacobite Ballads of Scotland' (by 'W[?illiam] A[?lexander]'), AFP, 22 Oct 1867-12 Nov 1867, p 4. Correspondence concerning the street singer Johnny Milne of Leevat's Glen, PJ,

12 Nov, 19 Nov, 3 Dec, 1870, 11 Feb 1871; 'The Ballads and Songs of Scotland', *Glasgow Weekly Herald*, 22 Nov 1878–10 July 1880, p 8 [the earliest example I know of that pleasant Victorian invention, the 'song-exchange', which involved readers sending in on postcards words and music of songs they knew in return for ones they didn't, supplied by other readers. This one specialised in texts and variants of high traditional ballads; it printed music too]; 'Notes on the Cultivation of Scottish Music', *WFP*, 7 Jan–14 Jan 1888; 'The Carle he cam' o'er the Craft', *WFP*, 25 Feb 1888, p 2 [text from oral tradition, with note appealing for variants], *see also* 10 March 1888, p 2, 24 March 1888, p 2; 'The Bothy Ballads of Scotland', by Robert Ford, *PJ*, 10 April 1897–9 July 1898, p 5 [Another song-exchange: 'Readers are respectfully invited to send in copies of Songs and Ballads of the Bothy class with which they are familiar'—quotes fragments of texts and then appeals to readers for the remainder; lists contributors by name], *see also* 3 Dec, 1898, p 5; 'The Ballads and Songs of Fife' *Fifeshire Advertiser*, 24 Jan 1903 *ff*; 'The Auld Scotch Sangs', *PJ*, 27 Oct 1906 *ff*; [a song-exchange based on The Poet's Box, 203 Overgate, Dundee—this gave long and detailed lists of correspondents and constitutes a first-rate source for studying the currency of material of every sort from music-hall songs to high ballads in the popular-song culture of early twentieth century Scotland. Latterly it continued under the title 'Songs for Readers'; it ended 30 Jan 1909; for a period it printed music in staff and sol-fa notation]; 'Lilts of Scottish Song of Byegone Days. By Fra. Brown, Paisley' in *Paisley & Renfrewshire Gazette*, 29 Aug 1908–12 June 1909 [issue for 1 May 1909 notes 'My esteemed friend Mr Gavin Greig, MA, sends me "The Pedlar" and some other old ditties for which I am much obliged—F.B.']; 'Scottish Folk Song in Canada. By James M Taylor', *WFP*, 18 April 1914, p 12 [warm appreciation of work of Gavin Greig and the way it is changing the popular perception of folk song]. Greig, of course, ran the most famous folk-song column of all, in the *Buchan Observer*, during the opening years of the twentieth century, republished in book form as *Folk-Song of the North-East* (2 Vols Peterhead 1909, 1914; reprinted Hatboro, Pennsylvania 1963).

18   Alasdair Gray, *Lanark* (Edinburgh 1981), p 243.

19   Sixty-three Scottish papers are known to have carried Tillotson fiction at one time or another, Turner 'Syndication of Fiction in Provincial Newspapers ...' op.cit., Appendix 11.

Glossary

As the ability to read Scots varies widely I have made the following word list as full as possible. A proper understanding of the evidence—much of which is in Scots—is essential to the argument of this book. Readers who find it annoyingly simplistic may accept my apologies in advance.

a I
a' all
ablach fool
aboon above
aboot/apoot about
ace ash
acquent familiar
adee to do
ae one
aeditur editor
afore before
ahin behind
aichty eighty
aifter after
ain own
ain-a-dees experience difficulty
aince/ance once
airt art, direction
airt and pairt implicated in
aither either
aiven even
aiven-doon sheer
aixtree axle
aizle cinder
alairm alarm
alane alone
alang along
alicht alight
alood aloud
alooin' allowing
ambeeshin ambition
amplush nonplussed
an' if
ance erran' especially
ane one
aneuch enough
anither another
appresheate appreciate
arles engagement money

aroon around
a' thegither altogether
attenit attended
attinshin attention
attiteed attitude
atween between
aucht/auchty eight, eighty
auld old
ava at all
awa away
awat an interjection
awee a little
aweel exclamation—'oh well'
awgent agent, solicitor
aw'm I'm
ay yes
aye always
ayenoo just now

ba by
baillie senior magistrate in a Scottish burgh
bairn child
bairnly childish
baith both
bann't swore
bar-bil't overheated
bauld bold
bather bother
bauk strip of fallow ground
baun band
bawbee halfpenny
bawsand with a flash (as of a horse)
beast horse
beets boots
begood began
behaudden beholden
belang belong
bellum bellow

Beltane 1 May
beuk book
bide stay
billys experts
binna be not
birsen overheated by exertion
birse' t-en's: shoemakers' thread
bit but
blate slow, stupid
blaw blow
bleck scoundrel
bleed blood
bletherin garrulous
body/buddie person
Bools were rowin': how things were developing
boon bound
boord board
born days life
brae hill
braid broad
braig brag
brainches branches
brak break
brawer superior
brawly very well
breeks trousers
breem-knowes broom-covered hills
breeshle rush
breet brute
brig bridge
brither brother
Broch 'the Broch', familiar name for Fraserburgh
brocht brought
brodmill brood
broolyie a struggle
broon brown
brunt burned
bubbly running
buckle wi engage with
buik book
busses bushes

ca' call, knock
caip/cyap cap
cairt cart
callant boy
cam' came
canna can not
carl man

carritch catechism; *put through his carritches* questioned closely
catecheesin questioning
cauld cold
caums *in's ain caums'* after his own fashion
Cawml Campbell
cep except
chafts jaws
chaitit cheated; *sair chaitit* much deceived
cheena china
cheenge change
chiel man
choppie shop
chowks cheeks
chucks chickens
claes/claise/clase clothes
clatters loose conversation
cleukin into supported by
clockin' brooding
cloods clouds
clossie alley
coblie small boat
cockernonie a kind of mutch
coft bought
collies lamps
complowsible amenable
coont count
coonter counter
coof fool
coorse rough, malign
couldna could not
cowpit overturned
craag/craig neck, throat
crackin' conversing
crap crop
craturs creatures, children
craw in their craps stick in their throats
crockanition pieces, destruction
crood crowd
croon crown
cry a demand; *a cry in* a brief visit
cud could
cuist cast
cun can
curn a few

daachter daughter
dae/dee do

dael deal
dakkert searched
dambrod draughts, hence, by extension, 'checkered'
daur dare
davoorin' davouring
debush't debauched
dee die
deed indeed
deen done
deil devil
dekyn expert; hence *gryte dekyn* very expert
deleerit crazed, demented
denner lunch
dicht wipe; *dicht it up* present it
dinna do not
disna does not
displenish to sell off contents of house, etc, by roup
div do
divin don't
diz does
dizna does not
dizzen dozen
dod an exclamation
dominie a schoolmaster
doon down
doot/doobt conclude, doubt
dother daughter
douce soft, sedate
drap drop
dreed dread
dreel hustle
drucken drunken
dunnies cellars

easht east
edder either
e'e eye
eemage image
een eyes, one
eence once
eerins ear-rings
eese use
eild age
elbucks elbows
elekshin election
eneuch enough
e'noo just now
en's ends
ereckit erected
ettlin at attempting

fa' fall
facks facts
faddoms fathoms
fader father
fae/frae from
fail-dyke turf wall
failt enfeebled
faimily family
fash fret, annoy
fat/faht what
faur where, far
faut fault
feared/feart afraid
feedle field
fecht fight
feck number; as in *maist feck* the greater number; most
fegs an exclamation
feenally finally
feint devil; used idiomatically as in *feint a* devil a; *feint haet* devil take it
fell very
ferlie a wonder
ferra very
fesh fetch, fetched
fesn't secured
Fiersday Thursday
fin/fan when
fit foot
fite white
fittininment concern
flare/flure floor
flee fly, flea
flicht flight, escape
flichterin' rapidly moving
flit move house
flooer flower
fobbin panting
foggage grass
foo how
fool-moo't blasphemous
foondit as in *feint foondit* not a thing
footer worthless person
forbye as well
forder further
forgie forgive
fornent opposite
forrat/forrit forward
foulk/fowk folk
fowre four
frauchtie cargo

freend friend
fricht fright
frowdy mutch a woman's cap
fu how
fule fool
fummlin fumbling
fun/fund found
furt for it
fusionless weak, enfeebled
futher whether
fyow few

gae go
gae an' very
gaen gone
gairdener gardener
gang go
gar force or compel
gate road
gate-en' locality
gaun/gawn going
gawpus idiot
geet child
gey very
geyan very
gengyies ?'geylies', pretty well
gi'e give
gif if
gillie male servant
gin if
glampit clambered
gled glad
gleg active, agile
gless glass
gleyed squint
glimsh look
glint glance
gloamin dusk
gou taste
gowan daisy; to *cow the gowan* be
   easily pre-eminent
gowd gold
gowff-sticks golf-clubs
gowk/gowck fool, idiot
gowpin' gaping
graith rubbish
granein groaning
'gree agree
greeting weeping, complaining
gret/gryte great, large
grices piglets

grou grow
grun ground
grup grip
gude/gweed good, God
gudeman/gweedman married man
gudewife married woman
gyan going, gone
gyang go
gyte mad

Haave heave
hae/ha'e have, have to
haibits habits
haill/hale whole
haimmer hammer
hairm harm
hairst harvest
haivens parts
halfin' half
halian rascal
haly holy
hame home
hamely homely
han's hands
hanfi handful
hantle quantity
haud hold
haud yer jaw/haud yer peace be silent
hause-pipe wind-pipe
haverin' speaking nonsense
he-al here (child usage)
hearse hoarse
hedder heather
heely wait
heemlin humbling
heer hear
heich high, hight
heid head
heid-heicht climax
heid-room independence
heowin hoeing
hereawa hereabouts
herschip robbery
het hot
hid/hed had
Hielan' Highland
hilliebuloo hue and cry
hin' rear
hinna have not
hinch haunch
hinner hinder

hit it
hiz has
hod hidden
hollan's gin
hoo how
hoose house
hoosomdever however
hoots an exclamation
houp hope
hove threw
howffin dolt
humphin' carrying with effort
hunder hundred
hurl excursion

ill bad
ill-grown stunted
ill-lucken ugly
ill-natur't cross, disagreeable
ilk/ilka every
immedantly immediately
in if
ingans onions
ingleneuk fireside
intull into
inveetors stock
irr are
ither other
itt that
ivery every
ivver ever

jaantin jaunting
jalouse infer, conclude or detect
jantry gentry
jist/joost just
jouket dodged

Kail throu the rikk idiomatic phrase
  implying merited reproach
keepit kept
keep's an exclamation
ken know
keest cast
kibble nimble
kilmarnock blue bonnet
kitchie kitchen
kittle tricky
kittl't born
knablich chunk
knappin knocking

kwintraside countryside
kwite coat
kye cattle

lade load
lait laid
lair bog
lairge large
Lammas 1 August
lang long
lang win'et long winded
lat let
lave remainder
lear learning
lee lie
leeberty liberty
leein' lying
leems equipment
leen alone, self
leet let
leivin living
lek like
leppirt leopard
leuk/luik look
leukit consulted
leys pasture
licht light
lichtit upon discovered
lickers liquors
lift sky
linkin travelling light-heartedly
lippen trust
little bookit small beer
loaf saps bread steepies
loike like
lood loud
loon/loonie boy
losh an exclamation
lug ear
luggerie small lugger
lunt fire
lythe sheltered
lows't set free

mainners/menners manners
mair more
mairriet married
maist most
maitter matter
mak make
marrows matched, a pair

Martinmas   11 November
maugre i' maugre o' my neck   despite my attempts to prevent it
maun   must
meat/maet   food
maelie sids   ingredients for sowens
meen   moon
meenlicht   moonlight
meesery   misery
meikle   much
mengyie   party
mensless   thoughtless
Michael day   29 September
mid-al   mother (child usage)
midden   dung-heap
min   man
minet   minute
mink   noose
minnyster   minister
mintit   tried
mischanter   accident
mischievin'   coming a cropper
misleared   unaccommodating
mistak'   mistake
mitha   might have
mither   mother
mithna   might not
moniment   laughing stock
mony   many
moosis   mice
mooth   mouth
morn: the morn   tomorrow
mou'   mouth
muck   dung
muckle/meukle   large, much
muir   moor
murnins   mourning
my certie   an exclamation
myne   remember

na   no, not
nabal   a coarse grasping fellow
naething   nothing
naig   horse
nain   own
naitral   natural
natur   nature
nave   hub
needcessity   necessity
neen   none
neeps   turnips

neibor/neepour   neighbour
neist/neyst   next
neives   knuckles
nesty   nasty
newlins   nearly
newse   conversation
neuk   nook
nice   finical, over scrupulous
nicht   night
nickum   mischievous child
nittle't   nettled
nivver   never
no'/nae   not
nominat   nominated
noo   now
nor   than
noshuns   notions
nots   pounds
nowt   bullocks
nu   new

obleedged/opleeged   obliged
objeckit   objected
ocht   anything
ohn   without
ony   any
onything   anything
oor   hour, our
oorsels'   ourselves
oot   out
oot o' reel   beyond all measure, un-
   acceptable
ooter   outer
ootheady   rebellious
ootline   outline
opeenion   opinion
ordinar'   in the sense of *for ordinar'*,
   usually
orra   dirty, insanitary
ouk/ook   week
ower/owre   too, excessively
ower cas'en   overcast

painch   paunch
pairt   part
pairtner   partner
pairts   ability, intelligence
parritch   porridge
parrymyack   likeness
parteekler   particular
pech   sigh or pant

peer/puir poor
peerat pirate
peeweet lapwing
pentit painted
pey pay
pilget a contest
pinshin pension
pinsl pencil
pit put, bit
pitten put
pivvle ?nit-pick, as in *a pivvlin' kin' o' a body*
plash't splashed
plew stilts plough handles
pliskie trick
plyps flings
pooches pockets
pooer't poured
poother powder
pottach porridge
pran smack
prawly well
pree taste, sample
press cupboard
prievin' 'tak a prievin' sample
progues shoes
puckle/pickle small quantity
py by

quo' said

rade rode
rael real, really
raiths terms
rakken reckon
rape rope
rase rose
raw row
rax reach or stretch
redd stir up
reek smoke
reet root
reisk rough ground
requares requires
richt right
rig strip of cultivated ground
rin run
ringin doon derogating
rippet quarrel
rist rest
rizzen reason

roch rough
rock spinning wheel
rodd road, way
rot wrote
Rottra-Head Rattray Head
roun/roon round
Roy o' Aldivalloch famous character in Scottish song

sae so
saft soft
saicks sacks
saip soap
sair painful, excessively
sairin' serving
san' sand
sang song
sanna shall not
saul sold
sax six
scaup shelf
schaime scheme
schule/skule/squeel school
sclate slate
scouthered burned
scowder pace, speed
scran spoils
scug hide-out
seen/shin/shun soon
seer sure
sel' self
seyven seven
shackle-banes wrists
shak shake
shankit gone
shanks legs
shaper cheaper
share sure
sharger weakly
sharry contretemps
she lowland version of the emphatic form of the Gaelic first personal pronoun
sheen shoes
sheet shoot
sheilin spreading
shirra sheriff
shoon shoes
shootable suitable
shoothers shoulders
shune soon

shuttin shooting
sib related to
sic such
siccar safe, secure
sicht sight
sid should
sikkin wanting
siller/silder money
simmer summer
sin'/sine/syne then, since, ago
sins sons
sirple sip
skaith harm
skance a small portion
skirl shriek
skite slide rapidly
sklyte uncouth person
skraich screech
skraigh o' day first light
skryin advertising
sleumin' rumour
slung ill-made disreputable fellow
slype physically unpleasant person
sma' small
sma'est smallest
smore suffocate
sonsy attractive, in an ample sort of
   way
sooperweeser supervisor
soord/swird sword
soom sum
sooth south
sorra sorrow
soud should
spak spoke
sparry a sparrow
speer ask
spikk speak
spikkin speaking
spooley a spoil
sprauchin' toddling
spurtle stirrer
squeelin schooling
stachers staggers
stamack stomach
stane stone
stane-cast stone's throw
stannin/staunin standing
stap step
stappin' stepping
starn a handful

steed stood
steen stone
steenbrakkin stonebreaking
stemmer steamer
stickit swine pig with its throat cut
stirk bullock
stoitin' staggering
stoot robust
stowlins furtively
straucht straight
streen *the streen* yesterday night
sune soon
sunna shall not
swither doubt, faint

tacketie heavily nailed
tae one, also
taes toes
tak' take
takes in sets rapidly off along
takin' aff consuming
tane taken, took
tap top
taties potatoes
tats an exclamation
taul/telt told
tee too
teed indeed
teem empty
teens tunes
telt told
thackit thatched
thae those
the-al there (child usage)
thegidder/thegither together
thocht thought
thocht a little, as in *a wee thocht*
thochtna did not think
thoom thumb
thrapple throat
thraten't threatened
thraw wring, twist
throu/throw through
tibacca tobacco
tig-tire exhaustion
tie an exclamation
Tiesday Tuesday
tiet's tied his
till/tull to
timmer wooden
tinkler tinker

tint lost
tither other; *the tither*, the other
tocher dowry
toon town
torry-aten infested with the grub of the crane fly
toun farm
tow rope
traivel walk
transack trade
tree three
trow believe
trowth truth
truff turf
truggs an exclamation
trypal a large and coarsely made person
tull'm to him
twa two
twal twelve

ugsome repellent
unco very
uneducat' unschooled
upo' upon

vaig scamp
veesit visit
veeve vivid
verra very
vreetin writing
vrocht worked

wa' wall
wad wager
wad/wid/wud would
wae sorrowful
waesucks an exclamation
waired spent
war were
wardle/warld/worl world
wark work
warroch worthless insignificant person
warst worst

wa's ways; hence *cam's wa's* made his way
wast west
wauges wages
wauk walk
waur worse
weans children
wechty weighty
weel well
weerin wearing
weel-a-wat an exclamation
ween wind
wha who
whase whose
whaur where
wheen several
whilk which
whussle whistle
wid would
wikk week
wile vile
win'art windward
win'et winded
winna/wunna will not
wint want
wirr our
wither weather
wiz we; was
won got
woodie gallows
woor wore
wrang wrong
wullin willing
wuppin whipping
wus/wuss/wush wish
wut intelligence, sagacity
wye way
wyles twist together as in making a rope; spin out

yalla yellow
yaup hungry
ye you
yin/yun one
younker child

Index

Newspapers and periodicals are listed alphabetically by title; individual works discussed in the text appear in chronological order under authors' names. Reference is to published book editions where available, although readers should note that there are sometimes discrepancies between the titles of book and serial editions.

Aberdeen and North of Scotland Newspaper and Printing Co Ltd, 9–10, 96
Aberdeen Free Press, x, xi, 3, 5, 6, 7, 10, 15, 25, 38, 55, 101, 102, 108, 115, 120, 143
Aberdeen Herald, 7, 10, 19
Aberdeen Journal, xi, 1, 6, 7, 9–10, 19, 32, 64, 96, 97, 122
Aberdeenshire and Banffshire Mutual Instruction Union, 104–6
Adam, James, 7
Ainsworth, William Harrison, 91
'Airchie Tait' *see* Leatham, James
Airdrie & Coatbridge Advertiser, xi
Alexander, Henry, 5, 101–2
Alexander, William, x, xi, 6, 7, 15, 25, 61, 87, 101–44, 148
  'Sketches of Rural Life in Aberdeenshire', 15–16, 102, 106–8, 113, 143
  'The Authentic History of Peter Grundie', 102, 108–15, 143
  'The Laird of Drammochdyle and his Contemporaries', 102, 115–20, 122, 127
  'Ravenshowe and the Residenters Therein', 102, 120–5, 127, 143
  Johnny Gibb of Gushetneuk, x, 25, 101, 104, 122, 125, 127–8, 133, 134, 143, 144
  'Back to Macduff', 143
  Sketches of Life Among my Ain Folk, 101, 125, 128–32, 143
  Notes and Sketches Illustrative of Northern Rural Life in the Eighteenth Century, 101, 106, 121
  'My Uncle the Baillie', 102, 134–43
  'Isaac Ronald the Dominie', 104
  'Aberdeenshire Character and Characteristics Old and New', 126–7

Allardyce, Alexander, 106
America
  comic stereotypes of, 48–52
  popular literature of, 58–60
Anderson, Arthur, 54
Annand, James, 5
Anti-Corn Law League, 18
Anti-Taxes on Knowledge Association, 18
Ardrossan & Saltcoats Herald, xi
'Artemus Ward', *see* Browne, Charles Farrar
Atlanta Constitution, 59
Ayr Advertiser, xi
Ayrshire Post, xi
Aytoun, William Edmonstoune, x

Ballantine, James, x
Banffshire Journal, xi
Barrie, Sir James, xii, 145–8
  Auld Licht Idylls, 145–7
  A Window in Thrums, 145
  Margaret Ogilvie, 145
Bell, James, 5
Berwick Advertiser, 73
Besant, Walter, 100
'Josh Billings', *see* Shaw, Henry Wheeler
Black, William, 100
Blackwood's Edinburgh Magazine, x, 9, 106
Blake, George, 87
Blairgowrie Advertiser, xi
Blatchford, Robert, 65
Bolton Journal & Guardian, 96–7
Braddon, Mary Elisabeth, 96, 100
Bradford Chronicle, 9
Brechin Advertiser, 18
British Weekly, 145–6

Browne, Charles Farrar ('Artemus Ward'), 59
Buchanan, Robert, 96
Buchan Clown, 15, 73-6
Buchan Observer, xi, 5, 64
Buchan, Peter, 64
Burgess, Alexander ('Poute'), 59-60
Burns, Robert, 35, 38
The Buteman, xi, 4

Caledonian Mercury, x
Campbell, John McLeod, 79
Carruthers, Robert, 7
Carter, Ian, 133
Chambers's Edinburgh Journal, 14
Chambers, William, 14, 24, 83
Chapbooks, 4, 35-6, 81
Chartism, 18, 28
Christian Advocate, 82
Clarion, 65
Clemens, Samuel ('Mark Twain'), 59
Cleveland Plain Dealer, 59
Collins, Wilkie, 96
Cornhill Magazine, 9
Crockett, Samuel Rutherford, 145-8

Daily Telegraph, 106
'Desperate Dan', 51
Dickens, Charles, 32, 64
Dostoevsky, Feodor, 134
Drummond, Peter, 81
Dumfries & Galloway Courier, xi
Dumfries & Galloway Standard, xi
Dumfriesshire & Galloway Herald, xi
Dundee Advertiser, xi, 1-2, 5, 6, 11, 23-9, 88
Dundee & Perth Saturday Post, xi
Dunfermline Press, 87

East Fife Record, xi, 56
Edinburgh Christian Magazine, 82
Edinburgh Courant, x
Edinburgh Evening Courant, x
Edinburgh Herald, 72
Edinburgh Review, x
Edinburgh Weekly Chronicle, 5
Edinburgh Weekly Journal, x, 73
Edwards, David Hershell, 18
Elgin Courier, 73
Ellis, Alexander John, 54
Eskdale & Liddesdale Advertiser, xi

Evening Express, xi
Evening Gazette, xi
Evening Telegraph, xi, 26

Falkirk Herald, 3, 5, 14
Ferdinand II, King of Naples, 42
Fergusson, Robert, 35
Fife Free Press, 97
Fife Herald, 28
Fifeshire Advertiser, xi
Forsyth, William, 6-10

Galt, John, 46
Gilfillan, George, 29-30
Gillies, Archibald, 9-10
Glasgow Citizen, 5, 34
Glasgow Herald, xi, 1, 6, 99
Glasgow Weekly Mail, xi, 61-4
Good Words, 34
Grant, Thomas, 77
Gray, Alasdair, 149
Greenwood, Frederick, 145
Gregor, Walter, 36
Greig, Gavin, 38
Grieve, Christopher Murray ('Hugh MacDairmid'), x

Hamilton Advertiser, xi, 4, 5, 53, 97
Harris, Joel Chandler ('Uncle Remus'), 59
Hart, Francis Russell, 87
Hedderwick, James, 5, 34
Hogg, James, x, 35
Hogg's Instructor, 28
Hyndman, H M, 65

'Ian Maclaren', *see* Watson, Dr John
Innes, Col Thomas of Learney, 9
Inverness Courier, xi, 7
Irving, Edward, 79

John O'Groat Journal, xi
Johnston, Ebenezer, 81

Kailyard School, xii, 145-8
Kelso Mail, x
Kilmarnock Standard, xi
King, Jessie, 33
Kirkcaldy Times, xi

Latto, William D, ('Tammas Bodkin'), 5, 17, 28-34, 39-53, 58, 104, 148

Leatham, James, 53, 64–70
Leng, Sir John, xi, 11, 14, 24, 28, 30, 33, 88
Leng, Sir William, 95, 99
'Lewis Grassic Gibbon', see Mitchell, James Leslie
Lindsay, William, 18–21, 25
Lippincott's Monthly Magazine, 99
Littlejohn, James, 24–5
Lockhart, John Gibson, x
Lytton, Edward George Earle Lytton Bulwer-, 91

Macallan, David, 7
Macdonnell, James, 106
MacLeod, Dr Norman, 34
Macnie, William, 81
Manchester Times, 99
'Mark Twain', see Clemens, Samuel
McCombie, William, 5–6, 101, 105–6
Middlesborough News, 85
Millar, John Hepburn, 133
Miller, Hugh, x, 105
Mitchell, James Leslie ('Lewis Grassic Gibbon'), x
Moir, David Macbeth, 46–7
Montrose Review, x, 5
Morison, James, 79

Naismith, William, 5
National Association of United Trades, 19
New Ashford Eagle, 59
Newspapers
  acquisition of copy, 6–7, 95–7
  capitalisation of, 4, 9
  distribution and circulation, 6, 23–8
  editors and their responsibilities, 5–7
  impact of 'the new journalism', 33, 149
  localism of, 4–5, 53
  national distinctiveness of Scottish press, 14
  payment of contributors, 96
  penetration of working-class market, 3, 11, 14
  politics and, 6, 9–10, 25, 28
  press agencies, 5, 95
  reader participation in, 14, 30–3
  recruitment and personnel, 5–7, 53–4
  restrictions on the press, 2–3
  social awareness of, 42, 47–8
  support for popular culture, 29–30, 60
  syndication, 95–6
  technical change, ix, 5, 9, 10, 24–5
Nicoll, Sir William Robertson, 145–7
North Briton, xi, 14, 77, 85
North-Eastern Gazette, 99
Northern Advertiser, xi
Northern Co-Operative Company, 19
Northern Daily News, 65
Northern Daily Telegraph, 99–100
Northern Ensign, xi
Northern Figaro, 53
Northern News, 9
Northern Warder, 28–9
North of Scotland Gazette, 104
Nottingham Journal, 145

Orcadian, xi, 4–5
Orkney & Shetland Chronicle, 4
Orkney & Shetland Journal, 54
Outram, George, 1
Owen, Robert, 92–3

Pae, David, 77–100
  'Drumclog', 79
  'The Next of Kin', 79
  'Mrs McGregor's Levee', 79
  The Coming Struggle among the Nations of the Earth, 80
  George Sandford; or, the Draper's Assistant, 80–1
  Jessie Melville; or, the Double Sacrifice, 77, 83–6
  'Frederick the Foundling and Ellen Campbell: or, Lights and Shades of City Life', 97
  Lucy the Factory Girl; or, the Secrets of the Tontine Close, 88–95
  Two Years After and Onwards; or, The Approaching War Among the States of Europe, 87
  'The Lost Heir of Glencorran: or, The Emigrants', 97–8
Pagan, James, 1
Palmerston, Lord, 42
Paisley & Renfrewshire Gazette, xi, 97
Payn, James, 100
People's Friend, xi, 26, 32–33, 85, 95

People's Journal, ix, xi, 5, 11, 14, 17, 18, 21-34, 38-9, 45, 47, 48, 53, 76, 77, 95-97, 115, 149
Perthshire Advertiser, xi, 5, 33
Perthshire Courier, 24
Peterhead Sentinel, xi, 5, 53, 64-70
Philip, Rev W M, 96
Pitman, Sir Isaac, 54
Popular Literary Market
  availability of reading matter, 16, 18-21, 30, 35
  extension of literacy, ix, 17-18, 30
  provision of schooling, 16, 18, 36-7, 39-41, 55-6, 104
  rise of new reading public, ix, 21, 96-7 99, 143-4, 148
  self-improvement, 20-3
  Useful Knowledge Movement, 14-15, 73
Power, William, 87
Punch, 9

Ragged Schools Movement, 18
Ramsay, Allan, 35
Randall, Charles, 4
Reid, Sir Hugh Gilzean, 5
Reid, Thomas, 105-6
Religious Tract and Book Society of Scotland, 81
Rintoul, R S, 5
Ruddiman, Thomas, x
Rural Echo, 105-6
Russel, Alexander, 2, 3

St James's Gazette, 145
San Francisco Examiner, 33
Scotsman, 2, 6
Scott, David, 64, 65, 69-70
Scott, Sir Walter, x, 35, 64, 72
Scottish Colportage Society, 81
Scottish Conservative Association, 10
Scottish Forty Shilling Freehold Association, 19
Scottish Land and Labour League, 64
Seestu, 56-8
Shaw, Henry Wheeler ('Josh Billings'), 59-60

Sheffield Telegraph, 95
Sheridan, Thomas, 35
Sinclair, Alexander, 1, 3
Social Democratic Federation, 64-5
Socialist League, 64
Society for the Diffusion of Useful Knowledge, 15
The Squib, 35
Stevenson, Robert Louis, 35
Stewart, Andrew, 77, 85, 95
Stirling Observer, 3-4, 81
Stirling Tract Enterprise, 81

'Tammas Bodkin', *see* Latto, William D
'Tam O'Shanter', 54, 72
Telford, Thomas, 97
Territorial Enterprise, 59
Thomson, John, 9-10
Tillotson, Frederic, 96-7, 99
The Times, 106
Tolstoy, Leo, 134
Tractarian Movement, 81-2
Turgenev, Ivan, 134

'Uncle Remus', *see* Harris, Joel Chandler
Uncle Tom's Cabin, 86

Watson, James, x
Watson, Dr John ('Ian Maclaren'), xii, 145-7
Webster, George, 61
Weekly Dispatch, 19
Westall, William, 99
Westwood, Alexander, 24
Whamond, Alexander, 53
Wilson, Prof John, x
Wilson, John Mackay, 73
Wishaw Press & Advertiser, xi
The Witness, x
Workers' Herald, 65
The Workman, 14
Workmen's Peace Association, 19

Zola, Emile, 134